YA CAN't Let CANCeR RUiN YouR DAY

Foreword by Tom Hanks Honorary Patron for The James Fund for Neuroblastoma Research

THe JAMeS EmAiLS

by Syd Birrell

GREEN TRAIN BOOKS

*Many thanks to Christina Langlois
for her encouragement
and her invaluable assistance in editing this book.*

All Scripture quotations, unless otherwise specified, are taken from the New King James Version. Copyright © 1979, 1980, 1982. Thomas Nelson Inc., Publishers. Scripture marked NIV are taken from the HOLY BIBLE, NEW INTERNATIONAL VERSION ®. Copyright © 1973, 1978, 1984 by International Bible Society. Used by permission of Zondervan Publishing House. All rights reserved.

Cover Design by Jim Whitney of Naked Creative Consultancy, Toronto, ON

Printed at Essence Publishing, Belleville, ON, Canada
Copyright © 2005, Canadian Edition

Library and Archives Canada Cataloguing in Publication
Birrell, Syd, 1953-
        Ya can't let cancer ruin your day: the James emails / Syd Birrell.
ISBN 0-9738080-0-4

        1. Birrell, James, 1993-2001--Health. 2. Neuroblastoma--Patients--Canada--Biography. I. Title.
RC281.C4B57 2005   362.198'929948'0092   C2005-902997-8

**For more information or
to order additional copies, please contact:**
E-mail: info@greentrainbooks.com
Internet: www.greentrainbooks.com

GREEN TRAIN BOOKS

A Division of Swell to Great Inc.

TABLE OF CONTENTS

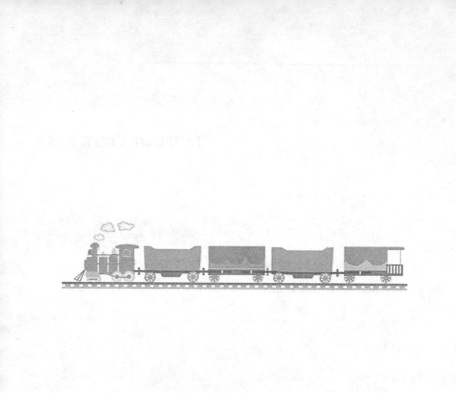

For James,

a boy who taught us to laugh when we
thought we could only cry.

James Birrell
October 2001

FOREWORD
BY TOM HANKS

Over the telephone, the voice of a little boy carries only his enthusiasm for the subject of the conversation—rocket ships, movies, railroad trains, and the other stuff that boys find fascinating. There is not talk of the doctor reports, the statistics, or the schedule of treatments—just the questions and opinions that blurt forth from the mouth and mind of a little boy like James Birrell.

The photographs will give you hints of his struggle, some more evident than others. But even in the pictures you can spot the obvious signs of a happy kid in love with life as much as he is in love with his family—the sunbeam smile, the cocked engineer's cap, and the look of satisfaction for a well-made snowman. The whole family is there as well: Syd and Pam, Ben and Rebecca. And James.

This book of the emails about James will tell you his story from all 360 degrees of perspective. And yes, some days and nights were so painful that you would not wish them on anyone. But there are other times—magical days and God-given nights of love, beauty, laughter, and awe— that will make you wish that you were one of the Birrell family. You will get to know all the Birrells, as well as plenty of people in their community, all of whom have come to know that their lives have been made a bit more special because James has become a part of their hearts.

And even better, these emails will allow you the pleasure of getting to know the little boy behind the cocked engineer's cap. He'll find a place in your heart as well. And like all great loves, James will be there forever.

Tom Hanks
January 2004

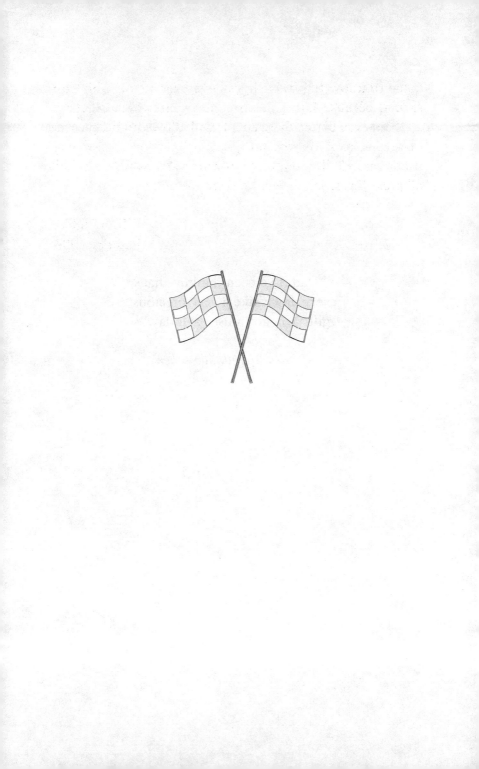

"Dad, I've been thinkin' that every day is like a very precious gift. You gotta use each day."

–James Birrell, age seven

PREFACE

What you are holding in your hands is a series of emails sent at a time of great challenge for our family. We had hoped that our five-year-old son had beaten cancer, but in the fall of 1997 James became ill once again, and our worst fears were confirmed. James had relapsed. I had recently signed up for my first email account, and to keep friends and family up to date on the medical situation I began to write email updates, most often typed in the middle of the night. Never for a moment did I dream that within months tens of thousands of readers would be logging on anxiously every day to read the latest update on James' heroic battle with recurrent neuroblastoma. And certainly I had no intent to create material for a future book.

Twenty-six months after he relapsed, James died. By then his story was receiving national coverage in the press, and a worldwide cyberspace community had become deeply involved in the life and death of one young boy. Why, I asked myself, would anyone be interested in what is clearly a tragedy? Here's what one stranger said:

"James, I never knew you. But your valiant fight and that of your family has touched me very deeply.

Go in peace to a better place—one free of pain and torment, of needles and nurses, of tears and pain. Go to the light that is there for you, and be a force of peace for your loving family. Thank you for touching my life and for reminding me of what is really important. Life, love, and family. I miss you."

Yes, James, I miss you too. But I don't want your brave, exciting, inspiring story to be forgotten. I still find myself waking up in the middle of the night, looking for answers. Unable to sleep, I still head downstairs to the computer and begin typing. Here's the book.

INTRODUCTION

My name is Syd. I am a church organist. You know—walk into a church on a Sunday morning and I'm the guy playing the organ and directing the choir. I have always had a passion for classical music in general and organ music in particular. Mastering a Bach fugue gives me great satisfaction. Waving my hands in front of a choir feeds my soul. Engineering was my other big interest, but when it came to the crunch, music won. I trained at the Royal College of Music in London, England, got various pieces of paper to prove it, and then returned home to pursue my career. I settled in a small city called Peterborough, where life treated me well and I was able to make a living in my chosen profession. I am still fascinated by engineering, and I love to read detailed books on building bridges or my father's *Engineering Review* magazines. I guess I came by these two interests honestly, for my father was a professional engineer who played the organ at church on Sundays.

I don't recall the first time I met Pamela, for she was one of my music students, and I used to have lots of those. She was studying business at university at the time, but singing was her real interest, and she had come to me to take some theory lessons. Well, one thing led to another, and rather quickly I married Pamela, ten years younger than I am, before her mother and her five older brothers could change her mind.

Rebecca was our first child. I had found myself curiously detached during Pam's pregnancy, unable to connect with the baby supposedly growing within. I duly attended those classes for eager first-time pregnant moms and their partners, and we learned how to relax and breathe and bond with each other and all that stuff. What really bothered me was the New Age music they played while we lay on the floor doing something important that I forget, music that drove me increasingly frantic as it melted from chord I to chord III and back again—that was it, no harmonic development at all, no rhythm, certainly no melody, just chord I and chord III. It all ended rather abruptly in the birthing room when Pam screamed at me to turn off the *!*!*!* music, and so Rebecca did not benefit from chord I and chord III as she was thrust into the world. Motherhood had come over a period of months for Pam, but fatherhood began right then—bang!— and I was smitten from the instant Rebecca was born, her eyes bright and curious, me changed forever.

James arrived sixteen months later, followed two years later by Benjamin. The kidless couple was now a family of five. It was exhausting; it was great; it was chaos; it was everything we wanted. Rebecca was a delightfully precocious little girl. James could charm anyone with his big, brown, mischievous eyes. And Ben was busy showing us once again that babies take a lot of work.

And then it happens. Pamela. Young, beautiful, healthy. Breast cancer. That 2.5-cm lump is nothing to do with being a nursing mom. Surgery. More bad news. Not one lump, but many. Nodal involvement. Right breast removed. Pathology report not good. Cancer type highly aggressive. Pamela not expected to make it. Six months of debilitating chemotherapy.

Pamela and Syd with Rebecca, James, and baby Ben

We are shattered. What to tell the children? We conclude that it is most important that they maintain their trust of us, so we decide we will tell them the truth, as much as their little minds can understand. "Mommy has a bad thing in her boobie. It's called cancer. Mommy will have an operation, and the doctor will take out the cancer." *Cancer*, a new word for our three year old and our four year old. Children are resilient, and for them the world of fighting cancer becomes normal. They listen; they see; they ask questions; and then they get on with their childhood. Lots of babysitters, because Mommy can't look after them any more, and if they get sick they have to go stay with their Nanny so Mommy won't catch their bug. Baby Ben is often shipped out for days at a time. But they are well looked after, and they continue to laugh and play. Pam and I are in shock, devastated by the thought that these adorable children may soon lose their mother.

Ben, Rebecca, and James

Slowly we begin to adapt to living with an unknown future. Pam's treatment involves two weeks of chemo and then two weeks of recovery. Repeat. During the chemo time she grows progressively weaker, loses ten pounds in weight, constantly fights nausea, and is more or less bed bound. In the good two weeks she leaves the bedroom, gains weight, and spends time with the children. But because of her compromised immune system we have to keep her sheltered from sick people; we can't go to places like shopping malls; and we all constantly wash our hands with antibacterial soap.

We have an idea: Pam starts a dream file. During the bad time, Pam writes in the file all the things she would like to do during her two good weeks. And then in the good two weeks we do it. "Why don't we all start dream files?" So we do. We start to fight back and begin to discover that the death threat of cancer is teaching us how to live. One day Rebecca tells us, "Just because you have cancer doesn't mean you stop having good times."

Never have we been so happy; never have we been so sad. We wonder how other families cope. Inevitably you start to compare your situation with the challenges others find themselves facing. One day we take comfort by saying, "Oh well, a parent having cancer is not as bad as your child having cancer."

Pam completes her course of treatment, and it appears that she is free of disease. The miracle has happened. It's summertime, and we soak up the sunshine; we enjoy summer as we never have before.

But adorable, cute, brown-eyed, curly-haired James is not well. He has frequent fevers. Now and then he vomits. His legs hurt. Finally he stops walking. And eating. And drinking. We come to the worst day of our lives. The unthinkable has come to pass. Little James, not quite four years old, has cancer. We hear the word *neuroblastoma* for the first time. Just as we are congratulating ourselves on completing the marathon, we find that in fact we have only just begun. It seems that Pam's illness was just the training camp. I take Rebecca to the toy store, and I show her the stuffed animal section. "Choose the one you like the best." And she chooses a soft, cuddly puppy called

Patches. "Rebecca, I love you very much, and every time you hug Patches I want you to remember that, because soon I am going to have to be away quite a lot, at the hospital in Toronto with James."

Devastating is the word that springs to mind. The odds that Pam faced were not good. The odds for James are just terrible. Desperately we claw our way through chemo, surgeries, radiation, bone marrow transplant, and one day we hear the magic word *remission*. As it turns out, we have eighteen months until relapse. Neuroblastoma relapse is particularly difficult, as there is now no hope. Always terminal. We begin palliative care. "We can probably give you one year, but not two." Actually, James carved out twenty-six months, packed full of living life to the fullest.

I wrote. Sleep was difficult. Jerked awake, my mind full of fears, I would head on down to the computer. There I would face the enemy in my own mind. Type, type, type, and then the wonderful release as I clicked the Send button. And then, sleep. In the morning all those wonderful replies would be waiting, the encouragement and wisdom required to face the next impossible day.

I think that's enough of an introduction. Let's go to Christmas Eve, 1999.

For the first time since the terrible news of James' relapse, I have not taken my bedtime sleeping pill. Instead, I find myself still wide awake at midnight, admiring our very beautiful Christmas tree, casting my eye over the dozens of gifts piled high round about. One gift, however, is missing, and that gift is James, sleeping soundly in his bedroom upstairs, in remarkably good health, in very good spirits, and eagerly looking forward to opening all those presents. He has had a very busy day: a nurse's visit for blood work after breakfast, making a fort with Rebecca and Ben in the just-tidied-up-for-Christmas guest room, several pages of homework, baking cookies for Santa, a visit to the corner store for treats, delivering flowers to his school principal, visiting Uncle Tony and brushing his dog, to the hardware store to buy a plastic funnel to play with at bath time, to the pet store to get a cat gift, a car ride to admire the Christmas lights, drawing a graph of his platelet and red blood cell count, a visit to the McCrackens to see Zeppo the cat, a wild romp on the bed with Rebecca and Ben, reading a chapter of his new *Arthur* book all by himself, 9 p.m. bedtime.

21

The Christmas Tree 1999

In his thoughtful moments, James, as usual, chatted about his cancer. Today he spoke of the time of the "Great Pain" before his chemo started. Later he encouraged the lady at the corner store who is about to begin chemotherapy. He is very aware that much more treatment lies ahead of him, yet he remains his cheerful self. Many people have spoken of the inspiration that James gives. Tonight, at our Christmas Eve church service, James lit the Christmas candle. I was privileged to stand with him along with the rest of my family, but the bigger privilege to me is this: throughout this ordeal we have seen the light of Christ, sometimes faintly, sometimes brightly, always conscious that our family has been surrounded by the love of God. Thank you for being a part of that gift.   Syd and family

SUBJECT: BACK TO THE FRONT LINES
SENT: JANUARY 7, 2000 2:27 PM

James' visit to the Hospital for Sick Children earlier this week brought us back to the front lines of cancer treatment once again. James underwent a bone scan; then the next day he was anesthetized for a bone marrow aspirate and a bone marrow biopsy. We met with his oncologist, Dr. Baruchel, and are able to report as follows:

The good news: James has responded superbly to the two rounds of chemo (called "ICE") that he received in November/December. It looks like we have achieved a temporary remission.

The bad news: James has not been cured. There is still no cure for recurrent neuroblastoma. If the bone marrow transplant protocol could not permanently eliminate the disease, then nothing else will either. Without further chemotherapy, James will relapse again very quickly.

The plan: Once-a-month chemo for the rest of his life. This will take place at the cancer clinic in Peterborough (Saint Joseph's) on an outpatient basis. It is hoped that this milder chemo will control the residual disease for twelve to eighteen months. Meanwhile we will look at various clinical trials happening around the world, with a view to participating in any that might offer a cure for James before time runs out.

In conclusion: Although the long-term prognosis is dismal, in the short-term we have seen another example of the extraordinary ability James has of beating the odds. The family has had a delightful Christmas holiday, and James is in terrific shape. Although some difficult decisions about future treatment lie ahead, we take comfort in the thought that to date we have made the right moves. The trick for the year 2000 will be how to emphasize quality of life for the whole family while keeping up with the demands of permanent cancer treatment.   Syd

SUBJECT: LONG HAUL AHEAD
SENT: JANUARY 27, 2000 6:35 AM

James has sailed through his first round of the "gentler" chemo. It is a mix of topotecan and cyclophosphomide and is administered daily over the course of two hours, through his central line, for five days. This is done at the oncology clinic at St. Jo's right here in Peterborough, which is very convenient. We are extremely grateful to all those in the local medical world who have made this possible. James goes to school when feasible and always gets a warm welcome from everybody. At home he plays noisily with his brother and sister, laughs at his own jokes, feeds the hamster, and lifts everyone's spirits with his joyous attitude.

Although to all outward appearances James looks just great, the results of his latest set of scans tell a different story:

1. Cancer can be found more or less throughout his body (widespread metastatic disease).

2. When compared with the scans of ten weeks ago, it is apparent that there is less cancer in certain areas (e.g., abdomen) but more in other areas (e.g., bones).

3. The recent bone biopsy was positive for neuroblastoma (James' type of cancer).

All of this is a stark reminder that a relapse of stage IV neuroblastoma post bone-marrow transplant is no picnic. The Hospital for Sick Children is at the forefront of worldwide research into neuroblastoma, but the sad truth is that none of the many clinical trials going on around the globe have found a cure. We know that HSC will facilitate any treatment worth doing.

Your support and friendship continue to mean a great deal through these difficult times, and we continue to be inspired by your prayers and expressions of love. We are planning another time of prayer and laying on of hands. Thank you for helping to make every day a gift.   Syd and family

P.S. we continue to appreciate soups and fruit salads, especially during times when we're at the hospital.

SUBJECT: THREE WISHES
SENT: FEBRUARY 9, 2000 8:23 AM

It's funny how cancer gets you doing the things that really matter while leaving much of your normal life in tatters. Last week we asked the children what each would really like to do for a special treat. Rebecca asked for a mommy-daughter sleepover. Ben chose to spend the night at the

McCrackens. James opted for a night on a train. So last Friday Pam and Rebecca went off to Winston's for a gourmet meal (rack of lamb, Caesar salad, and a Shirley Temple), having first gone shopping for a new "house on the prairies" nightgown. (Rebecca's comment on her wish: "That was the best evening of my life!") Later they moved upstairs to one of Winston's charming suites, did some crafts, slept well, and had an enormous English breakfast when they woke up. Ben went off to Bean's hockey game, drank black pop, ate fries, and then played with Zeppo the cat before heading to bed. Ben's summary of the whole thing: "Awesome!"

James' story is longer, because I was there. We started our trip rolling by phoning VIA Rail for information.

"Where are you going?"

"It doesn't matter, as long as it's overnight."

"But I can't sell you a ticket if you don't tell me where you're going."

"How about New York?"

"It's much cheaper to fly to New York."

I gave up and explained James' situation.

"Oh...I see." That's when the wheels started turning.

So, the next day we hopped on the GO Train to Toronto. We went to Rosie's house, had a huge nap, played with Thomas' train set until 8:30, and then we caught the subway to Union Station. After trying out crazy faces in the photo booth, we went to the waiting room, where it became apparent that VIA had been doing some work behind the scenes. "You must be James," they said as we entered the waiting room. "Please wait here a moment." And so we sat down in the first-class lounge and drank orange pop. Then the conductor arrived and let us get on the train early.

"We are looking for room 'C,'" said James.

"That's right, but we've moved you to room 'A.'"

"Wow, Dad, they gave us the biggest compartment in the train!" It being 10 p.m., I thought it was bedtime, but James had other plans. "Let's go to the dome car!" And there we found more surprises from VIA: a train whistle, VIA hats, badges, goodies, special VIA bags. Now James knew all about dome cars from books and videos, but to see a six year old check it out in real life was priceless. We were still upstairs at midnight as the train pulled out.

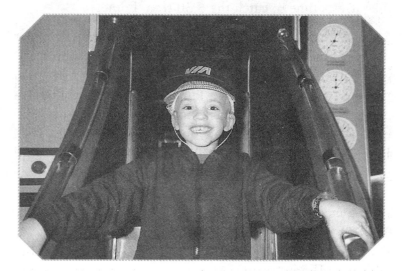

James on the steps to the dome car

Then Michelle the conductor set up the bunks, and we slept. Next morning while we ate breakfast up in the dome car, we could see the outline of Montreal. Soon we were at the station, where once again VIA couldn't do enough to help us. And there at the gate was Uncle Rodney, our chaperone for the day. First we went to his office in Place Ville Marie, and because it was Saturday and nobody was there, we played golf in the reception area.

Then we went to the Biodome and saw animals in their natural habitats. The crocodile and the penguins were the best.

Then we went to the planetarium. James already knew it all from "Magic Schoolbus," as it turned out. Then we looked at ships at the port before going to Rodney and Veronica's house in Hudson. We wrecked their beautiful home for a couple of hours, scared their cats, built a snow fort, and then it was time to catch the 6:30 train home.

Because Pam was not with us, we were able to order bologna sandwiches on white enriched bread for supper and gum balls for dessert. The train ride back was great! Brian was the conductor, and he let James make the PA announcement: "Ladies and gentlemen, boys and girls, it is ten minutes to Prescott!" Everyone on the train clapped. Then James got to speak on the walkie-talkie to the engineer. All too soon we arrived in Cobourg, where Peggy Two was waiting to drive us home.

"Bye, James!" Brian shouted as the train pulled out, and so ended a magical thirty-six hours.   Syd

Sorry, no cute stories, just some good news arising from James' latest round of routine tests at the Hospital for Sick Children. Here goes:

1. The MIBG scan shows "much improvement" since the last scan in January. The dozens of cancer sites visible last time are much reduced in size and number.

2. The bone aspirate was negative (good).

3. Other non-specific indicators such as the LDH and VMA were normal. The ferritin figure was still high (522) but better than last time.

4. Outwardly James appears very healthy, very energetic, and pain free. However, at times he is very badly behaved and quite a handful (i.e., a normal six-year-old boy?).

5. Although this cannot be interpreted as a cure, it is very encouraging in the short-term. It means that the recent cocktail of chemotherapy is working and is worth continuing. Next round starts Monday in Peterborough if James' blood counts have returned to satisfactory levels by then.

6. There appears to be a glimmer of hope for a cure, courtesy of James' very own oncologist, Dr. Sylvain Baruchel. His work on stopping angiogenesis (the growth of blood vessels that feed the cancer tumors) is resulting in mice being cured of neuroblastoma. "Will it work in humans?" is the big question, and clinical trials may start soon.

In conclusion: In view of James' excellent response to recent chemos, it seems best to continue in the present direction rather than launching into high-risk experimental treatment immediately. Another difficult decision; hope it's the right one! Syd and family

I want to tell you about two James events that I found quite moving this last week. To begin with, James lost his first tooth, which I suspect is fairly commonplace for a six year old but I take as a great achievement. Yaboo! to cancer that has tried to snuff out his short life and has not succeeded yet. I find something very defiant in the toothless smile on James' face and in his newfound ability to suck up spaghetti through clenched teeth. (Look, Dad!)

The other story involves buying new bikes for the children, as they have outgrown their old clunkers. "But what's the point in spending money on one for James if he's going to be dead by year end?" spoke one of the voices in my head. Well, I ignored that voice and listened to the one that said, "Buy that nice, shiny red one over there with the training wheels."

James tried it out in the store, got things all adjusted nicely, and, it being a warm spring day, we went to the park to try it out. "Careful! Your platelets are low; you mustn't get a cut or bruise; stay on the right side of the path!" Then winter returned, so it wasn't till yesterday that we were able to go bike riding again.

Off we went. With great confidence James zoomed around, and as he zoomed he said, "Dad, when can I take my training wheels off?"

James and Pam

"Right now," I said quickly, before the sensible voice in my head could register an objection. Off came the wheels, and then came that back-killer business for the parent where you grip the saddle and stagger along, desperately trying to avert disaster. So far, so good. All the time I'm thinking, *He's on Acutane; his skin is compromised from the drug; can we afford a spill, a scraped knee, hand, or face?* But his platelet count was good that week, so I took courage and let go. This, I suppose, is a priceless moment for all parents because the letting go goes far further than just the bike-riding thing, but for me and James the stakes seemed so much higher. I watched, enchanted, aghast at my foolhardiness, thrilled at my daring, convinced that a terrible accident was seconds away, savoring the moment. But James just kept riding around the parking lot, feeding instructions to the non-existent dad behind him, until he looked up and saw me on the other side of the parking lot. "Dad, you're there and I'm here!" "Dad, I can ride without training wheels all by myself!" "Look at me, Dad!"

Have a great day!   Syd

SUBJECT: JAMES VISITS THE KRATT BROTHERS
SENT: MARCH 31, 2000 3:40 AM

Last November James' cancer had returned, and while lying in hospital paralyzed by the pain of widespread metastatic disease, he received a call of encouragement from Chris Kratt of "Kratt's Creatures" kid-TV fame.

James was thrilled, and instead of a five minute call, they spoke for half an hour. An invitation followed to visit Chris, Martin, and the gang on the set in Montreal. Susan, the executive director, had recently lost a young nephew in tragic circumstances, and she wanted to make the trip possible. When a date in March was mentioned, we said yes, please, but privately I saw little hope of James lasting that long, given the current situation. But James got better, and we made the trip. Here is what Susan had to say on our return from Montreal:

> I'm so glad you had a good time. While sorry I didn't get to go with you, I knew you were in good hands; we've got a great cast and crew.
>
> Your visit closed a circle for me: I'd like to think that my nephew Eric, who died a couple of days before he was to join us on set and meet Chris and Martin, was with you in spirit. And if there was

32

laughter (and I'm sure there was), then I know he was with you.

Best, Susan

Here's the story:

Have you noticed that if you travel by plane your holiday begins when you finally make the connection between your luggage, your destination, and your bleary body, whereas a holiday by train starts the moment you get on board? No check-in two hours before departure, no frantic "which terminal do we want?" no embarrassing emptying of pockets at security, no sardine seating, no waiting forever for luggage, etc. Our family tried this older method of travel last week when we visited Montreal courtesy of some very special people who wanted to give us a bit of a lift in between James' chemo treatments.

And so it was that, at a very civilized hour on a Thursday morning, all five of us hopped on the train at Cobourg for a very entertaining ride to Montreal. James soon was able to note that when you flush the toilet you can see the track whizzing by underneath. After exhaustively testing the little tables that pop up out of your armrest, we dined on food that definitely beat out our last plane ride. We arrived, picked up our rental minivan (thank you, Budget!) and checked into the Delta Hotel. The rooms were quite sumptuous (thank you, Delta!) with a perfect view of the passenger trains coming and going. Always choose the middle west elevator when planning an elevator ride at the Delta, as it gives a marvelous view of the city as you zoom upwards. Another tip: as you zoom downwards, there comes a point where the elevator dives back into the building. Immediately following this is the indoor swimming pool, momentarily visible in all its blueness through the glass wall. The effect is quite stimulating. We returned to the twenty-eighth floor several times to rerun the whole business.

Rebecca assigned everyone their beds, drawers, and closet space, supervised the unpacking, and made sure all the Beanie Babies got comfortably settled in. James decided he liked the taste of the little bottles of mouthwash in the bathroom. Ben discovered that the beds were awesome for jumping on.

Supper was upstairs in the exotic revolving restaurant, where guests are encouraged to respect the dress code. After a while I stopped worrying about the children dashing off every few moments and sprinting around the restaurant, as they inevitably ended up back at our table, having taken in another 360-degree view of Montreal. Out of consideration for our fellow guests, we had booked in early, thus avoiding possible reproving glances of appropriately attired adults sans les kids. Although four of the Birrells ate like pigs, number five, Ben, craved only orange slices, and this is why subsequent diners found strange gaps in otherwise magnificently displayed buffet items. We said "*merci*" to the unsmiling waiters, rode on the middle west elevator for a while, and went to bed.

Next morning we were joined by Uncle Rodney, dressed in a classy suit that would surely have satisfied those unsmiling waiters, and we set off for the highlight of our trip. We had been invited to spend a day on the set of "Zoboomafoo," one of the hottest kids' shows currently running, and meet the stars Martin and Chris Kratt. It was to be a day of surprises.

Having arrived early at what appeared to be a large warehouse, we tentatively and apologetically approached the first person in sight, who loudly announced, "The VIPs are here!" Chris and Martin's personal assistant, Annick, took us under her wing, and the fun started. She handed us the call sheet for Day Twenty, a kind of "Bible of the day" that tells every one of the fifty or so personnel in attendance their who, what, where, and when. Today's props: bikes, helmets, backpacks, monster robot, smoke, mud puddle. General crew call 8:00 a.m.; estimated wrap-up time 7:00 p.m. A long day? "No, eleven hours is the norm, and usually we go overtime. Yesterday ended fifteen minutes early, which is unheard of." Okay, we'll try not to waste their time.

First up was the animal holding area. Here we admired the animals booked to appear on the set that day. A large tortoise was placed on the floor, and after a decent pause he stuck out his head and gave us the beady eye. James and Rebecca put on leather gloves, and a great horned owl (cast member #24) clamped onto their arms. A big and very fierce looking water monitor (cast member #109) we were content to leave in his cage, keeping our distance while he glared and periodically flashed out a long forked tongue at us. Note: fatal attacks on humans by water monitors have been recorded.

Annick's headphone squawked, summoning us to the set. Soon we were waiting outside the set for the "filming in progress" light to go off. "It's off!" shouted Ben, and in we went. (Thank goodness Uncle Rodney was there: adult/kid ratio was a manageable one-on-one.) And there we were, in surroundings perfectly familiar to us from watching the show on TV, Chris and Martin approaching us with those great big welcoming smiles, wearing, of course, their trademark T-shirts. Later I thought about this moment a lot, trying to decide whether we were watching the show at home and suddenly we had all stepped into the TV or if the TV screen had magically expanded so as to include us all. Was it a case of us barging in or of them reaching out to us?

The set is a brilliant flourish of imagination, a medley of kid whimsy. I've come to think of a movie set as a very fake affair—all's well as long as the camera points the right way—but this one is quite different. It is a complete entity— no gaps; point the camera where you will and it still looks great. It's a fort, a tree house, a play structure; it's got a ladder, a cave, a pond, swinging doors, a jumping-outside window, a mystery closet, a swinging vine, a clunky wooden snack machine; it's colorful and exciting; and it says unmistakably, "Let's have fun!" That sentiment obviously is shared by Rebecca, James, and Ben, who immediately resurrect the restaurant theme by madly dashing around the set, much encouraged by Chris, Martin, and several dozen studio personnel. Being a good parent, I am mortified by their behavior, convinced that they are about to break something, sure that we are adding expensive studio time, fearful that we will shortly be kicked out. But no; everyone is smiling, and I begin to get a feel for the business at hand. Out of seeming chaos, the words "one, two, three, action!" are heard; everyone shuts up and the cameras roll. Chris and Martin fall off their bikes, or the tortoise pokes his head out of his shell, or Zoboo lands in the mud puddle, or whatever, then "Cut!" and we all start to play again. Then Pierre the director says, "Do it again!" and the whole procedure repeats itself.

"Animal coming!" we hear. Consulting my call sheet, I see that cast member #109, the man-eating water monitor, is about to arrive. (We later read that water monitors can run at speeds of up to ten miles per hour.) We must leave the set and take shelter in the director's booth. Doors swing shut, and the "wrangler" appears, clutching a disgruntled #109, and then it's all eyes to the TV monitors as we watch the next take unfold. This time Zoboo the puppet is on (alias Gordon Robertson, the brave puppeteer).

I think a short diversion at this point is in order. I had been wondering how the children would respond to the revelation that Zoboo, the adorable, quick-talking, bouncy third member of the show, is actually a puppet on the end of the arm of a man of extraordinary talent, the above-mentioned Gordon. Well, there was indeed a moment of shock and disbelief, but for maybe thirty seconds and no more. I was later informed that a good puppeteer strives to become a nonperson, everything being transferred to the puppet. So skilled is this man that you cannot keep your eyes on his face as he talks. His lips move; you know the sound is coming from his mouth; but, try as you might, you relate to the puppet, not the man. Zoboo speaks, and you look the puppet in the eye and respond to the puppet. Moments after meeting Zoboo, Ben is being urged by Chris to run over to Zoboo and tickle him. Off Ben goes; tickle fight ensues, with hoots of laughter; James joins in; man on other end of puppet might as well be invisible for all the attention he gets. (Note: definitely got some sermon material here; must speak to Pastor Jim.)

To continue, Pierre pops James onto the director's chair in front of the TV screens, starts the countdown, and motions to James, who shouts out, "Action!" It's Chris, Martin,

Zoboo, and the uncooperative water monitor...and "Cut!" as a hand appears on the screen to haul the wayward lizard back into position yet again. One begins to see the challenge of keeping to any sort of schedule with guest artists like #109. But apparently this is nothing. During a previous shoot, the crocodile hopped into the pond, and there he stayed. It was two hours before filming could resume. I wonder if Uncle Rodney is calculating the cost overrun caused by one belligerent croc. I digress. Patience and a sense of humor seem to be a prerequisite for this game.

At last it is lunch time. Mind you, everyone has been snacking all along, not least of all the Birrells. But first Chris, Martin, and the cameraman do us a special favor. James' class at Armour Height's School has sent a list of questions, and it has been decided to answer these on camera so the class can view the answers on a VCR. Rebecca reads: "Chris, do you like Martin's driving?" "Are you two really brothers?"

Lunch is a delight. James sits with Chris, Ben with Martin, and Rebecca with Cheryl the producer. I don't see any sliced oranges, but Ben finds something to eat. Marvelous gift packs arrive for the children. I am coming to some pretty firm conclusions about my earlier question. No, we are not barging in; they are reaching out. No, we are not intruding; they all are delighted to have us.

Pam tells a crew member, "You have no idea how much all this means to our family."

"On the contrary," is the response. "Having your family here makes this the most important day of the year for all of us here."

The Birrell family meets the Kratt brothers on the set in Montreal

Once again the Birrell family is bowled over by acts of kindness that we can't even begin to reciprocate. But the day is not over yet. Next stop: the park, for some film footage of Rebecca, James, and Ben playing, to be used on a future show. (No, Nanny, we don't have a date.) Then back to the studio to meet the next animal guest. Bach-O (being an organist by trade, I gravitate to this spelling of the name) is an English mastiff weighing in at 208 pounds, all smiles, licks, and tail wagging. Ben frantically looks for the middle-west-elevator button, sees me instead, and claws his way up to my shoulders. Dog wanders around, politely wagging his tail—whack! whack!—leaving path of destruction. Vaguely wish Bach-O had accompanied us to dinner last night to intimidate unsmiling waiters. Or, even better, joined in 360 dash around restaurant. Back to the set, where Chris and Martin shoot a few scenes romping with the dog, and then, all too soon, it's time for big hugs with everyone. Later Ben informs me, "Hugs are how you show people that you love them." Good one, Ben.

Pierre announces, "Our guests are leaving!" Big round of applause from cast and crew. Thanks, everyone! *Merci!* Thanks, Susan!

James can have the last word: "This is the best day of my life!"

The end.

Hello everyone, again! Pam usually leaves the scriptwriting to me, so I was nicely surprised to find the following on the kitchen table on my return to town tonight. I want to share it with you.   Syd

PAMELA'S REFLECTIONS ON THE BEST DAY OF JAMES' LIFE

As a cancer survivor myself, I am honored with special glimpses into my six-year-old son's world. A world of nausea, baldness, constipation, diarrhea, mouth ulcers, and needles. A world of clowns, trains, bikes, dreams, wishes, and friends, new and old, who make the journey bearable and sometimes wonderful.

James frequently shares thoughts with me that no one else gets to hear. We have our own mini cancer support group. I try to be very respectful of his confidences, but I know that others sometimes need to hear his thoughtful reflections. So often his thoughts lift the burden and pain of those watching him suffer, those who love him very much.

After James and I look at the photos of our recent trip to Montreal, where we spent a day on the set of the wildly popular kids' show "Zoboomafoo" (me hiding the tears I get every time I look at the pictures), James starts talking. "Mom, that was the best day of my life!" We giggle and laugh as we remember tickle fights with Zoboo, swinging on the vines, getting bubble gum from the snack machine, having lunch with Chris and Martin, filming in the park, giant freezies, and meeting really cool animals. (Mom hides more tears as she fears losing the memories of the "best day.")

James becomes more reflective and informs me that he really doesn't want to die. "I'm too young."

I grasp for a response. "I don't want you to die, either. Yes, you are far too young. But sometimes children do die. Sometimes mommies and daddies die. Sometimes life is really hard, and sometimes life is the 'best day.'"

I stumble and fall on my inadequate words. But I am encouraged when I remember our conversation last fall, in the middle of the night when James was completely immobilized by the pain of cancer in his bones. James and I were talking about heaven. James quickly demonstrated how well he has everything figured out by informing me that "Jesus is building a house for me in heaven." (Mom hides her tears yet again.)

I was finishing Dave Dravecky's book Do Not Lose Heart *last night, and I read Dave's thoughts on heaven. I quote: "Think of the best day you've ever had. Remember the joy? The thrill? The sheer happiness that welled up in your heart and burst into uncontrollable laughter and ear-to-ear smiles? Well, that was good, but heaven is better." I now have some new ideas to share with James about heaven. "Hey, James, do you remember that day with Chris and Martin and Zoboo? Well, you know what, James? Heaven will be even better than that day." But I hope that both of us have some more "best days" here first.   Pam*

A brief word to all our wonderful friends and family to say that the latest round of tests show that James' cancer is once again returning. This news is hardly unexpected but is nevertheless disappointing. Any particular neuroblastoma chemo tends to lose its effectiveness after a while. James is experiencing some mild leg pain but is still attending school, playing outside with his friends, having a busy and happy time. On Monday he will start a new regimen of chemo, once again five days of treatment followed by three weeks off, minimal side effects predicted. Please keep praying.   Syd and family

A short note. Reprieve. James has completed five days of what for him is a new chemo, irinotecan. It has reversed the downward trend of the previous ten days. He is without significant leg pain, is walking, running, and generally going wild playing outside with his friends.

Perhaps I could add an anecdote. We had a famous composer, Srul Irving Glick, to dinner this week, prior to his conducting a rehearsal of my Peterborough Singers that night. Mr. Glick is also battling cancer, so he and Pam and James had much to share during his visit. At one point Mr. Glick commented how important it is to have friends who can help you get through cancer, to which James added, "Yes, and friends are like very valuable treasure." So to all you valuable treasures, thank you once again for your friendship.   Syd

To our many friends:

We want to tell you that James is doing very well today. This week's chemo (round two of the new one) has gone well. James took a fairly advanced Technic Lego toy ("Mom, this is a big-boy Lego, ages nine to fourteen!") to assemble while plugged into the chemo IV line. He loves these part-machine, part-monster, part-spaceship items. This one is in two pieces: the "puncher," which when you squeeze the levers pops out a pair of articulated mini boxing gloves, and a "spider space-ship," which randomly scoots around the floor until you hit it in the right place with the "puncher." Ben went with James to chemo, which certainly livened up the oncology unit, most specifically when James sent the "spider" down the hall with Ben in pursuit, aggressively wielding the "puncher." After chemo, James watched the *Apollo 13* movie again, very intrigued with the technical challenges of bringing back the astronauts safely. Then, although it was still only 3:30 p.m., he got dressed for his 6:30 soccer game. James is very excited about playing soccer, as are Rebecca and Ben, and fortunately the rain held off. James played enthusiastically for the first half, and then the chemo barfiness feeling caught up with him, and he sat with Pam and cheered his team on for the second half. A very satisfactory day, free of pain, lots of fun, lots of friends; life is good.

Which once again makes it all the harder for our family to deal with this disease. Many of you ask ever so nicely how we are coping, and I think you would like us to share the not-so-pleasant with you. The unpalatable truth of the matter is that at any given moment James may start experiencing bone pain and need Tylenol; a week later not even morphine will be adequate; by week three essential bodily functions shut down; week four is the funeral. Neuroblastoma is the fastest-growing solid tumor cancer and, so far, is always terminal for post-bone-marrow-transplant relapses. One of the hardest things in the world is to see your child suffer the worst pain imaginable and to be unable to pick him up, cuddle him, comfort him, because that same pain causes him to shrink away from you in fear of even greater pain if you were to do so. Twice we have been to this place.

"You probably have one year, but not two, after relapse." How do you plan family life, sitting on this information? True, we are hoping that the new cure that works in mice and should soon be available for Phase One study in children will turn this deadly disease into a chronic but manageable one, but there are no guarantees.

All of which leaves you in quite a dilemma when it comes to decision making and planning. Questions: Should you take that family summer holiday now in case August is too late? Do you spend the day with James, or should you take advantage of professional or business opportunities as they present themselves? How long will the present chemo keep working? How important is employment? How often every day are you allowed to think about James' mortality? Is it normal to quietly shed tears several times a day? Why is it so hard to watch James having the time of his life every day of his life? Are we spoiling our family by doing too many nice things together? Are we too focused on James, to the detriment of the rest of the family? Each day brings new questions.

But every day is a great day for James. And there is no doubt that cancer has enriched all of our lives immeasurably. The words *friend* and *family* have taken on such a new and deeper meaning. Looking back on the difficult decisions we have had to make, we recognize the hand of God.

Looking around us, we see the love of God in the people who share our burden. Thank you for staying with us on this long journey to an unknown destination.   Syd, Pam, and family

P.S. If you've got any books on the Apollo space program that are going begging, James would love them. So would I, actually.   Syd

SUBJECT: BOYS, ROCKETS, REBECCA TURNS EIGHT
SENT: JUNE 21, 2000 6:44 PM

Since the last report, James has had two rounds of chemo and the usual bimonthly battery of tests at Sick Kids. These show very little change from two months ago. There are still many cancer sites throughout his body. However, there are no new lesions (good), and the biopsies show the cancer cells to be mature and differentiated (also good; not growing).

James is in no pain and is very active, playing soccer, riding his bike, outside playing street hockey with the neighborhood kids, attending school, and generally having a good time. The cancer for now is being held in check by the latest chemo. When this chemo fails, we hope that the experimental "mouse medicine" they are working on at HSC will have been approved and that James will be eligible and able to start that treatment. Currently there are no other worthwhile treatment options to follow the present chemo.

We have had one tricky decision to make regarding James' central line. This is the little tube thing that hangs out of his chest, with a port in the end through which medicine can be painlessly injected, chemo run, and blood drawn out. Very handy, but it must be kept sterile under a special dressing (don't get it wet!), and generally we have to be careful not to bump it. This is a great hardship for James, as he loves swimming and playing on the beach at the cottage. So we have decided—or, I should say, James has decided—to replace the lumen with a port-a-cath. This device sits under the skin of the chest, where it is connected up to his arteries somewhere or other, and is accessed by poking a special needle through the skin and through the rubber membrane of the port. When not being accessed, James can do what he likes; in addition, the risk of infection is eliminated. It is a bit more of a bother to use, but the benefits at this stage outweigh the disadvantages. James had a port-a-cath thirty months ago for the first six months of treatment. Surgery to insert the new line has been booked for next Tuesday, June 27th. Twelve days later he will be clear to swim.

So much for the medical stuff.

The Apollo 13 theme continues to flourish. Both boys now have homemade Apollo 13 rockets; however, James added an escape tower to the top of his, ostensibly for the sake of authenticity but really just to make his taller than Ben's. Some Apollo 13 books have arrived courtesy of our email friends, and James has been soaking up the technical details (why couldn't they reopen the reac valves after they closed them?). On the carbon dioxide buildup, we had the following dialogue:

James: "And I know why there was too much carbon dioxide!"

Syd: "Why?"

James: "Because there were four astronauts on Apollo 13 instead of the three there were supposed to be."

Syd: "Who was the fourth astronaut? There's only three in the movie."

James: "Well, it was the one who was holding the camera to make the movie, silly Dad!"

In other news, Rebecca has turned eight and is planning a sleepover birthday party at the cottage this weekend. Ben is enjoying soccer and just finished this year's gymnastic classes with an entertaining open house. Pamela has moved up to the next level at yoga class and completed a course in therapeutic touch. Recently Pam visited her oncologist for a checkup and received a good report. Now that the choir season is over, I am enjoying evenings at home with the family, especially the "Read me a story!" at bedtime part. Rental and administrative duties remain heavy. Rest assured that we are having lots of family fun.

Thank you for your prayers.   Syd and family

In haste: James' surgery to insert a port-a-cath yesterday went very well. There was very little bleeding despite some serious concerns about his poor blood clotting. Due to endless delays, James went for surgery five hours late, James without food and drink since the day before. This also means Syd without food, as James and I have a gentleman's agreement on this matter. James spent most of his waiting time reviewing his postop menu: "I always have spaghetti and meatballs with cherry Coke after my operations." Fortunately for both of us, we were spared the other test of solidarity, the scratch-and-bleed clotting test, at the last minute after the lab admitted to blundering on the blood work. Syd and James ended up spending the night post-surgery at Sick Kids (sans toothbrush, sleeping pills, razor, deodorant, five pillows––poor Syd, feeling sorry for myself). Later in the evening we got to eat, summed up on our return home with the words, "I got to eat my breakfast, lunch, and dinner all at the same time!"

This morning's dressing change proved to be very painful for James. I confess to buying James another unreasonably expensive Lego toy to staunch the tears. However, the incision site did look good, so we are cleared to head off to the cottage ASAP. James once again showed his determination to get the job done. He wants to spend his summer swimming, and if that means surgery, missing school, IV pokes, whatever, he just does it. A couple of days ago I found James grinning from ear to ear, lying on the floor, saying, "Dad, when I get my port-a-cath in, I'm going to be lying down in the water like this, getting my whole body wet, even my chest; it will feel so good!" With luck, he'll be all healed up in a week and in the lake with the other kids. Syd and family

I often wonder what to say when people ask, "How is James?" Usually I include the *today* word in my response, as in, "Today, James is doing very well," because the timetable for this disease is anyone's guess. I very much like the rather dry phrase used by James' Peterborough oncologist, "The prognosis remains guarded," a phrase that leaves room for hope in the face of statistical evidence to the contrary. There have been three crises during James' battle with neuroblastoma when Pam and I were left with no hope for his immediate survival, and it is a terrible place to be. I better understand why hope is part of the great biblical trilogy: "And now abide faith, hope, love, these three" (1 Corinthians 13:13). So, although we are living with a "guarded" prognosis for both James and Pam, I am pleased to report that our summer to date has been quite delightful.

Central to the last eight weeks are two things: James' surgery to implant a port-a-cath so as to allow swimming, and our cottage on Tangamong Lake, with its beautiful beach. Every spare moment, we are there. No electricity (ha! no TV, no computer!), no phone, lots of family time instead. The possibilities are endless. I very much like the idea that successful parenting includes creating memories for your children that they can carry with them throughout their lives. James' memories of the summer are: "catching seventy-seven minnows, building the tree house, swimming every day, learning to drive the boat, playing crazy eights with my brother and sister, learning to do plumbing with my dad, sailing in the sailboat, playing chess with Ben, having lots of fun with our friends, lighting the fireplace, going to Peck's Camp to buy candy, reading books with my mom and dad, making crafts, playing tennis [yes, two of our neighbors have tennis courts], playing hide-and-seek, surfing behind the Zerker's motorboat, watching the sun go down, playing Water World at the beach, going fishing."

James driving the boat at the cottage

James and Rebecca on the screened-in porch at the cottage

It is wonderful to watch our children playing so well together, enjoying each other, living life to the fullest. As you may have noticed, the weather this summer has been somewhat bizarre. At our cottage there seems to be something of a Great Divide. When the daily thunderstorm arrives, it is as though the center of the lake forms a meteorological barrier: just to the west, brilliant sunshine, while overhead and to the east, torrential rain pours down. It's a violent thunderstorm and a beautiful sunny day all at the same time. Although it's cancer for two of our family along with that guarded prognosis, for the Birrell family one could hardly imagine life being better. We are having a wonderful summer. I hope you are too.   Syd and family

P.S. James was voted Most Valuable Player at soccer last week!

For some time I have been meaning to let all you James News readers know how encouraging it is to Pam and I to receive your responses to the updates. Your thoughts give us strength to continue. Thanks!   Syd

Author's Note: After much thought, I have left this email untouched, written a year and a week before the World Trade Towers lost their innocence.

James' health being superb right now, I want to share with you a nice thing that happened as a result of a not so nice foul-up.

CHAPTER ONE: THE BAD PART

This story starts with Lugol, 0.25 mls, to be taken orally, leading up to and following an MIBG scan. Lugol has an appalling taste that initially burns your mouth, stains your tongue and throat, and then lingers for the rest of the day, reminding you, according to James, of rotting apples and tomatoes and other very bad things. We have all tried it, just the smallest drop on the tip of a toothpick, and it has the foulest imaginable taste, and we think that anyone who prescribes this medicine ought to try it themselves first. There is an excellent reason for taking Lugol, as it protects the thyroid from being damaged by the MIBG isotope. We just wish there was a better way of taking the Lugol. Please don't bother writing to suggest jam, ice cream, mushed bananas, Kool-Aid, what your grandmother used to do, etc., because nothing works.

MIBG is the short form of a very long word that even the nuclear medicine technicians sometimes forget. It's a diagnostic tool that is particularly useful if you are looking for soft tumors. From a layman's perspective: a radioactive isotope with a thirteen-hour half-life is injected into your body; it tends to collect in any cancer tumors; and a day or so later you lie very still on a movable table while two fancy camera things (called Freddie and Eddie) close in and pick up the radiation emitting from various parts of your body. Each image takes ten minutes, so a full body scan takes an hour or two. Now you know enough background to pick up the story as of August 16th, the day before his scheduled MIBG scan.

While James was contemplating a dose of Lugol, the MIBG isotope was being prepared in a particle accelerator in Vancouver. While James was getting ready for bed, couriers for the drug company MDS Nordion were rushing the isotope with its thirteen-hour half-life to Vancouver airport. While James slept, the specially marked package was put on an Air Canada cargo flight to Toronto. While James breakfasted, the shipment moved by courier to Toronto General Hospital. While James glared at the next dose of Lugol, Dr. Reilly was performing quality control checks on the newly arrived batch. While James traveled to Sick Kids in Toronto, Dr. Reilly was putting the final touches on this very expensive dose of MIBG.

At least this was the plan. What actually happened was that Air Canada goofed and sent the shipment to Calgary instead.

First news of the missing shipment reached us from Sick Kids just as James and I were heading out the door to Toronto. I am glad they caught us in time. It was bad enough to have Lugol twice to no purpose and to cut short our holiday time at the cottage, without a wasted trip to Toronto.

Now you may have wondered how I came to know the game plan outlined above. One thing the cancer business has taught us is that you don't just roll over and die; you do something about it. So I called nuclear medicine at Sick Kids and asked who made this drug. I then phoned the manufacturer, MDS Nordion, and spoke with a very helpful manager called Selma. Armed with a waybill number, I then phoned Air Canada Cargo. After speaking with Air Canada personnel in Calgary and Montreal, I reached the office of the vice president of Air Canada Cargo. I explained somewhat irately that this was not about a lost shipment but about a six-year-old boy called James with cancer and that James deserved some answers.

Chapter Two: The Good Part

The following week, James received a parcel from the vice president of Air Canada Cargo. In it was a model of an Air Canada plane and, more importantly, a letter addressed to James, apologizing for the lost shipment. And then came a phone call from Air Canada Flight Training. Would James, along with his brother and sister, like to try out the Airbus simulator? So it was that Syd, Rebecca, James, and Ben zipped down to Toronto last week (Pam stayed at the cottage to enjoy the heat wave) to be welcomed by Captain Burns aboard one of those incredible examples of technology, for a very exciting hour of simulator time. In the words of Ben: "A simulator is the front part of an airplane on some legs that move, but the back part of the airplane is not there." Not bad for a four year old. You board the simulator via a drawbridge that lifts out of the way once you're on board. You close the door and find yourself in a replica of the Airbus cockpit, perfect to the last detail. Behind the pilot and copilot seats are jump seats for instructors and the like, along with a computer screen that allows the instructor to monitor the pilot while throwing the odd wrench in the works, such as, let's pretend your wheels are stuck up or an engine just fell off. And as you look ahead through the cockpit windows, you see just what you would see parked at the terminal building in Toronto.

I was a little anxious that Rebecca might not find the simulator business quite her thing but was pleasantly surprised by her immediate reaction: "Wow, this is so-ooo cool!" Ben hopped into the copilot's seat first while we strapped in behind. Ben's flight started at the terminal building.

After a zillion preflight checks, we feel a little jerk as the tug begins pushing us away. Out the windows we see the building slowly recede. We gently lurch to one side as the nose wheel turns and the plane turns away from the dock. Another bump as we stop to disconnect from the tug. We receive clearance from the control tower to begin taxiing, so Ben and Captain Burns push forward on the two throttle levers. The engines can be heard revving up. Every little bump in the tarmac is faithfully transmitted to us as we move towards the runway. The view out the windows is unbelievably real. We stop and watch another plane ahead of us take off. The control tower clears us for takeoff, and we move into position on the runway. Then it's throttles full forward; the engines roar; we are pushed back in our seats; and off we go. At 146 knots Ben helps pull back on the stick, and up we go. Pull up the landing gear, Ben! We throttle back and settle in for a cruise around Toronto at 2000 feet. The air is only a mildly turbulent today. The city is laid out below us in great detail; we even see the headlights of cars moving along the highways. Look! there's the CN Tower. Oh no! Ben has decided to fly us into the CN Tower! We descend a little and start lining up with the tower restaurant. We take in the Island Airport, the Skydome, the downtown skyscrapers, but it is the CN Tower that is racing towards us. Wham! We smash through and miraculously emerge in clear skies. Back to the airport for a totally realistic landing. I have great difficulty keeping Rebecca on my lap as we brake sharply with the reverse thrust full on.

James in the Airbus simulator

James' turn. "Where to, James?"

"New York!"

"Okay, set up the computer for New York."

Once again we taxi to the end of the runway, line up, and off we go! Then we cheat a little, and Captain Burns asks for warp speed, and before we know it the children see New York for the first time. There's the Empire State Building; there's the World Trade Towers.

"What are you doing, James?"

"We're gonna fly right between those two towers!"

We bank sharply. We can see the individual windows of the building now, closer and closer.

"We're not going to make it!" and we don't, but it's only a simulator, and we land safely.

Rebecca straps in, and we prepare for our return trip to Toronto. We take off. "Can we fly under the Brooklyn Bridge?" I guess Captain Burns doesn't often fly under bridges, but he agrees and down we go. Lower and lower we fly over the river. Alarms sound as we fly too low.

"Terrain!" speaks the plane's computer urgently, but we continue down.

"There's the bridge!" and we flash underneath.

All too soon, it is time to land at Toronto. "Landing gear down, Rebecca!" But what's this? Our flight instructor is busy setting up a challenge for Rebecca. Lights blink and alarms sound—the port engine is on fire! Rebecca quickly throttles back the engine. The plane slews to one side. James activates the fire extinguisher. Ben—oh no, Ben has fallen asleep. We'll have to manage without him. It's going to be a tricky landing, but Captain Burns lines us up nicely and we make a safe landing. Whew!

I'm not sure what the moral of this story is, but I am very glad that a big company employing thousands of people still has time for a small boy. Thank you, Air Canada! And thank you to all the unnamed people in chapter one who helped get us to chapter two.   Syd and family

SUBJECT: OCTOBER AGAIN
SENT: OCTOBER 2, 2000 4:26 AM

The computer man is coming in a few hours to upgrade the RAM, and having a practical, once-burned, twice-shy kind of attitude towards these things, I thought I better communicate before it's too late. You never know.

I am pleased to report that to all external appearances James looks to be in great health. As you will know from previous reports, the scans show widespread disease throughout his body, but the cancer is "sleeping," as James says. No pain, gaining weight, happy (is it possible for a child to be happier than James is?), life is peachy. The only complaint James carries is the ongoing lack of a dog in the Birrell household, a burden shared by Rebecca and Ben but not by Pam and Syd, who remain appalled by the thought of yet one more complication at 96 Dufferin St. "But we will feed him and walk him and look after him!" Sounds very much like the pre-hamster resolutions, which proved as elusive as peace in the Middle East.

"When did you last feed the hamster?"

"Mom, it's very stinky over here by Butterscotch's cage."
No wonder the late Butterscotch drew blood every time you
put your hand in his/her cage. The matter of gender, by the
way, remains another unsolved mystery.

On a subject infinitely more challenging than dog owner-
ship, perhaps I could share with you a personal load that
Pam and I cannot avoid at this time of year. It looks like this:

OCTOBER 1996: Pamela diagnosed with breast cancer

OCTOBER 1997: James diagnosed with neuroblastoma

OCTOBER 1998: Pamela diagnosed with clinical depression

OCTOBER 1999: James relapsed—neuroblastoma

OCTOBER 2000: ?

I think about this a lot, especially at night, and I take comfort from the deeper meaning we have found in life since
October 1996, the extraordinary new friendships we have
found, and the remarkable adventures we have shared. I
think we have learned to focus better on what's important
in life and have learned a bit about creative confrontation
and pursuing goals. Maybe there's been an improvement in
time management, too. Another deeply moving thing has
been to hear that our story has been of help to others. But
the problem of October disasters still faces us. Now the
Birrells are blessed with an exceptionally talented support
group, so I shared my phobia with my good friend Patrick,
an Anglican priest, but still human, whose response was so
helpful to me that I want to pass it on. I hope that others
may find the message equally encouraging. Here it is:

First, some analysis. The fear is understandable! Lurking behind our Christian consciousness is a vast sea of primitive fears that pagan religions address. These are ancient principalities and powers. One is the old "fate"; somehow there is something predetermined about you, and you neither know it nor can control it, and it is vaguely ominous.

There is another side that crosses many cultures, a variation on fate that is often named "the jealousy of the gods." Or "balance of fate." There is a belief that when something is going well and you acknowledge it, your "luck" will change.

I think the way out of it is partly in insisting on believing rightly; after all, orthodoxy is right worship. That is where we start. We believe in the sovereignty of God; he alone holds our future. We also believe that in Jesus Christ it is revealed that his will for us, even in this fallen world before the final consummation, is always abundant life! So you need to insist on dealing with the future that is in the hand of this God, the Father of Jesus, who has made captive principalities and powers.

But that need not land you in some kind of denial of pain and even your aversion to it. What happened, as my children would say, sucks! I think that you can draw heavily on the psalms—full of honest talk to God, full of protest, full of frank descriptions, but pleading of deliverance and ending in hope.

When you write about James, it is clear that you can discern between the framework of affliction and the good within it. No one can say what befalls one in any given future time. But you must resist the idea of fate, for if you believe it, you allow it to be a curse for you.

I often find it helpful to turn something I know or believe into something I live by, through meditative repetition. Let me make a suggestion: four years of disaster out of how many years of blessing? Whenever the image of the last years surface (they are strong!), can you locate in your memory the best fall ever and think about that fall as well? (Not necessarily instead of, but you need the emotional resource of "good" falls to put the other in perspective.)

This is off the top, practicing psychology without a license. But what is psychology if not the art of the soul?

Blessing. Patrick

Well, I did as Patrick suggested, and an odd thing happened: I found that the last four "disaster" falls were also the best falls. The pain makes you appreciate the good so much more. Maybe we should get a dog. Have a good October!   Syd

SUBJECT: RECURRENCE
SENT: OCTOBER 5, 2000 7:11 AM

I am sorry to report that the last four days have brought a change in James' health. Monday night's leg pain was noted but written off as a way of not going to school. Tuesday's leg pain was there only when specifically questioned about it. Wednesday it hurt at the birthday party. Thursday morning James asked for a piggyback and spread his arms wide out when asked how much his legs hurt. But he still wants to slip over to school for today's pizza lunch.

For James and many other children with neuroblastoma, leg pain is one of the first signs of a recurrence. It would appear that the present chemo, irinotecan, is no longer effective.

Tomorrow we will travel to Sick Kids for a bone scan and other tests, then meet with his wonderful oncologist, Dr. Baruchel. Some difficult decisions will have to be made about future treatment, which will undoubtedly be in the experimental category. Following our Toronto visit we will go to the cottage for a family weekend. We would especially appreciate your prayers (and homemade soups!) at this time.   Syd and family

SUBJECT: BONE SCAN
SENT: OCTOBER 6, 2000 1:31 PM

A short note to you all following our visit to HSC today. We took advantage of the school holiday to bring Rebecca and Ben, so as to include them in James' ongoing treatment. James had a bone scan, which we are pleased to say shows no catastrophic new cancer sites. There is no doubt that the "come and go" leg pain indicates something is up, so next week will include an MIBG scan, an MRI, and a bone marrow biopsy and aspirate. A conference with Dr. Baruchel is planned for Wednesday morning, to discuss and plan further treatment. On a lighter note, we were all able to visit Dr. Reilly's research lab while waiting for James' bone scan contrast to do its stuff.

James was very radioactive and sent the Geiger counter right off the scale; we all got to see cancer cells under the microscope; and Dr. R did some fancy science experiments with the children. We also got the head technician of nuclear med to try some Lugol, along with some other HSC personnel. They don't like it! Dr. Baruchel was too chicken to taste it ("It's not ethical for a doctor to have kid medicine"), and he just had one of our delicious post-Lugol chocolates instead.

We remain very concerned about the situation and hope to have some answers next week. Thanks for your encouragement.   Syd

---

SUBJECT: MOUSE MEDICINE
SENT: OCTOBER 13, 2000 2:08 PM

James is feeling pretty good today as he heads back home after three days of tests at Sick Kids. To recap: over the last twelve days James has had some leg pain; we did a bunch of tests: bone scan clear, MIBG shows disease but unchanged, bone aspirate clear, LDH and ferritin normal, nothing obvious showed up. Nevertheless, leg pain is a pretty big red flag when dealing with neuroblastoma, so it was generally agreed that it was time to explore new treatment options. We met with Dr. Baruchel (I like the way James and Dr. Baruchel begin every checkup with a big hug), and here's what we came up with:

—Irinotecan, the chemo we have been using lately, is probably losing its efficacy.

—There is no other standard known therapy to try. We've used them all up.

—We do not have a lot of time.

Now, as I mentioned in earlier updates, one of the most promising new protocols comes out of Dr. Baruchel's own research group, and it's called "A Pilot Phase I/II Study of Low Dose Chemotherapy and Cyclo-Oxygenase-2 Inhibitor as Anti-Angiogenic Therapy"—but we call it the "mouse medicine," just to be different. Dr. B is very good at explaining this project, but I forgot to invite you all to attend last Wednesday's consultation, so here's my understanding of it all:

First you take a lot of lab mice and surgically implant live neuroblastoma tumors. Then you divide the mice into four groups as follows and see what happens:

GROUP 1. Control group; no treatment given: mice all dead in 25 days

GROUP 2. Mice receive low-dose chemo: mice dead in 60 days

GROUP 3. Mice given drug very similar to Celebrex, an arthritis drug: mice all dead in 80 days

GROUP 4. Mice given low-dose chemo and Celebrex substitute: mice still alive after 180 days, and tumors have disappeared

As you might guess, the Group 4 therapy grabs your attention. The thinking behind this treatment is contrary to normal chemo strategy, which involves big blasts of chemo to kill as many cancer cells as possible, followed by a rest period to allow the patient to recover from the some pretty major side effects. Here, instead, the idea is to cut the growth of new blood vessels that a tumor needs to grow, using a constant dose of the two medicines. It's called metronomic chemo (like a metronome—it just keeps ticking away). Apparently tumors give off two hormones that stimulate the growth of new blood vessels, bVGF and VEGF, along with two molecules called PGE2 and V-CAM 1. The treatment aims to stop or slow down these guys and consequently starve the tumor. James will have ongoing blood work to track this quartet. The nice thing about this protocol is the lack of any side effects, because the chemo is very low dose. The pain-in-the-butt side of this treatment is that chemo will be three times a week, forever (a five-minute procedure at St. Jo's). Celebrex morning and night is quite manageable.

So we have signed up for this new treatment, and James will be the fourth child on the Phase I study at HSC. The study started this August, so it is too soon to know how effective it is, but it sure looks good to us, especially in view of the lack of alternatives. To launch James into the program we will be in Toronto frequently over the next two weeks, so all those soups you have been sending are most welcome.

I must say that we feel very good now that we have a plan, even if it is a journey into the unknown. On a different tack, let me close with a short anecdote. We were driving James to Sick Kids, going down Avenue Road in Toronto, when I remembered that we were driving by the street where our friend Srul Irving Glick, the composer, lives. Srul has just successfully completed a bone marrow transplant, and he and James are buddies. Srul's house is full of magical things, like a real merry-go-round horse, and a hidden silver tea set that appears when you press the remote control, and lots of other fascinating things. So I asked James what he liked best in Srul's house. His answer was, "My favorite thing in that house is not a thing; it is Mr. Glick!" Bye for now.   Syd and family

The last few days have seen the pain disappear and James zooming around like any other six year old. Monday through Thursday, James attended Sick Kids to give countless blood samples geared at monitoring the levels of the new (for James) drug Celebrex in his bloodstream. We stayed at Rosie's nice house nearby and cluttered up the place with Hot Wheels track. James and I also discovered Toronto's most economical kid entertainment: for $2.50, father and son were able to ride in the front seat of numerous subway trains for most of the afternoon. The part where you go over the Don Valley Bridge we did four times in a row.

Next Monday we return to Toronto for three days to begin the chemo part of the mouse medicine, which once again requires frequent blood work.

Thereafter the treatment reverts to Peterborough, with quick chemos on Mondays, Wednesdays, and Fridays, forever, and Celebrex pills twice daily. No side effects are expected. One item to note: James' refusal to swallow the Celebrex capsules whole has been cause for mounting concern at HSC, as no one knows if sprinkling the contents on ice cream or your tongue compromises the dose. Unfortunately no amount of scientific reasoning could persuade James. However Nanny solved the problem speedily with a five dollar bill, so thank you, Nanny! And thank you, everyone, for all your support, prayers and encouragement. Syd

SUBJECT: TELEMARKETING AND A MOVIE STAR
SENT: OCTOBER 27, 2000 2:29 PM

FROM LAST NIGHT:

Phone rings.

Pam: "Hello?"

Voice: "Is this the Birrell residence?"

Pam: "Yes." Deep suspicion. *What are they trying to sell me this time? Telemarketing scam?*

Voice: "I am calling at the request of Susan M, and I wish to speak with James."

Pam: "I'm sorry, James is not in. Is…is this Tom Hanks?"

Voice: "That's right; you just won the prize!"

And that's how the latest Birrell adventure began. Next day Tom called again, but James had gone to school for the first full day in three weeks, so Syd got to yak. The third call found all the children at home, with Deb, our homemaker from Red Cross, busy in the background and very anxious to see James' face when he talked with Tom. Rebecca was first, and spoke for ten minutes about school, Armour Heights, music, science, and acting. Tom found out all about Rebecca's upcoming performance in *Oliver* and told her that his niece took part in *Oliver* just last year. (Hello, St. James Players, Tom Hanks knows about your *Oliver*!) Rebecca said "bye" and immediately called her best friend, the other Rebecca, on the other phone line. "I just talked with Tom Hanks, and he's a famous movie star!"

Ben was next, but Ben is only four years old and was too shy. Tom Hanks said that was all right; his own five year old never used to talk on the phone when he was four. So James took the phone.

Now James has no difficulty chatting with anyone, so he and Tom covered a lot of ground fast. Soon Tom was firing off *Apollo 13* questions for James to answer:

"What did we call the Lunar Module?"

"The LEM."

"What was running out in the spacecraft?"

"Oxygen."

"What did they use to make water?"

"Hydrogen and oxygen."

They chatted about Halloween. "What are you going to dress up as?"

"A spider! And that's because my sister is really scared of spiders!"

Twenty-five minutes later, it was time to say good-bye. But I had one last request: "Tom, would you say hi to Deb?"

and I thrust the receiver into Deb's hands and reached for the camera.

Tom is never at a loss for words, either. "Hi, Deb, how do you fit into the picture?"

Poor Deb; eyes popping out, she's a quivering wreck. Meanwhile Deb's pager is paging. Photo op. "I...I...I'm James' homemaker."

Tom did his best and smoothest, and soon Deb was talking with him about how wonderful the children were. And then in her consternation she blurted out, "You must come to Peterborough and meet them."

"Where's Peterborough, Deb? Is it near Toronto?"

"I don't know!" wailed a beautifully flustered Deb, long-time Peterborough resident. Photo op 2. (Note: overheard Deb talking to Red Cross a little later: "I couldn't call back sooner because I was talking to Tom Hanks...It's true!...I am not lying...I was so!")

Well, we're off for a much needed weekend break; James is pain free; and we seem to have successfully launched the mouse medicine protocol.

Thank you, Susan and Tom, for making our day!   Syd

SUBJECT: "YOU'VE GOT MAIL"
SENT: NOVEMBER 11, 2000 1:52 PM

A little card arrived to tell us we had a parcel down at the post office. Pam went to investigate. It was a large package. From Tom Hanks. For all of us. With individual letters, on

Tom Hanks stationary, typed on a real, old-fashioned type-writer. I didn't know anyone used those things any more.

"You've got mail!" What has Tom Hanks sent us?

"Dear Rebecca,

I can't believe you are actually in a production of *Oliver* and you are only eight years old. I was not in a play until the fifth grade, and that was only a short play we did at school." Lots more, but I feel reluctant to share a private letter verbatim.

"Dear James,

I greatly enjoyed talking to you on the phone, just a couple of days, really, before your birthday. To be seven years old is a great thing, so much more wisdom than being a mere six."

"Dear Pam and Syd,

You have two pretty swell kids there. I will give shy Ben the benefit of the doubt and assume he is swell, too...Give Ben my best regards."

Ben was too shy to talk last week when Tom phoned. He was the only Birrell not to get a letter and has decided from now on he will not be shy on the phone. Lesson learned.

And some gifts: a complete set of the video series "From the Earth to the Moon" and a toy astronaut.

"I hope you enjoy this astronaut I have sent along to you. It's from the Gemini 4 mission. A friend of mine gave me this toy, but I have not been able to play with it much, so I want you to have it."

One can't help musing on Tom Hanks's willingness to share his time in this way. Somehow his thoughtfulness doesn't fit the picture that the press leaves us of the super-rich film star flitting from one glamorous party to the next. Like the manual typewriter, it's an idea that seems very old-fashioned and out of place in the new millennium. But in the face of arguments to the contrary, it fits, this "retro" personal touch, this reaching out from a family man to another family, with a bit of encouragement. Syd

P.S. Tom spelled my name right!

I thought you might be interested in the ups and downs of a typical week with James at Sick Kids Hospital, so here goes. Believe it or not, this is a very abbreviated version.

This week marked the end of two months on the new antiangiogenic treatment (the mouse medicine), so James and I returned to Sick Kids on Monday and Wednesday and Thursday for tests, scans, blood work, and a visit with Dr. Baruchel. Although we have no results to report yet, I thought you might like to know what happens on a typical visit to the hospital.

We always plan to include some nice things on these trips, to make up for the yucky stuff. So James decided we should drive as far as Oshawa on Monday morning and then catch the GO Train to Toronto, an inspired decision in view of the impending snowstorm. As you know, trains are a big deal for James, and we went right to the front car so we could talk with the engineer. The first car is actually the last car when traveling west, because the train doesn't turn around at the end of the line; it just returns backwards. We found out that the coaches only weigh forty-four tons because they are built of aluminum and that the driver can enter the station at sixty miles per hour and still stop in time because of the dynamic braking. This trip proved to be immensely satisfying, because the train broke down shortly after departure. We got to listen as the engineer talked with the repair guys as they traced the problem to a brake connection between coaches one and two.

But now we were running late, so at Union Station we hopped lickety-split onto a subway train, where a nice lady gave up her seat at the front of the train so James could look out on to the track as we zoomed through the tunnel. Run, run, we mustn't be late for the MRI…and we made it just in time.

"Yes, we are running on time today, maybe five or ten minutes behind," said the receptionist. And now it's time to ponder on that adage of seasoned hospital visitors, "Hurry up and wait!" for we were to wait an hour and three-quarters before moving on to the scan. We sat down on the floor and made a giant truck with sixteen wheels out of Duplo blocks. It didn't drive very well, so we discussed the scrubbing of tires on transport trucks as they turn, and reassembled it as an articulated giant truck. It then drove very nicely around the waiting room, filled as usual with worried-looking parents.

The MRI (magnetic resonance imaging, I think) is James' favorite scan, because it is very noisy, and you have to wear hearing protection, and there is lots of vibration, and you are strapped tightly onto a moving bed that pops in and out of this huge magnet thing, and it's very much like being an astronaut on Apollo 13. The magnet is so strong that it can rip bullets right out of your body. James had to fill out a form ahead of time, promising he had no bullets in his body that he was aware of and that he was not a welder by profession (small bits of metal in your eyes, in case you were wondering). In the event, James fell asleep for the hour it took to do the MRI. The snow was falling heavily as we left the hospital, and it was a great pleasure to look out the GO Train window at some monumental traffic jams as we sped back to Oshawa. Then home to Peterborough in our trusty all-wheel-drive Subaru.

On Wednesday we returned for "Hurry up and wait" #2. Dr. Baruchel was only forty-five minutes behind schedule, which we figure is pretty good for a doctor. His nurse (manager? handler?) is Janet Gammon, and it looked as if she had her work cut out for her as she ushered him down the hallway to our consult room. Unless she is vigilant, Dr. B tends to wander off. James was assigned to Dr. B a year ago when the cancer returned, to receive palliative care under Dr. B's program, with special emphasis on quality of life.

Janet's job is to make everything happen the way it should with regard to James' treatment, but she also spends a lot of time handholding when Pam and I are on edge about things, which is most of the time.

Anyway, Dr. Baruchel walked in, and first thing, as always, he went to James, shook his hand, smiled and greeted him, and took a good look at him. Now some medical people have a different style with kid patients, and they first read the charts, then ask the parents some questions, and basically ignore the child. James does not respond well to that method, and neither do his parents. It makes you feel like your child is a recurrent neuroblastoma Stage IV instead of a person. Dr. B leaves you with the feeling that his business is the whole person and not just the disease.

Today's consult was a pretty happy affair, with James clearly in great shape, gaining weight, pain free, full of energy, and enjoying life to the fullest.

Next we went to the IV room, where nurse Claire and James quickly became friends and discussed the best way of getting an IV into James' hand.

"Do you like to count one, two, three before the needle goes in, James?"

"Yup."

With a skilled nurse who relates well with kids, this whole business is a no-brainer, and so it was today. James helped himself to candies, and off we went to diagnostic imaging.

The MIBG scan is in two stages. Today James was to be injected with the radioactive substance, which then collects in the tumors and lesions, ready to be scanned twenty-four hours later. Another "Hurry up and wait," the hour-and-a-half wait being long enough to watch a full episode of *Tom Sawyer*, which James really liked, especially when Injun Joe fell to his well-deserved death in the cave. After the injection, we decided to go look for Dr. Reilly, head of radiopharmaceuticals over at Toronto General Hospital. Deep down under the downtown hospitals is a network of tunnels connecting them, so we took that route for a change, and it proved quite a challenge to find our way. We had to get past a rather stern looking nurse guarding nuclear medicine, but then there was Dr. Reilly, who had figured out we might be over, waiting to welcome us.

Ever since Air Canada lost the MIBG shipment, Dr. Reilly has been "scientist at large" for our children. Today he had ordered up a cage of mice from the lab to show James. These are the special mice that are used for cancer research, called "nude mice" (thirty dollars each), with no fur and no immune system. They have no T-cells, so if you inject them with live cancer cells, a tumor quickly grows. If they catch a cold, they die. James used a sterile glove to pick one up, making very sure not to get bitten by its very sharp teeth. Then we moved on to an experiment that Rebecca thought up. We got out the dirty penny she had chosen and put it in a Petri dish to see what kind of bacteria would grow. James shoved his thumb in as well, to see what that would produce. Note: Rebecca got top mark in a recent science test at school. How come? "I got really interested in science when I visited Dr. Reilly's lab."

On our return to HSC via the tunnels, James stunned me by recalling in reverse precisely how to navigate back through the maze of tunnels. Now we had a bit of time, so we went and found Rita, one of James' favorite nurses at HSC. Rita had nursed James as he lay close to death last November and then had watched him turn the corner in December. But she hadn't seen him since his return to good health, and this was a James twenty pounds heavier, bursting with energy. Time for big hugs, big smiles. Rita is one of many who have given so much of themselves to make James better.

Thursday we returned for the MIBG scan. We were bumped by a high-priority patient, so we phoned Deborah in Public Affairs and invited her for coffee. Deborah is putting together a big do next week to recognize a large private donation to the hospital, and James has been invited to attend as an example of what can be achieved with your research dollar. We sat by the indoor fountain and visited while James threw pennies into the waterfalls. Soon James was fishing out the silver coins, turning them in for pennies at the cafeteria, and returning to toss in handfuls of pennies. Then an outraged parent appeared with James in tow, asking if we were his parents, and did we know he was climbing on the fountain and stealing the money? Time to go.

MIBG scan next. And then, as James lay down, everything instantly changed as he casually said, "Every day it is always hurting at the back of my head." The back of his head was the primary site of the "Great Pain" of a year ago.

77

Is the lesion growing again? Is the cancer on the move? Please, not another crisis.

The scan proceeds, and sure enough, a big white hot spot at the back of the head materializes on the monitor. A hot spot can mean many things, good or bad. Reading the scans is a highly skilled task that is reserved for the radiologists, and their reports usually take a week or so to trickle back to the parents. I returned with James to Peterborough with a heavy heart, fearing the worst, and settled into the waiting game that we know all too well.

So there you have it, a round of ongoing tests at the Hospital For Sick Children. (James decided long ago that it should be called the Hospital For Better Children, because that's what they do for kids, make them better.) Each visit is always a time of frustrating delays interspersed with great moments of love, wonderful people to meet, plenty of fun, and times of absolute panic. Pam and I always return home from HSC exhausted and need a few days to process all that's happened. And as I wind up this update, Janet calls with good news: The scans are fine; the disease is stable; stop worrying; and have a good weekend. Thanks, Janet, for a speedy report! We shall go to the movies with the kids and watch *The Grinch*. All the best!   Syd

SUBJECT: GIVING BACK
SENT: DECEMBER 20, 2000 8:10 PM

The Birrell family has benefitted in a big way from the support of our community as we faced the double cancer challenge. Strangers and friends alike have reached out to help carry the load. Pamela and I have made sure that our children understand how much we have received and have encouraged our children to give something back when opportunity presents itself. So I was pleased when Rebecca and James decided to raise some money to buy books for their classes at Armour Heights School. In case you're not up on this issue, you should know that many school boards do not have the budget to properly equip schools with all the new resource books that the new curriculum requires. The school council suggested that $1000 would go a long way to filling the gap in the primary division. We said we would try to help.

And so it was that I gave the children a short lecture on fund-raising at bedtime last night. This morning we all put on nice-looking clothes, practiced shaking hands, reminded ourselves about being polite and saying "thank you," and off we went. We visited a number of local businesses and industries and each time were warmly welcomed and ushered into the boss's office. There Rebecca, or James, or sometimes both, made a brief presentation, picked up a check, shook hands, and said "thank you." Rebecca was extremely eloquent, while James was somewhat more unorthodox at times: "I only got a 'B' on my report card for reading 'cause we don't have any hard books in my class!" Well, James was due at chemo at 11:30, so we didn't have a lot of time, but nevertheless we managed nine visits, and Rebecca made several solicitations on the car phone while we drove. This story ends at lunchtime, by which time James and Rebecca had exceeded their target nicely, with $1200 in checks made payable to the Kawartha Pine Ridge District School Board. By suppertime even more money was arriving.

I think my children learned some useful lessons today. Pam and I feel proud of them and wanted to share the feeling with you. Hope you don't mind. It's nice for our family to be giving something back.   Syd

P.S. We are off to Sick Kids tomorrow. It's a non-medical visit, and it's a secret, but I can say that by Thursday night all will be revealed.

SUBJECT: JAMES MEETS THE PRESS
SENT: DECEMBER 22, 2000 2:55 AM

Hello, everyone,

Our family was invited to be a part of a ceremony at Sick Kids Hospital yesterday afternoon, at which a large donation was made to pediatric oncology. Have you ever seen a pencil with "Hillroy" written on it? Mr. Roy Hill (get it?), having made a nice pile of money supplying children with school supplies, established a charitable foundation before his death, and his heirs recently decided that it could hardly be more appropriate than to give some of that money to help kids with cancer. James was one of three kids attending who have benefitted from the extraordinary expertise of Sick Kids Hospital in treating kid cancer. The donation was enormous, and afterwards Rebecca and James cornered the official holding the envelope and got her to pull out the check. Oddly enough, the Birrells had never seen $5,000,000 before (later James asked me why there are two commas in five million: an observant boy when so inclined), and I freely admit it does give you a bit of a gooey feeling to see it with your own eyes.

The occasion was suitably formal and attended by the oncology doctors who have done so much for James, along with all sorts of important hospital officials and, of course, members of the Roy Hill dynasty. I guess we were there to put a human face on the whole business of fighting cancer in kids, although I did warn Public Affairs that James can be a terror at times. We were interviewed and filmed by the press. If they were looking for evidence of sick children returning to good health, they got it. Why can't they make a silent version of those folding seats you find in auditoriums? Or, better still, supply them with restraining straps. James tried out all possible ways of sitting/climbing on a seat, all the while adjusting the noisy attached folding table. He made faces at the TV people every time they panned in on him, and I recall seeing James, at a serious moment during the speeches, wriggling across the floor until his nose touched the lens of a TV camera. He has come a long way from the little boy who was lying paralyzed and on life support a year ago.

Afterwards we got to say thank you to the Hill family, and James gave the elderly matriarch a big, long hug that was worth at least five million dollars. And I must say, it was very novel to go to the Hospital for Sick Children for non-medical reasons. A first for us, for sure, but I hope not the last.   Syd

SUBJECT: CHRISTMAS EVE PRAYER
SENT DECEMBER 25, 2000 12:13 AM

To our friends,

I write this note with great difficulty, not wishing to dampen your holiday cheer. I have spent several minutes debating whether it is right to share this burden with you at this time, but we do seem to be in another crisis, and we do believe in the power of prayer, and judging by your responses in the past, I think you would like to receive this Christmas Eve email.

James awoke shortly after bedtime, crying because of the pain in his head. This follows a couple of days of headache. We gave him painkillers, but he awoke again, whimpering and clutching his head. More codeine. Then he laughed because it's after midnight and he noticed that his stocking is full of toys. Then, "I think this pain in my head is because there is a tumor growing in my head." Yes, that is our fear, though we have no proof of it yet. "I think I should have a MIBG scan of my head."

Would you have a moment in the midst of your celebrations to pray for James? I take comfort from a verse in Psalm 91:

"You shall not fear the terror by night." Meanwhile, we will seek to tread that path many have walked already and try to celebrate amidst fear and sorrow. Rebecca, James, and Ben have been eagerly waiting for Christmas morning. Thank you.   Syd

SUBJECT: ANSWERED PRAYER
SENT: DECEMBER 25, 2000 5:13 AM

Best Christmas present! James awoke this morning and immediately said in a big excited voice, "The pain in my head is gone!" Thanks for your prayers.

Pam and I are a little emotional this morning, to say the least. It's a very good feeling.   Syd

A short note to thank you all for your prayers. James is once again in fine shape, free of pain and full of bounce. Pam and I are very relieved. We leave town tomorrow, as it has become our custom to celebrate New Year's Day pioneer style at our cottage. There's no phone or electricity, which leaves us without a multitude of distractions when we are aiming for high-quality family time. Besides, long ago we declared our cottage a "Cancer-Free Zone," and we feel the need for a bit of that right now.

Sincerely,   Syd

Well, James and Pam and Ben and Nanny traveled to Toronto on Wednesday to visit Janet and Dr. Baruchel for James' three-month checkup, and it was a good day. I wasn't allowed to go because I took far too much time off over the holidays, had far too much fun, and now I am paying for my sins, trying hard to catch up with work. James' holiday headaches were a hot topic, so Dr. B knocked and tapped and prodded without slightest complaint from James, who has been mentioning the headaches less and less of late. Dr. B could find nothing nasty, which is a big relief for all of us. Ben really enjoyed coming along. We have always felt it important to involve Rebecca and Ben in as much as they wish of the medical business, and we encourage them to ask as many questions as they like. Ben made the sensational discovery that those twirly licorice sticks are now available in his favorite color, blue. Later I made the more predictable discovery that, once licked, they stick to our furniture.

The three-month mark on the new anti-angiogenesis treatment is a good point to take stock of the situation. In October the previous chemo was showing signs of failing, so it was decided to enroll James in the new experimental program. Once a recurrence is under way, experience tells us that without effective treatment the funeral is just three or four weeks away. The new treatment has given us twelve weeks to date, which is very exciting, to say the least. There is still widespread disease throughout James' body, but it is stable, not growing, and perhaps in places beginning to shrink. We are now entering that period where in the animal studies the tide begins to turn and the cancer starts disappearing. That is our fervent hope for James, and for all the other kids facing recurrent neuroblastoma, until now stubbornly terminal. It works in mice; does it work in people?

The thing that astounds me is how lucky we are to have such a high quality of life in between the nasty bits. Whether it's on the medical front or on the home front, we are surrounded by exceptional people. We keep having memorable family adventures, and we keep meeting extraordinary people. Just last week we all went off to Toronto to see *Peter Pan* with some close friends, and I don't know what gave more pleasure, the show itself or witnessing the utter delight of our children as they watched and participated. And of course after the show James got to go back stage and chat with Ernie Coombs (Mr. Dressup, one of the cast), who had painted James a special picture when he was very sick. Christmas was as about as sweet as it can be, full of family meals and visits, with James once again smiling and excited, having rebounded from the head pain of the night before. Our time at our cozy cottage over the New Year was perfect, with fireworks on New Year's Eve, skating on the lake, tobogganing, building igloos, cross-country skiing, friends visiting, and gourmet cooking. We even set a new (unofficial as yet) world record for getting water from the lake while standing on fourteen inches of ice: twenty-eight seconds from the moment we started turning the hand auger to walking away with a full bucket of water. Keep your eyes on *Cottage Life* magazine for a full report.

For Ben, now five, cancer has become a way of life, the good and the bad, he being just ten months old when Pam was diagnosed. At breakfast the other day, Ben brought me James' Celebrex (part of the new treatment) in the child-proof pill bottle and very earnestly said, "Dad, I want you to show me how to open this so when I'm an adult if my kid has cancer I will know how to do it."

Thank you for sticking with us! Happy New Year!   Syd

SUBJECT: LEG PAIN
SENT: JANUARY 20, 2001 1:20 PM

Pam and I would value your prayers just now. Without a lot of warning, the kind of leg pain James experienced during earlier relapses has returned, once again in the right femur. Both the suddenness and the severity of the pain has come as quite a shock to us all. Will keep you posted.   Syd

I am afraid that James' situation has worsened. We are off to Sick Kids where James will be admitted for tests, including a bone scan and an MRI. In haste, Syd

It's Monday night and we've just returned from Toronto. Sick Kids moved very quickly on this latest crisis. Did blood work and a bone scan and met with Dr. Baruchel. James' leg pain remains unexplained. The good news is that neither the blood work nor the bone scan show any new disease. As of now we cannot say that the pain is due to cancer. We will return on Thursday/Friday for an MIBG scan, which is a more powerful tool when it comes to detecting active neuroblastoma. Everyone is puzzled; the pain is very real; and James will continue on codeine and morphine. He is using a wheelchair and a walker to get around and is in much better spirits than Pam and I, though we are improving. Perhaps solving this mystery involves looking at possible side effects of the Celebrex. Thanks for being with us. Pam and Syd

Hello to all of our faithful supporters.
Today we completed round two of the investigation into

James' week-old leg pain. We took the GO Train, James in a very cool kids' wheelchair that he drives around very independently and accompanied by his good friend Bean.

The MIBG scan done today is inconclusive, so we move on to round three for further tests over the next two weeks.

Today's MIBG scan shows no new disease that might obviously explain the pain in his legs. The lesion at the back of his head might look a little bigger, but maybe not; it's open to debate. However, the general opinion is that there are signs of new disease on his vertebrae, and this needs to be investigated; hence the need to move on to round three. This will include an MRI of the leg and spine and an ultrasound (or was it a CT?) of the abdomen. It is possible that disease on or near the spine could produce leg pain. But so could many other things, like influenza, Celebrex side effects, etc.

James is in a lot of pain, but it is now in the left leg and not the right. He takes codeine every four hours, morphine now being held in reserve. His appetite is off, and he has lost three pounds. He has not been to school this week. If things look good tomorrow morning, Dr. Baruchel wants us to go to our cancer-free zone (the cottage) for the weekend and stop worrying for a couple of days. It's been a very difficult week, and that sounds like a good idea to all of us. Our friends at Sick Kids have been very good to us as we grapple with this latest challenge to James' health. I would like to say how much your recent responses have encouraged us. Our sincere thanks.   Syd

Sunday evening news: With great trepidation we set off to the cottage on Saturday afternoon, wondering if we would find ourselves miles from help with a sudden deterioration in James' situation. As is our custom, we stopped at Dad's Donuts in Havelock. James came in too, in his wheelchair, but couldn't see the ice cream selections, so he stood up to see. He made his choice, then realized it wasn't hurting his leg and tried a step or two. To cut a long story short, James is better, pain free, walking, running, jumping, eating, and in great spirits, and off pain meds completely. We had a terrific time at the cottage, and now we're trying to figure out just what all this means. Seven days of pain, heartbreak, terror, insomnia, questions, adrenaline—we just can't get our heads around the whole business. Thanks for standing by us.   Syd

Hello! All five Birrells have recently been interviewed by a wonderfully compassionate psychologist at Sick Kids, called Norma. The idea is to talk about the experiences of a family going through cancer and then use the findings to better help future families though the ordeal. We each talked to Norma individually, and although the conversations were confidential, we were allowed to share in one priceless thought Ben came up with. Ben is now five and has grown up with cancer pretty much a permanent fixture, as he was just ten months old when Pam was diagnosed. When

Norma asked him, right off the bat, what it was like to have someone in the family have cancer, he instantly said, "It's a lot of fun!" Certainly not the way Pam and I see it, but it gave us great comfort to hear our youngest come up with that kind of response. I guess we do try hard to make sure there are exceptionally good times to make up for the exceptionally bad times.

Last weekend was full of memorable events. James climbed up the ladder to help me shovel snow off the roof of our house. Then Ben, James, and I went to Granny and Papa's and managed to include a dog sled ride and a hot air balloon ride in between playing with Granny's cats and all those fabulous toys in her house. Rebecca and Pam went out for a very proper afternoon tea and tried on fancy dresses. Pam and I went to see the movie *Cast Away* and then on to a nice dinner out. Now, if Tom Hanks calls again, we can truthfully tell him how much we liked his latest movie. On Sunday night James and I traveled to Toronto so as to be able to make Monday morning's ultrasound appointment at Sick Kids, and we stayed at Rosie's house overnight. We set up the train set and had a blast, and then Mike brought up his old Lionel train set from the basement. It's fifty-plus years old, so we cleaned it a bit, set up some track, crossed our fingers, and plugged it in. It worked! and James was in seventh heaven. Cancer is lots of fun, right, Ben?

So Monday by contrast was not fun. James (and that of course means me, too—gentleman's agreement, remember?) was not allowed to eat breakfast and instead went off for an abdominal ultrasound. They push hard on your empty stomach with these devices that look like a computer mouse. Here the proceedings were darkened by some black spots on James' liver. After the technician had done her business, the radiologist joined us and spent a good bit of time looking at the liver himself, and despite his cheerful manner, it was clear he didn't like what he was seeing. The official word came later from Dr. Baruchel, and it is that there are three or four small lumps (6 or 7 mm) in James liver, and what they are we do not yet know. Maybe there has been an infection; maybe it's cancer. Further testing is indicated. We will return Wednesday for a bone biopsy and aspirate.

The next scan was an MRI of the right femur. And then after a two hour wait we returned for an MRI of the spine. This scan went on much longer than predicted, which probably also means bad news is coming, but by this time James had been subjected to over five hours of scans in one day, a new record for James, so we took off quick for Peterborough. Later James asked, ever so politely, "I wonder when I will be finished having cancer treatment?" Another "Black Monday" seemed to be a good description of the day, the weekend fun in another century by now. But then I remembered Ben's "It's a lot of fun!" How could I redeem what was left of this day?

Well, as I hit Peterborough I asked James, "How would you like me to buy you a can of shaving cream for your bath tonight?"

"Just for me to use?"

"Yes."

"Wow!" So the yucky day ended very nicely after all, with James and me in the big tub, wasting a whole can of

Gillette's Foamy Shaving Cream. We threw a bunch of medical supplies in the bath and got to work. We filled up an IV bag with shaving cream and then smushed it and watched shaving cream fly everywhere. Then we filled up syringes with it and injected it into the interlink ports and watched it flow down the tubing. We wound up the clockwork Titanic toy and watched it plow through giant shaving cream icebergs. We made shaving cream soup, and James went to bed a happy boy. I am glad Ben reminded us that cancer is supposed to be fun. We will try to claim that concept as we dig deeper into James' present disturbing situation. Good night!   Syd

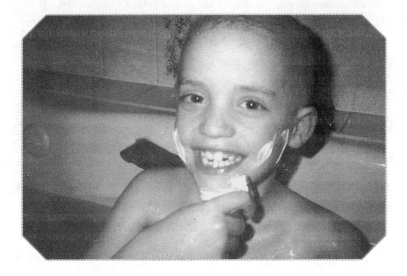

Today James, Pam and I traveled to Sick Kids, where James underwent what he calls the "Butt Poke" procedure. While anesthetized, bone biopsy samples were taken from his pelvic bones and sent off for analysis to see if neuroblastoma is on the move in the bone marrow or not. Results are expected in a few days. Pam and I met with Dr. Baruchel while James was asleep, to talk over the confusing events of the last three weeks. James has undergone many tests lately, and some suggest (maybe) evidence of new disease while others show none. Meanwhile James has rebounded from his week in a wheelchair with severe leg pain and is back to school, in great shape, and pain free. Today's conclusion is that James is back on track, so let's keep on the mouse medicine. We have no evidence to show that the protocol has failed, so there is no reason to change the game plan. Maybe some ups and downs are par for the course. The Birrell position on all this is that we are pleased and encouraged by today's news.

The other piece of good news arrived by courier this morning. It's a marvelous piece of music commissioned by The Peterborough Singers (I'm the conductor), written by Paul Halley, a Grammy-Award-winning Canadian composer. Paul is coming to Peterborough to conduct (and record) the first performance of the work at our upcoming Feb 24th concert. Rather than trying to explain, I think I had better just quote the inscription found on the song, which is called "A House In Heaven." Here it is: "Commissioned by the Peterborough Singers for James Birrell, a boy who showed us we could sing when we thought we could only cry." And on the cover we read: "James Birrell, just six years old, lay close to death. He was suffering from a rare childhood cancer called neuroblastoma. As he lay in great pain, unable to move, he whispered to his mother the words 'Jesus is building me a house in heaven.'" Finally, our friend Tom wrote: "By purchasing this CD you are taking part in a great cause—that of the James Birrell Fund for Neuroblastoma Research. And you are receiving wonderful music that celebrates the joy and spirit of one extraordinary young man. Thank you. Tom Hanks"

There is more to come on the story of this song, because it keeps growing as the days unfold, and it includes a local company that makes dental products, hundreds of dentists across Canada, actor Tom Hanks, funds for neuroblastoma research at Sick Kids, and funds, too, for the new hospital in Peterborough. I will have to save news of this for another email, because choir practice is fifteen minutes away. I hope I don't get too emotional rehearsing this song with the choir for the first time.   Syd

SUBJECT: DIFFICULT DECISION
SENT: FEBRUARY 12, 2001 12:37 PM

It would seem that once again we have come to a crossroad with regards to James' life. The bright, cheerful, energetic boy we put to bed on Friday woke up with a headache on Saturday. By Sunday night he was in great pain, and by Monday morning James was cradling his head with his hands, not turning his neck at all, unable to keep food down, and lying carefully on the sofa all day. Meanwhile both the bone aspirate and bone biopsy have returned positive for neuroblastoma. It would seem highly likely that the pain is due to disease. So tomorrow, barring a turn for the better, Pam and I will talk to James about a decision that only he can make. Does he wish to try a round of aggressive chemo, or does he wish to go to his "house in heaven"? The chemo known as ICE was very effective fourteen months ago and might buy some more time, possibly giving the anti-angiogenic treatment a second chance to work. But it is very toxic, and we will face once again hospital stays, hair loss, transfusions, fevers, etc. Please pray that we all might be given wisdom for this tough time.   Rebecca, James, Benjamin, Pamela, and Syd

---

SUBJECT: BACK HOME BRIEFLY
SENT: FEBRUARY 13, 2001 1:27 AM

Just after writing my short note to you a few hours ago, we dashed down to Sick Kids, thinking we might have got it all confused, as James was showing all the signs of meningitis. After a very thorough examination and blood work and a CT scan, we must have been the first parents in the world to be disappointed that our son did not in fact have meningitis. It really does look like neuroblastoma at work in his head. In one the quiet moments of the evening, while James sat cuddled on Pam's lap, we had a very intimate conversation with James that I am not ready to share the details of just yet. In general we spoke about the choice he needed to make, whether it was time to stop treatment and think about his "house in heaven" or whether it was time to do a big chemo. But I can tell you that James has decided tonight that he will keep fighting cancer and have the big "ICE" chemo. We discussed all those nasty side effects, the barfing, the transfusions, but what is really bothering him is the thought of losing his hair again. I was able to phone home to Rebecca and tell her of James' decision, and she gave a huge sigh of relief and was then too choked up to say much more. By 11 p.m. we were free to go, and we returned home for the night. Tomorrow—actually I think that's today by now—we will return for a consultation and likely start a few days of intensive in-house chemo. Sorry this email lacks coherence; it's past my bedtime. I'll sign off now.   Syd

SUBJECT: OFF WE GO
SENT: FEBRUARY 14, 2001 3:47 PM

A bed has become available, so we are on our way to Sick Kids later tonight. Tomorrow morning James will start the ICE chemo. From James: "I may be weak on the outside of my body, but inside I am very strong and ready to do my chemo." Off we go.   Syd

SUBJECT: HOME
SENT: FEBRUARY 17, 2001 7:31 PM

It's a great thing to come home from Sick Kids, even if that hospital is one of the best in the world. Things went so well (not counting paperwork foul-ups) that James was discharged this morning. All his pain has gone. Compared to fourteen months ago, this round of the "ICE" chemo was a breeze. We were expecting lots of vomiting, so James took down a brand new green "barf bucket" to use during those unpleasant moments, specially inscribed on the inside bottom with "Aim Here!" by his friend Steve. To our amazement, the new bucket only got used once. As usual ,James was looked after by a fabulous set of nurses. I must admit that when the nurse walks into the room and James, recognizing her from his stay fourteen months ago, says, "I missed you so much, Tina!" it does get things off to a good start. Uncle Rodney joined us from Montreal, and that gave Pam and I a bit of breathing space. I did the sleepovers with James in his room while Pam and Rod stayed at Rosie's. We always rig a piece of string from James' bed up to the curtain track on the ceiling and back down to the sofa bed where I sleep and attach an antique bell, so during the night James can wake me melodiously for assistance. Another tip: bring masking tape and disposable diapers to cover the PA speakers in your room. That way you can get the decibels down to an acceptable level. They work even better if you moisten the diapers first. With water.

We have noticed in the past that James often stops eating and walking while in hospital, and this visit followed along those lines. I suppose that's because he's usually in rough shape by the time we are admitted, but I think there's also a bit of the "you're in hospital because you're sick, so act sick while you're there." The interesting thing is how fast all that changes once James leaves the hospital. He began walking again just ten minutes after leaving, the better to check out the candy selection at Candy Island. By the time we reached Peterborough, he was mobile, managed the staircase, and made a good start on the eating. About three weeks from now we will return for an assessment and decide on a game plan. The mouse medicine has worked well for a time and has been the least invasive of all the treatments to date. Maybe we can tinker with it to improve its efficacy. However if yesterday's MRI of the head showed new disease, we may want to try a new drug. There are so many "successful for a while" treatments for neuroblastoma that you can't help thinking that if some serious funding and awareness was given to this disease, a cure would soon follow. Meanwhile, we take it as a good sign that his head pain has disappeared.

The chemo has left him absolutely wiped. Pam's description from her own chemo experience is "your veins feel full of lead; all you can do is lie down; opening your eyes becomes an effort." Which I confess is my state right now, so good night, and thank you for all those encouraging emails, notes, letters, phone calls, soups and casseroles, and child-care, all of which helped us through the week.   Syd

SUBJECT: BACK TO LIFE
SENT: FEBRUARY 22, 2001 12:54 AM

If you can take today by itself and ignore the huge challenges James faces to make it through the next few months, then today was one of the best of days. Today was the day the old James really came roaring back to life. He has been in poor shape after the return of the disease over the last three weeks and was completely wiped by the chemotherapy of last week. There have been lots of days of pain with no walking, no eating, no smiling, no playing. Until James gets up, the morning tends to be fraught with anxiety for the parents. There is always that dread feeling that the new day will bring further deterioration, new symptoms, new pain. But today James surprised us all by bouncing down to breakfast, laughing because he was not the last person up. Then he laughed because the brown sugar had a giant lump in it. Then he laughed because for some reason we were all sitting in the wrong places at the breakfast table. At that point it hit me that I might learn something if I watched James today. He had just been given his life back again, and the way he looked at the world around him was a treat to observe. And he was laughing.

Now it was our expectation that school for James would be out of the picture for some time. But yesterday's blood counts were surprisingly good: "Becca, do you know what my white blood count is? It's 2.5!" Another laugh. "Can I go to school, Mom?" And so we agreed to try the morning at school. It went well, and he was delighted to see all his friends and catch up on some science. Lunch was another occasion to laugh. Because of the Birrell obsession with not sharing our contagious diseases with one another, double-dipping of carrot sticks in the veggie dip is not allowed. With a laugh, James introduced us to his latest invention, the "dip flip," whereby you dip your carrot stick, flip the remainder around, and dip the unbitten end into the dish, and keep your germs to yourself. Good one, James!

Some pretty exciting things happened today, like the TV people interviewing James about the "House in Heaven" song that my Peterborough Singers are premiering in concert this Saturday. And he did get a new Lego set from Uncle Tom. But what challenged me personally today was James' way of looking at what I would label the "daily grind" and taking such pleasure in the simplest of things. And laughing. Somehow it seems so wrong that a child who can embrace a day so wholeheartedly should be denied a future. Yet I cannot deny that he showed me a thing or two today about leaving tomorrow's worries for tomorrow and getting on with the gift of today. Another late night email; I hope it's not too incoherent. Good night.   Syd

SUBJECT: AIR RAIDS
SENT: FEBRUARY 28, 2001 6:48 AM

Sometimes I feel our situation is very like those who lived through the air raids of the Second World War. You hear the air raid sirens; you hope it's a false alarm but you dash for cover; the bombs start falling; you pray they won't fall on your shelter; maybe you sing to keep your spirits up; the all-clear sounds; and you cautiously emerge to survey the damage. Here's our latest air raid: early Saturday morning, James developed a fever. The immune system takes quite a beating from the ICE chemo, and one is very susceptible to serious complications, so we dashed off to the Peterborough hospital and found a safe room where he wouldn't be exposed to sick people with flu bugs and the like. Blood work was done; the IV was hooked up; and an antibiotic was started. James was feeling hungry so they ordered up breakfast, but I had heard that one before, so I slipped out and drove over to the IGA to buy some Lucky Charms cereal and milk. The breakfast tray never did appear. A bed was found, and James was welcomed back by all his nurse friends in pediatrics who have looked after him so well over the years.

Now the weekend was already a busy one for Pam and I, with my Peterborough Singers doing a recording session and two concerts, plus me playing the organ at church and

Pam off to Swan Lake in Toronto with Rebecca, so I was relieved later in the day when James said Pam or I didn't have to sleep overnight at the hospital with him. Of course by 7 a.m. next morning I was feeling very guilty about this, so I whipped over to the hospital to rescue him, only to find James holding court with no less than five nurses, who were sitting on his bed, chatting and playing with him.

The concerts were very moving and ended with the "House In Heaven" song my Peterborough Singers choir had commissioned. The local dentists paid for it, bless them. This is the piece we commissioned from Paul Halley, Grammy-Award-winning composer, and he was there playing the piano for the first performance. I have probably mentioned in previous emails that the song is based on James' words whispered to Pam when we thought we were losing him, "Jesus is building me a house in heaven." Paul has combined this idea with some words from the psalms, the children's hymn "This Is My Father's World," and some very appropriate Canadian poetry. It's a powerful and moving piece, as the one thousand people who attended will attest. It was recorded, and the CD will soon be ready. (I've listened to the pre-edit, and it's very exciting. James grins every time I play it and says, "That's my song!") This is the CD that actor Tom Hanks is going to sign the first 100 copies of, with the proceeds going to the oncology unit of Peterborough's new hospital.

Included in the concert was another Grammy Award winner, flutist Rhonda Larson, who blew us all away with her virtuosity, her musicianship, and her presence, not to mention her stunning good looks. Her role in the show was not immediately apparent, but partway through the first half, as the organ was gently playing, it seemed that Paul Halley was creating new sounds on the organ. Well, he wasn't; it was Rhonda, dressed in some heavenly white outfit, floating down the aisle, playing like an angel all the while. The effect was magical beyond belief.

After the concert, Rhonda asks, "Can we go and see James?" I make a phone call, and off we go. Now, to help protect James from the bugs of other sick children, he was given the last room at the end of the corridor. We arrive; we step out of the elevator, and Rhonda begins to play her flute. The sound floats down the corridor, and once again she begins her enchanting walk down the aisle. Faces pop out of the doors, grinning kids and little babies charmed alike, while James listens from his room. After serenading every patient and peeking in each room, Rhonda makes it to James. Of course they are instantly friends, lounging together on the bed. It's forty minutes before I can drag Rhonda away.

By Monday morning, James was ready to leave hospital. He is now cheerfully busy around the house. He had several blood transfusions over the weekend, and this morning's blood work, I hope, will indicate no more are necessary. The ICE chemo sets back bone marrow production of blood cells in a pretty major way. And this morning the inevitable happened: James' hair is falling out in big clumps. He's laughing about it. Next week it will be time to run some scans and decide what treatment to use next. There's no doubt the air raid siren will sound again and the bombs will start falling; we just hope they keep missing James.   Syd

Somehow I found this brief little scene at the cottage with James and Ben very touching. "I'm having a bad-hair day" happens for thousands of cancer patients undergoing chemotherapy around the world every day. This version takes place in the boys' bedroom at bedtime by the light of an oil lamp, our cottage being delightfully without electricity. I was catching up on paperwork at the time, and so I was able to jot down the conversation as it happened. The mood shifts between hilarious and quietly serious, but mostly the former. B is for Ben and J is for James.

J: "Whenever my head gets really itchy like this, it's time for my hair to fall out."

James gives a trial tug and drops a chunk of hair onto the floor. It comes out very easily. A bald patch appears on his head. Ben watches with the calm acceptance of a five year old. James pulls out another chunk. Then, I guess, Ben senses an unusual opportunity.

B: "James, can I help you pull it out?"

J: "Yes."

Ben reaches over and tentatively pulls.

B: "Nice big mess on the floor!"

J: "Hey! Quit pulling so hard!"

B: "Like that? Nice and slow…This is fun. I'm getting a big load!"

J: "Nuggy!"

B: "It's nice and fluffy!"

J: "Thanks for helping, Ben."

B: " It looks like you're getting a buzz cut, but it's a finger cut."

J: "Nuggy!"

B: "Soon you're not gonna need a haircut for a long time!"

J: "I like it when my hair falls out 'cause then I only have to have my head wiped with a warm wet cloth and no more shampoos!"

B: "James, you look like Captain Hook."

J: "Nuggy!"

B. "What does *nuggy* mean?"

J: "It means, don't pull so hard!"

B: "You look funny, James!"

J: "It is fun to pull your hair out, but it is not funny."

Pause.

B: "James, we missed some over here."

J: "**Dapoo!**"

B: "What's that mean?"

J: "Time to spit some hair out of my mouth!"

Come to think of it, pulling hair out is a very messy business. It gets in your eyes, ears, mouth, and all over everything. Quite regularly the hair puller can be seen with tongue sticking out, groping with fingers for that elusive strand of hair. Spitting is quicker.

J: "Hair tastes really awful!"

B: "Can we use your hair for crafts?"

J: "No way! I'm gonna keep it in an envelope."

B: "Dapoo!"

Fifteen minutes later and we're done. Definitely a nice big pile on the floor. A new look for James. Offhand, we can't figure out if this is the third or fourth time James has lost his hair.

As I type this email, the boys come in and demand that I read it to them. They think it's very funny, and they hoot with laughter, especially at the *Dapoo!* word. I print up a copy, and now they're in the rec room reading it noisily together and playing with the plastic sandwich bag containing his hair. I wasn't looking forward to James losing his hair all over again, but it seems the boys have got the right attitude. **Dapoo!**   Syd

SUBJECT: INTRUDER
SENT: MARCH 15, 2001 2:55 AM

It's 3:30 a.m., and pretty well on schedule I've woken up to have my nightly worry session. It's always some kind of cancer worry, usually a James worry, but often a Pam worry too. The arrival of the worry is much like the "Waz that noise?" you think might be a burglar in your living room, so you jerk instantly awake and alert, straining to hear the intruder. But this week James is in terrific shape, so much so

106

that without Pam or me, he has gone off with Rebecca and Ben for a holiday at Peggy Three's parents' place in Picton. Dr. Baruchel calls it a chemo vacation; ICE has done its work, and for a few days no treatment is necessary, no visits to hospital, no blood work; life is peachy.

Unfortunately the intruder does have an agenda. Tonight the intruder is reminding me for the thousandth time that young Eric has just died, after a lengthy and courageous fight with neuroblastoma. Eric, who always pulled up short of the precipice; Eric, another brave boy who loved life as much as any of us; Eric, who defied the neuroblastoma odds for so long; Eric, whose parents, both PhDs, were always ready to explain the latest innovative treatment to us; Eric, who cheerfully joined us for an energetic romp in the park one summer's day despite the debilitating effects of recent chemo; Eric, tearing around our cottage with his brothers and sister, dressed up as pirates.

Eric's parents also get this email. Thank you, Meg and Paul, for sharing your family's story with us over the months and years that you have faced this dreadful disease. You have been a great source of strength and encouragement.

I don't know how to deal with the intruder tonight, with his stark reminder of the harsh reality of recurrent neuroblastoma. James' chemo vacation/cancer vacation has allowed me to step back and look at him in a more normal light for the last week or so. The medical spotlight has been switched off (I know, just temporarily), and I'm noticing all these interesting details of James. Speaking as a former piano teacher myself, I can say he's a very promising piano player. And his paper airplanes are the envy of the junior choir, with all the other kids asking him to make one for them. His reading skills are quite exceptional for his age, but what I didn't realize is that he can also read his books perfectly well upside down. His grade two teacher at school related how James gave a lecture on structural engineering to the grade threes, drawing bridges on the blackboard to illustrate struts, braces, beams, triangulation. "James is a fabulous structural engineer!" said one kid.

So I'm left to ponder on the legacy of children like James and Eric. So much potential. They give so much to the world. They capture our hearts. They challenge us to give of our best. They lift us beyond the trivial. Tonight's intruder has gone now; I will return to my bed.   Syd

SUBJECT: A MATTER OF MONEY. THE JAMES FUND
SENT: MARCH 16, 2001 1:29 PM

Some time ago I had a late-night hospital hallway chat with an oncologist whose name I have forgotten, but I remember his words distinctly: "A few decades ago, childhood leukemias left 85 percent of the kids dead. We threw a lot of money into research and now 85 percent survive. We need to do the same thing with neuroblastoma."

And more recently I heard the following: "I'm one of thirty-six oncologists that sit on a review board that doles out money for cancer research. Just three of us are pediatric oncologists. Breast cancer, colon cancer, prostate cancer…they get a lot of money and deservedly so. Neuroblastoma?…"

James was one of the twenty-five children diagnosed with neuroblastoma in Ontario in 1997. Many of those kids are now dead; most of the rest have relapsed; and few have hope of five-year survival. James is still alive, thanks to some innovative treatment pioneered by the Hospital for Sick Children, including what James calls "the mouse medicine," which worked well for one hundred days before failing. Intravenous vitamin C is a hot topic in the last month. The acne medicine Acutane has had some success in treating neuroblastoma. There are many tantalizing leads to chase, and it all needs research money. Pam and I have been provoked to try and do something to help. So in conjunction with the Hospital for Sick Children Foundation and with a lot of help from our friends, we have set up the James Birrell Fund for Neuroblastoma Research. It's been set up as what is called a restricted fund.

Unlike an endowment, where only the interest is used, all the money donated to the James Fund must be used immediately for neuroblastoma research at Sick Kids Hospital. The real live launch of the fund takes place on Monday, March 19th, in Peterborough, and I am delighted to report that James' very own oncologist, Dr. Baruchel, will be the guest speaker. (By the way, did you know that his CV/résumé is twenty-eight pages long? Ran out of fax paper.) Murray St. Baptist Church, 7 p.m. Please come if you are able, and bring your checkbook.

These emails I send out have a special place in my heart, and using them to ask for money goes against my feelings about their purpose. It took a great deal of thought and much discussion with friends before I was willing to put out this information in a James letter. My hesitation arose out of the fact that the emails have become very therapeutic for me and my family, and I did not want to complicate that by giving it any other other purpose or by trading on the enormous goodwill of the many people who seem to read these letters. However, Pam and I are convinced that kick-starting some additional research will improve the quality of life for children like James and increase their chance of survival. To be frank, we'd prefer to see "In Honor Of" and not "In Memory Of."

"Please help me fight cancer"
www.JamesBirrell.ca

We have set up a Web site at www.jamesbirrell.ca to raise awareness and to facilitate fund-raising. It's up and running now, so do have a look. Because it's linked to the Sick Kids Foundation site, donations can be made on-line or by the old-fashioned method. And I can't help mentioning that over $27,500 has been pledged since we decided ten days ago to start the fund.

Support comes in so many wonderful ways, and we have been overwhelmed by the caring responses that James' story has brought our way. Thank you.   Syd and Pam

James is very well today. For two weeks he has been striding forward, seizing each day with the exuberance of any happy and active seven-year-old boy—not the slightest hint of disease, full of fun, looking to the future—life is good. The terrifying pain he suffered a few weeks ago and the assault of the ICE chemo has been forgotten. It is not possible to look at James and think terminal cancer.

But Rebecca is right. At bedtime she told me, "I'm really scared, because James has a very rare kind of children's cancer and most of the kids who have it die." The CT scan of James' head, done after the ICE chemo, shows that the old lesion at the back of his skull is still there, dormant perhaps for the moment but threatening at any time to spread to the brain.

Of course there are many other sites of the cancer throughout his body, but this spot is of the most immediate concern. So, in a preemptive move, Dr. Baruchel has advised a chemo not previously used for neuroblastoma but for cancers of the brain, called temozolomide, or Temadol for short. Getting a chemo to cross the blood brain barrier can be a problem, but Temadol can do this, and James began taking it a week ago, four pills a day for forty-two days. Low dose, metronomic, no side effects, no nausea, no hospital visits.

Janet warned us about one possible side effect—fatigue. Observed side effects in James: increased stamina, less sleep required. James always seems to be different.

So once again we are experiencing the neuroblastoma roller coaster, this time the good bit. I guess the Birrell family has seized this moment to move ahead. Rebecca and Pam are moving into the final rehearsals of *Snow White*. We went to the maple sugar farm. We went horse riding. Pam and I had a night off at a wonderful bed and breakfast. And the big focus has been the launch of the James Fund. It involved us all, and in two short weeks we had an event, a Web site, $40,000 in donations, and Ben's first speech in public. The launch night was supposed to be about money, but instead it was all about courage, hope, determination, and love. Who could forget the scene where James took the mike and said, "Ladies and gentlemen, boys and girls, this is my good friend, Dr. Baruchel!" and then two people running across the stage towards each other, James jumping into Dr. Baruchel's arms, big hugs, big smiles, traveling the road together, not as doctor and patient but as friends facing a common enemy.

Dr. Baruchel spoke about "living with the enemy" and asked the question, "Do we have to use a nuclear weapon to destroy a mosquito?" Much of the experimental treatment James has received, such as the mouse medicine, is designed to avoid the major side effects of standard treatments. And then Dr. B had some closing words for James: "Together we are fighting cancer. You are fighting for you.

You are fighting for the others. You are helping us fight cancer. We need you, James. I know there is a house in heaven for you, but you know, somehow I think it's not ready yet...there have been delays in the construction...you know there are always problems with the contractors. Stay with us." We are so lucky to be under the care of Dr. B and his team.

My friend John asked me a question: "What are your battles?" A very helpful question. I think my quick and short response was:

1. Get James though cancer.

2. Get Pam through cancer.

3. Keep Rebecca and Ben nurtured, growing, fulfilling their potential.

4. Take care to look to matters of the soul.

My battles do not include my career right now, although I want to do the best I can in my various jobs. And the battle does not include RRSPs and net worth, although I want to keep the family fed and clothed, with a roof over our heads. The battle question is good, because living with the enemy means always asking the question, "What is important right now?" I think in a different life I recall the idea of waking up in the morning and thinking idly, "What shall I do today?" Now the question seems to be, "What shall I not do today?" Time is so short for James, and we are all learning to discard what is unessential.

I forgot to tell John about one other battle: I am trying to train myself to sleep through the night. Is it a Dr. Ferber I need to see?

Perhaps my children can tell me.   Syd

P.S. Don't forget to visit the James Web site at www.james-birrell.ca I love Rebecca's entry in the guest book. She doesn't use spell-check yet. "Dear James, Even if you are anoing I still pray for you every night."

SUBJECT: THE WIND BLOWS
SENT: APRIL 12, 2001 12:50 PM

My junior choir at our church is made up of sixteen lively and noisy children, including Rebecca, James, and Ben. The children are all very concerned about James, and at the end of last Thursday's practice the children gathered around and laid their hands on James and our pastor prayed for him. It was a simple but sweetly sincere ceremony, reminding me of the Scripture that begins "unless you...become like little children" (Matthew 18:3). My experience of childhood cancer to date has taught me that it's often the children who have the answers rather than the adults. One six-year-old girl stayed behind to tell me that every night she prays for James, that cancer will get better and then he won't die.

The last few weeks have been good ones for James. He has been gaining strength and weight, participating fully at school, playing outside with his friends. We were given tickets for a Blue Jays baseball game, and it did me good to see James hollering, "Go, Jays, go!" at the top of his voice.

And while we were in the neighborhood, our friends at VIA Rail gave us a behind-the-scenes tour of Toronto's Union Station. The boys loved it, especially the visit to the cab of a big diesel locomotive. Then we had a boys' night at the cottage, with campfires and marshmallows, while Rebecca and Pam had a fancy tea party back at home.

The first hiccup arrived last week when at bedtime James said to me, "Dad, in the last ten seconds my head has been hurting right here," pointing to a spot towards the back of his head suspiciously close to the lesion that we know about. Then the next night, "I don't know why I'm getting major headaches whenever I'm trying to go to sleep." I'm afraid I'm still not good at keeping cool when James drops these bombshells, so I go to the medicine cabinet and get a Tylenol for James and a sleeping pill for me.

Then it was Rebecca's turn. "When James gets sick, I feel like dirt. When he is sick, Ben and I don't even feel like we are part of the family." Now Pam and I try very hard to nurture all three children equally, but inevitably there are times of crisis where James becomes the center of attention. When people offer special outings or adventures for James, we turn them down unless the other children can be included. And we try to discourage gifts that are for James only, much as we appreciate people's generosity. Even Ben wants to know how come James gets all the presents.

So this week we have been thinking more carefully about Rebecca's needs, and we talked to teachers, professionals, and friends to seek their advice on the matter. And of course we talked directly to Rebecca. I think she's all right.

Meanwhile James' headaches went away, and Pam and I downgraded from Red Alert to whatever the level of concern below that is. Over the last couple of days James has had some leg pain now and then, which we try to dismiss as overexertion, but, needless to say, we have moved onto a war footing of sorts and have checked the stock of codeine and morphine and made sure the car is full of gas for middle-of-the-night trips. James has just arrived in from school, and when I asked how he felt, he said, "Great!...But my right femur is hurting." So there you are. Things are great but at the same time rather unsettling. James has got a new kite and is beckoning to me, so good-bye for now; we are going to take advantage of the wind while it blows. Syd and family

SUBJECT: REASSESSING
SENT: APRIL 16, 2001 5:13 PM

Today it seems to Pam and I that we are entering a new phase of James' illness where fighting pain is going to be an everyday event. Last week the pain returned in earnest. Over the long weekend Dr. Baruchel came up with the bright idea of restarting Celebrex, which quickly reduced the pain to a manageable level. We changed our plans and zoomed off to the cottage for the day, went for rides on the ice floes, lit bonfires, and had lots of cuddle time reading books. There is a certain "look" on James' face when he is in serious pain, and the Celebrex appears to have banished that look for now. So with the added help of codeine, James forgets about pain when he is busy, active, and having fun. It's only when he slows down, at bedtime for example, that he complains.

Rebecca and Ben joined us for today's trip to Sick Kids, as it is their wish (and ours too) that they be involved in James' ongoing treatment. For now the plan is to continue the daily dose of Temadol chemo along with Celebrex and codeine and see what happens. We don't have conclusive evidence that the present treatment has failed. If the head pain gets too bothersome, we will try a shot of radiation. A repeat of the ICE chemo remains a possibility. As always, the plan also includes family time, so after lunch today we moved on to Casa Loma for a bit of fun and adventure. For our non-Canadian friends, Casa Loma is Toronto's castle, the private endeavor of a wealthy industrialist early in the twentieth century, with suits of armor, towers and turrets, a great hall, secret passages, and suchlike. I'm afraid it doesn't compare with old world castles and country homes, but it was a pile of fun for the children.

I guess we will be reassessing priorities once more and adjusting to the increased demands of James' illness. The tension is to be preparing for the worst while still pushing hard for that elusive cure. Having heard too many horror stories of late about expensive out-of-country miracle treatments, we feel in very good hands with the team at Sick Kids. Thank you for your prayers.   Syd and family

SUBJECT: A SUMMARY OF THE WEEK TO DATE
SENT: APRIL 19, 2001 6:47 AM

MONDAY: James played street hockey with his friends for two hours.

TUESDAY: Right leg hurting, used a walker to get around.

WEDNESDAY: Pain in leg worse, graduated to wheelchair.

THURSDAY: Too much leg pain for transfer to wheelchair; stayed in bed; started using morphine. We are waiting for a response from Sick Kids with regards to another round of the ICE chemo.

On the plus side:

— Head pain is gone; maybe the Temadol chemo is working.

— James is in great spirits for much of the time.

— James was thrilled to chat with Apollo 13 astronaut Jim Lovell, who phoned yesterday. A very timely phone call, courtesy of our wonderful friends at Make-A-Wish.

— We combined all the model railway sets we have been given and built a giant layout in the basement. A great distraction.

In haste, Syd

SUBJECT: JAMES A DAY LATER
SENT: APRIL 20, 2001 11:05 AM

Yesterday was another example of how unpredictable life with cancer can be. Following a late afternoon telephone consultation with oncology where we discussed the fact that the pain was now only in the leg, we decided on a different approach, so instead of checking in for the ICE chemo, we made our way to Princess Margaret Hospital for 9 a.m. this morning.

At simulator B, James lay very still while his sore right leg was scanned and marked up with green marker pens, and then a short while later James cheerfully received 800 rads to the right femur. The radiation room is heavily shielded, and only the patient stays inside for the radiation treatment. This is fine with James, who enjoys these technological adventures, but I had a tearful moment waiting outside. The twelve-inch-thick door slid closed, and the green light reading "Please enter" changed to a red light "Do not enter—room in use." My difficulty lay in accepting that this was palliative treatment and that over the next sixty seconds permanent damage would be done to his right leg, stunting long-term growth and who knows what else. I knew the decision to irradiate was a good one and would control the pain quickly, but it was another step along a road none of us wish to take. Quality of life today got a big boost, while the hope of a cure felt even more distant.

So here we are, having just returned to Peterborough to a lovely spring day. Although the prediction was that James might need a couple of days postradiation before walking, I am pleased to say that he is out in the flower garden, already walking with the help of a cane, no wheelchair, having a great day. One day at a time.   Syd

SUBJECT: JAMES SIX HOURS LATER
SENT: APRIL 21, 2001 2:19 PM

Hello again. Am feeling a little numb, very sleepy, and lacking in initiative.

Yesterday afternoon turned out so well that we decided on another boys' night at the cottage. James, Ben, and I got packed, bought our favorite junk food at IGA, and arrived at the cottage after dark. The boys were asleep, so I lit the wood stove and carried them to bed. It was while I was contemplating which sleeping pill to take that I noticed that James was looking uncomfortable. He was twitching in his sleep; his breathing was laborious; and he had quite a high temperature. In the case of Rebecca and Ben, this means administer some Tylenol and keep the fluids going in. In the case of James, we always wish we could take similar action, and for about two minutes I tried to marshal the arguments for staying put and sitting it out.

So off we zoomed back to Peterborough, James making good use of his green barf bucket while I phoned Sick Kids for advice. Neutrapeanic fever, neuroblastoma on the loose, radiation sickness, food poisoning, and a few other new diseases that I just thought up were all buzzing through my head. Pam was not answering the phone, so I reached Peggy Two, who leapt into action, raced to our home, threw small stones at the bedroom window, and half woke Pam, who remained under the influence of her sleeping pills. I dropped off Ben, hoping he was not going to be traumatized by the night's events, grabbed some medical supplies, such as grippers, three-quarter inch, low profile, for accessing kid ports, and carried on to Emerg. The Peterborough hospital with its new name that I can never remember had everything ready for us except three-quarter-inch grippers, so blood work was quickly done, and number one on the list was ruled out. James' symptoms were very much what we have seen before during recurrences—lots of widespread pain— so we felt foolish thinking it was anything but number two. Face to face with the enemy once again. With great care we moved James up to the Pediatric Unit for the rest of the night, with James crying out in pain as we made the bed-to-bed transfers. By morning, plans were being made for an ambulance transfer to Sick Kids.

And then at 9:30 a.m. James woke up, winked at me, made a few silly faces at me, ate a freezie, ate twenty Cheerios, and said he was feeling much better. I blinked; the nurses blinked; and the pediatrician had a look and then sent us home. James has had a reasonably comfortable day in his wheelchair, doing the usual rainy-day stuff like playing with the train set, computer games, checkers with Ben, playing the piano, and of course, that trial for all parents, the latest Chipmunks video. I am not sure what all this means, but I suppose that as the disease progresses we are going to experience a lot more of these sudden crises. Every parent of a child with recurrent neuroblastoma can tell you similar stories. I have extraordinary respect for families who cope with situations worse than this, along with the medical community that cares for these families. Each time we visit Sick Kids I see children born with some terrible condition and wonder how the parents manage with a load that never ends.

Soup arrived at our doorstep at suppertime, for which we were very grateful. James, by the by, was given a teddy bear by one of the nurses at radiation yesterday, and Teddy has been a constant companion ever since.   Sincerely, Syd

SUBJECT: IN HASTE
SENT: APRIL 24, 2001 11:41 AM

In haste: James' pain has been steadily growing, despite morphine since the weekend, and has spread throughout his body. There is still no bed for him on the chemo floor at

Sick Kids to do the ICE chemo, so in desperation we are going through Emerg at Sick Kids to be admitted to another floor for pain control. We are told there is a serious shortage of nurses, and James is still way down the list for the chemo floor.   Syd

Ever so carefully I climb into James' hospital bed and cuddle up next to him. He is in frightful pain. "And now the pain that was below my sternum is in my sternum and above it too!" Each breath is a big effort and accompanied by a little moan. IV morphine was expected to control the pain, but it hasn't. The dose has been increased, yet the pain worsens.

"Please rub my leg." The nurse takes his blood pressure, and he weeps from the pain of the inflated cuff.

Then he tells me, "Ben And Becca are the best brother and sister in the whole world."

I warm up a beanbag for the back of his head.

It's 6 a.m., and it slowly filters through to me that perhaps it's time to call in the family.

Do we want Rebecca and Ben to see him like this? Yes, it is better than being denied a final good-bye. But then James always bounces back.

Won't he come back from the precipice again this time? I really hope so, but his appalling condition suggests otherwise.

A gap. Now it's ten a.m. James has improved and is a bit more comfortable.

The increased morphine dose seems to be helping. We have had a meeting with Dr. Baruchel, and James agrees to go for another round of the ICE chemo, to start immediately, as a palliative measure. Sorry this email is so emotional.

Four hours ago I thought we were near the end. Thanks for your support.　　Syd and family

SUBJECT: VERY SICK PATIENT...NOT!
SENT: APRIL 27, 2001 12:58 PM

I gather that my assistant Joan was able to send out a brief update on Wednesday. Let me pick up the story.

As you know, Wednesday was the day of the "Great Pain." Paulette was his nurse that day and was responsible for administering the ICE chemo, IV morphine, TPN (intravenous feeding plan), as well as caring for his personal needs. A dozen visitors arrived that day to help, and all contributed something to his well-being. His sister Rebecca was very sweet, helping mop his face with warm face cloths, holding his drink, and generally supplying tender loving care.

James began moving away from the brink as the chemo kicked in. Thursday morning arrived, and I was very glad that Paulette was again his day nurse, because I was beginning to doubt my sanity. At 7 a.m. she walked into his room, and her jaw dropped. There was James, sitting up, eating a bowl of Corn Pops; the green-gray pallor of his face was gone, normal color restored, a big smile on his face. "Look, Paulette, I can move my head!" and he shook his head vigorously. Then he lay on his back and kicked his feet in the air like a wild man. The change for the better was unbelievable.

"This is amazing!" were Paulette's words. James had just done a James again and got better again.

By the time Dr. Baruchel dropped by, there was a sign on his door saying, "Very sick patient...Not!" Dr. Baruchel commented that the proper words that they would use in today's medical report would be "Responded to treatment." But he then pointed to James, happily active on his bed, and said how totally inadequate "Responded to treatment" described what we were seeing. Everyone was very pleased, especially Rebecca, who had spent some time during the night hypnotizing the cancer cells to go away. By the time Pam and Rebecca arrived in from Rosie's, James was at the end of the hall on the sofa, where he could watch the demolition of the old hospital across the street. Posy the clown dropped by, and she and James had a ball together. So it was a good day.

By Thursday night, however, chemo reality had set in. Now James was no longer suffering from cancer but from the effects of high-dose chemo. Very barfy, very lethargic, bone tired, and completely out of it. Thursday night was difficult. Even a new toy cement mixer could not provide any distraction. This stage of chemo is a real trial to get through, and there is little that helps aside from a barrage of anti-nausea drugs. We cut back on the morphine, but I guess a little too fast, as the back of his head began hurting a bit and back up went the dose. The last chemo has now gone through, and once he is comfortable we will return to Peterborough, likely Saturday or Sunday. Will try to keep in touch.   Syd

Although you can see from above that this was emailed at a decent hour, it was actually penned as a nocturnal muse around 4 a.m. while still at Sick Kids. Here goes:

The storm seems to be over, and the waves that threatened to engulf our James have eased to a gentle swell. Maybe that's too literal, for James is still suffering from the odd wave of nausea. Now and then he reaches for his trusty green barf bucket, but then the feeling passes; we have a brief hug; and he settles back to sleep. For the first time since the latest flare-up of James' neuroblastoma (it hit on April 12th, my birthday—what a birthday present), there is peace. I am surprised to find that there are no items in my "Worry Inbox." For a change I can't sleep because, in a fit of reverse logic, there's nothing to fret about. Actually, I find myself very happy.

So it appears that James once again is back in business, Sick Kids having worked its magic. True, we need to get through the impending drop in his blood counts, the inevitable consequence of ICE, and there's a good chance we will need to dash to hospital for within-the-hour IV antibiotics if he develops a fever, but if history repeats itself, James has another forty days or so of good health before the disease hits again. We know that on the medical front Dr. Baruchel and his team are discussing the follow-up and weighing the options. For James and the family, the immediate challenge is, "What are we going to do with the forty days of new life we've just been given?" James has some ideas of his own and has just been sharing them with me as we lay together on his bed a few minutes ago. "I want to see my friend Austin; I want to have a sleepover with Rebecca in the guest room; I want to build the new Lego electric train set with Ben; I want to have a boys' night at the cottage and make a campfire; I want to raise some more money for the James Birrell Fund; I want to see my cousins."

For Pam and I, there is an overwhelming desire for quiet normalcy—no fireworks, no gut-wrenching crises, no life-and-death decision making. And more sobering, I guess we need to find a way around the nursing shortage at Sick Kids that left James waiting for a bed for a week of mounting agony. It is frightful for both family and our medical friends at Sick Kids alike to know that a child desperately needs treatment but a dozen or so other cancer kids need treatment even more urgently.

That's it for the 4 a.m. email. Now we are back in Peterborough, and the last word belongs to James: "I'm so glad to be home!"

SUBJECT: JAMES ON SUNDAY
SENT: APRIL 30, 2001 12:03 AM

How fast life moves in the world of James and his battle with cancer!

126

Apparently it was just yesterday that we returned from Sick Kids, and I believe it was just four days ago that we began the recent round of ICE chemo, but I must confess that neither Pam nor I can get our heads around the speed of this roller-coaster ride. We are both shattered emotionally and physically after the latest round. But not our James.

Today James was occasionally a little nauseated, not yet eating well, still thin and fragile and easily tired, but completely pain free, very cheerful, on the mend, and has had a great day. Today he began walking in earnest and surprised us by heading down to the neighbors' to play in their backyard. By the time I got my camera, he was playing Frisbee with the kids on the street. Then his good friend Austin arrived, and he had to delay his game of chess with Cam. I had a ridiculous thought and asked James if he would like to play in the end-of-year piano recital after all.

"Yup." So at 6:08 p.m. James played "Blue Bird Waltz" for the crowd (quite flawlessly, I might add) and then "Strolling Camels." I have no recollection of when it was that he last practiced these pieces and can only assume that he has inherited my own trait as a musician of performing well enough to fool most of the people most of the time, despite the absence of preparation. Obviously chemo does not affect musical ability, something we all noticed when Pam performed so well during her chemotherapy.

Rebecca performed right after James. (I puffed with parental pride when I overheard a little girl seated behind me whisper, "She's really good!" Perhaps all those tears at piano-practice time were worth it.) Then we sneaked off to the doughnut place to celebrate. I got my camera out and took a picture of James placing his order, then realized that perhaps this was a little unusual and tried to explain to the doughnut girl why I needed to take a picture of my son ordering a doughnut, but it didn't go over very well. She didn't get it, and I suddenly realized that there's no point in explaining. I don't get it either; I can't begin to grasp what is going on myself. Four days ago James was in uncontrollable pain and close to death, and yet today we are going to piano recitals and doughnut stores and playing Frisbee. We will keep fighting the enemy and accept the gift of more life. The first day of the forty has been good. Good night!

And thank you Dr. Baruchel, Janet Gammon, and all the others on the team!   Syd

SUBJECT: JAMES ARTICLE IN SATURDAY'S *NATIONAL POST*
SENT: MAY 3, 2001 12:38 PM

On Thursday James had a terrific chat with reporter Heather Sokoloff from the *National Post*, and we expect an article on page three of this Saturday's edition. I also spoke with Heather for an hour or two. It's funny that the more you talk, the more there is to talk about when it comes to our family's fight with cancer. It's a little difficult deciding just what the story is.

James is now in full recovery mode after his round of ICE. The first few days were shaky, but now James is eating like a horse. His blood counts have been dropping through the floor, so we have had transfusions of blood and platelets. White count is down to 0.2 instead of a normal 5 or so, platelets 13, and hemoglobin 71. We have to watch for fever quite carefully. With blood counts on his mind, it was interesting to hear James on the phone with reporter Heather's colleague Chris, who was sent to Florida to cover the recent space shuttle launch. "Chris, what do the white counts of the astronauts have to be to go into space?" Well, Chris is as well informed about space matters as anyone, but he didn't know the answer to that one. So he's going to talk to Dr. Williams, Canadian astronaut/medical doctor, and come up with some answers.

Around 11:30 this morning I saw a gap in the schedule appearing and figured that things have been a bit grim for the other two lately, so I gave our friends at the animal hospital a call, picked up Ben and Rebecca from school, and off we went for a frolic with four adorable kittens awaiting adoption. The children even got to give the kittens names, which were duly entered into the adoption papers. In other news: for a while we thought it wouldn't be happening, but here we are—it's opening night, and Pam and Rebecca are off to perform in *Snow White*. Pam is the wicked queen, and Rebecca is a dwarf.

Just saw James walking down the street to play croquet with the neighbors' kids. Must go and watch. Nice to be able to send a fairly worry-free email for a change!   Syd

SUBJECT: ANNOUNCEMENT: THE JAMES BIRRELL
NEUROBLASTOMA RESEARCH FUND
SENT: MAY 8, 2001 5:41 PM

The James Birrell Neuroblastoma Research Fund (JBRF) has been established at the Hospital For Sick Children (HSC) Foundation by the Birrell family to

generate knowledge leading to new therapies for the treatment of patients with neuroblastoma.

The JBRF is soliciting grant applications for the calendar year 2001-2002.

Funds up to $25,000 for one year are available to qualified applicants. Two proposals will be funded during this competition cycle, one in fundamental, longer-term research and one in translational/clinical research with immediate clinical applications.

The JBRF will accept grant applications from scientists, clinical scientists, and associate scientists from HSC and the University of Toronto.

OBJECTIVE:

The objective of The James Birrell Neuroblastoma Research Fund is to help HSC and University of Toronto researchers develop pilot data from feasibility studies to be subsequently used in new research grant proposals. The seed grant funding is specifically designed to advance translational research that could otherwise not compete successfully in external grant competitions as patient-based research without convincing pilot data. It is anticipated that the successful applications will lead to a rapid translation to clinical research or be immediately used as clinical research project.

DEFINITIONS:

Translational research will be interpreted in its widest scope. It includes, but is not limited to, genomics small molecule targeted therapy, preclinical pharma-

cology, clinical pharmacology immunotherapy, vaccine angiogenesis, bone marrow transplantation, differentiating agents. All projects need to be directly related to neuroblastoma. The ultimate goal of this funding initiative is to speed up the development of new therapies for neuroblastoma funding.

SUBJECT: SORE NECK
SENT: MAY 10, 2001 6:16 AM

Today I have a very sore neck—me, Syd, not James. This is because I drove the car backwards down the winding gravel road that continues from our cottage all the way to Peck's Camp at the other end of the lake. You see, James, Ben, and I had decided to pick up on our boys' night at the cottage that was so rudely interrupted by James' sudden deterioration a few weeks ago. Every time we go to the cottage, a voice whispers, "This is probably the last time for James," and the last time almost was the last time. Yesterday James had a platelet transfusion; his white count had doubled overnight; he was zooming back to health; and it seemed to be the right time to invalidate that whisper. So, as you can predict, we bought white bread and junk food at the IGA, visited Dad's Donuts for green ice cream, and before we knew it we were out on the lake in our ancient boat, testing our newly repaired six-horsepower motor. Supper was informal. (Ben: "We don't have to say 'excuse me' when we burp, 'cause there are no girls here!") James ate like a horse, while Ben feasted solely on spicy curly french fries dipped in pink pop.

It was the next morning that we heard the sound of heavy machinery and went outside to investigate. Joy, O joy! A

131

grader was fixing up the road, and we love watching graders, excavators, bulldozers, cranes, even more than we love the pink pop and doughnuts that we were eating for breakfast. And that's how I found myself reversing the car down Tangamong Lake Road, the rear hatch wide open, the boys in the cargo area, best seats in the house, following the grader as it justified our exorbitant property taxes. Also justifying our taxes was a supervisor relaxing in his parked truck, but I didn't notice him the first time we reversed by. The grader driver was concentrating on making a beautiful pile of gravel along the middle of the road—a thrilling sight to watch, judging by the excitement of James and Ben—and he didn't notice our friendly waving. Then he saw us and politely pulled over so we could pass, but we didn't, so he continued grading, a little nervously it seemed, and we followed him as he turned around and graded back down the road, past the relaxing supervisor. We waved to him, but he was unsmiling and unresponsive. Justifying taxes is serious business. That's when I noticed my neck was getting quite sore, so reluctantly we ended the chase.

I am pleased to report that we were very successful in chasing away the bad feelings of our previous cottage trip, with the bone pain, the high fever, and the mad middle-of-the-night dash to the hospital. The visit was less than a day, but even in that time you could see the improvement in James as he roared back to life. Back in Peterborough we are all enjoying the richness of life that is permitted when we are not in a cancer crisis. *Snow White* was terrific fun; Pam and Rebecca were superb as the wicked queen and a cute dwarf; and it was great to have the two Birrells on the stage with the other three of us in the audience, even if James' white count was low and he had to wear a surgical mask and we had to form a human shield of healthy friends and relatives around him. Our thanks to the special unnamed doctor who put quality of life ahead of medical correctness and told James to go. Every day, after the ICE chemo, James has an injection of very expensive GCSF, which stimulates blood cell production, but even so the counts were still low. Having survived another round of ICE without unduly severe side effects, it looks probable that we will do one more round. But first James wants to play in the opening soccer game of the season and go to his swimming lesson and go to school, and a million other things, and we all want to spend the long weekend at the cottage. And after ICE we will try something less invasive. There are so many treatments to choose from. Some work well for some kids some of the time, but there is not yet a magic bullet. The clock is ticking.

You probably noticed the fine article on James in the Saturday edition of the *National Post*, which has helped the research fund along nicely. The *Toronto Star* also did a telephone interview with us, and once I had confiscated the *Model Railroader* magazine that James was avidly reading, he paid attention and spoke very sincerely with the reporter. And now I will abruptly end this email and sleep.   Syd

SUBJECT: WHICH WAY IS THE WIND BLOWING?
SENT: MAY 22, 2001 12:11 AM

I am surprised to find that it's been almost two weeks since I last sent a James update. Two weeks filled with wonderful family times, all sorts of spontaneous adventures, and a feeling that just one of those days alone was worth the effort of going through the rigors of the recent round of chemo. James has been back to school (top of the class in his math test); soccer has started, and he made it to the first two games; we spent a morning tearing through Madeleine's forest paths on her ATV; we went to Cobourg railway station to watch trains and ended up taking the VIA train to Belleville and back just for fun; the children have discovered Monopoly, the real old-fashioned board game version, and love playing it together.

And then the cottage is another chapter: for weeks the boys have been planning the 2001 launch of "Water World," so with the sun blazing down and the dragonflies thoughtfully gobbling up the blackflies, we sallied forth to the beach with four-inch ABS pipe, laid out an underground system, and started pouring buckets of water into the protruding pipe till it formed a little pond at the bottom of the system. Then James and I carefully positioned ourselves in the lake, equipped with a length of old screening, while Ben waited attentively on the shore. "Now, Ben!" we shouted as a school of minnows swam by, and Ben dashed into the lake, driving dozens of minnows into our trap. What to do with all those flapping little fish? I am afraid to say that they get poured into the black pipe, to appear downstream looking very confused and unhappy. And then there is our tubby little sailboat, which James now sails confidently, one hand on the tiller and the other on the sheet, while I lounge in the bow trying to figure out where the wind is coming from.

Accompanying all these good times is the gnawing unknown of being eighteen months into recurrent neuroblastoma. "One year but not two" was the official word on what one might expect. James has reached a point where the only thing that is predictable is that every day is now unpredictable.

During the last few months, Pam and I have been coming to grips with what appears to be a contradiction: we work as hard as we can for a cure for James while at the same time we prepare for his death. Over the last few weeks the medical community has been working very hard to make sure that the best palliative care possible will be available for James at home in Peterborough. That is a huge challenge when you are dealing with neuroblastoma.

Three years ago, in the hours following surgery to remove the primary tumor, Pam and I sat next to James in the recovery room as things began to go terribly wrong. His nurse kept leaving to phone the surgeon. James thrashing. Heartbeat climbing over 200. Internal bleeding. Sometime after midnight, he went into cardiac arrest. Code blue. Nurses and doctors running, shouting. Paddles. Pam in hysterics. "Get the parents out of here!" Waiting in a darkened hallway. The longest, loneliest, and most terrifying time of our lives.

What we learned from that experience was that never again would we allow ourselves to be excluded. We want to be there when he dies just as much as we want to be there as he lives, and we want to be prepared in ourselves so that no one need shout, "Get the parents out of here!" That is why we are glad that so much thought is being given to getting James and our family through life's ultimate tragedy.

Although he is in great spirits, James has not recovered well from the latest round of ICE. He keeps needing transfusions, particularly platelets, and it would appear that his bone marrow has been hard hit by the cumulative effects of many chemotherapies. We cannot begin the round of ICE that was scheduled for today, yet James is beginning to experience pain in his left arm and shoulder, a sign that the disease is on the move. None of this is unexpected, but it is not what we want to see.

In conclusion: Pam has a dreadful cold and has long since gone to bed.

Rebecca is sleeping with me tonight in the guest room so as to be next to James' room in case he needs help during the night. Already Rebecca has been down once to get me from the computer, as James is crying out in his sleep, and she has been very sweet, helping give him Tylenol and tucking him in.

Thank you for allowing me to share these thoughts with you tonight. I find it good therapy, even if I don't know where the wind is blowing. You have been a great source of encouragement to our family. And thank you for your prayers.   Syd

SUBJECT: ANOTHER CRISIS
SENT: MAY 23, 2001 1:47 PM

The last hour has been another of the hardest of our lives as we discussed with Dr. Baruchel whether it is now time to let James go. Over the last twenty-four hours James has deteriorated rapidly. Yesterday he awoke with widespread pain, and this morning he was much worse, with no significant relief from oral morphine. He was not able to walk or even sit up. So we talked about whether it was right to prolong his suffering and about what we might achieve if we continued treatment, and we talked about what James wanted. The ICE chemo has been ruled out, as James has not been able to recover from the toxicity of the most recent round and keeps requiring blood transfusions. After much soul-searching, we woke James and asked him if he wished to try the chemo called irinotecan. "Yes," he said. This treatment can take place in Peterborough, so we will give it a go. Five doses, one a day for five days.   In haste, Syd

I guess this roller-coaster ride may soon be over, but not apparently today, as James has stabilized very well and is completely pain free, is eating well, is in good spirits, and has begun to walk again. He has been made very welcome in the Peterborough hospital whose new name I always forget but which is really still Civic Hospital. The pediatric nurses there have put a great deal of thought into providing the best possible palliative care for James, even though terminal neuroblastoma is outside their normal role. So he has been fixed up with a terrific room with an extra bed for me or Pam plus cots for Ben and Rebecca should they wish to sleep over. Actually, Rebecca is very keen to do this and share in looking after James. Ben, I fear, just wants to play with the fancy electric bed. It is an enormous relief to Pam and I that we need not be in Toronto, away from our family and support network, to receive the care James needs. The team of nurses that traveled from Sick Kids to Peterborough last week to help set up palliative care for James has clearly done a great job. We now know that if James does not make it then everything is in place right here in our Peterborough community. For some time Pam and I have been thinking of whether it would be better for James to die at home or in hospital, and now that we have seen the arrangements that have been made at Civic, we are inclined to move in that direction.

Most importantly, James is very much at home at Civic, surrounded by nurses that he knows and loves.

Where are we? Is this the final round for James? Why is he better today? Is it the pain patch? Is it the new/old chemo? Is it an answer to prayer? Is it the natural cycle of the disease? Is it James' own inner will to keep fighting? I have a lot of questions these days. Meanwhile James is having another great day, playing with his new electric toothbrush, making crafts, reading *Arthur* books, ordering up all his favorite foods, schmoozing with the nurses, phoning Uncle Steve and singing him "Happy Birthday" plus the bit about "you look like a monkey…"

Yesterday, following our discussion with James about whether to continue treatment or not, we somehow got him into the van and over to see his Peterborough oncologist, Dr. Wierzbicki, and for the first time since the latest "Great Pain" began, James sat up and, looking Dr. W straight in the eye, said with great emphasis, "I am *not* giving up!"

Well done, James!

A strange calm seems to have descended on James' situation, at least from my perspective. James is happy and well looked after in his room at the Peterborough hospital and has been pain free since Wednesday night.

One brief barf this morning, and then it was back to, "Dad, did you know that if you put a few drops of grape pop on your Rice Krispies it makes them taste really good?" We have had plenty of visitors, plenty of craft time, as well as lots of snuggly one-on-one reading time together. Today James asked that we read the story of raising Lazarus from the dead. Rebecca slept over for one night and helped look after James very nicely. James is quieter and less energetic today, which fits our previous experience with this chemo but which also fits progressive disease. The CT scan done on Friday shows cancer on the move at the back of his head, which of course concerns us, but this is not new, and there are plenty of other nasty things to worry about. Today James will receive the fourth of five doses of chemo, and after tomorrow's dose he is planning to go home. Making any plans at all these days seems a little presumptuous, but we will give it a go.

Yesterday night was the occasion of a family wedding, and Ben had the privilege of being the "ring burier," as he quaintly calls it. Actually the ring almost did get buried. It was tied on to the ribbon on the little white cushion as we left for the wedding, Ben happily swinging the thing around his head as we headed for the car. But the ring was missing when we arrived at the church! Panic, and some bad words too. Oh well, John and Kelly married, and we found the missing ring later after the wedding. Ben looked completely smashing in his little black tux. We were so glad that Ben for once was center stage and even gladder that James' health was stable enough for all of us to attend while he played with Bean at the hospital. During the afternoon, James received a beautiful VIA conductor's hat, the formal kind with the gold braid on it, and James sent it to the reception for Ben to wear, so as to be present in spirit though absent in person. Ben wore it very proudly.

James received a number of exciting gifts yesterday (so did the other children, I am glad to say), and one was a beautiful conductor's pocket watch on a gold chain. James is immensely impressed with it and is always reaching for it, checking the time, winding it up, and carefully putting it away. Last night I left the wedding reception before the dance and returned to the hospital at about 10 p.m., way past James' bedtime, but there he was, holding the pocket watch, waiting up for me to return so he could show it to me. So we cuddled up, and before we knew it he fell asleep. He looks so fragile as he lies sleeping, so pale and thin, IV pump humming away, and yet today as we cuddled and my thoughts moved in the direction of losing him, James said in a small, strong voice that left me in no doubt of his intentions: "When I have to make the choice, it will always be to keep battling cancer."

Towards the end of my phone conversation with Dr. Baruchel on Monday, I think I may have given him the impression that perhaps Syd is losing it.

We had nicely covered the serious medical stuff, the pressing need for radiation to the back of James' head, and we also touched on the fact that James had returned home pain free on Sunday night. And of course we are all desperately anxious to know if the recent chemo is working. But it was on the topic of future plans, in particular the soapbox derby, that we stopped understanding each other. You see, James insists on staying alive and healthy for the second weekend in September coming up, when the annual soapbox races will be held in Peterborough and which, contrary to all logic, he intends to participate in and win. Now I don't think Dr. Baruchel has any problem with kids planning to stay alive and to enjoy life, but I think the matter of the soapbox derby has left him confused, and others too, so let me explain.

Although the concept no longer fits in world-class cities like cosmopolitan Toronto, here in small-town Peterborough, with its quaint seven-digit phone numbers, we still like to take a wooden box, fit it with four wheels, add steering and maybe brakes, put a child inside, and look for a steep hill that can be closed to traffic for a day. Two at a time the children race each other down the slope, and by a slow process of elimination you eventually have a winner. Each year I sit with the children on the curb, eating junk food and watching the races. Ben and Rebecca are good for an hour or so, but James is really only satisfied by sitting out the whole thing. We discuss and analyze as we watch, predicting winners and losers at the pre-start inspection. We talk about frontal area, aerodynamics, wheel bearings, and weight, as well as styling and coloring.

James long ago set his heart on making his own soapbox racer and taking part. And during James' stay in hospital last week, he talked with one of the medical team, whose husband is an aeronautical engineer and who owns an airplane maintenance facility at the Peterborough Airport and who happens to love soapbox derby-ing and whose kids are now getting too old to race and who happens to be willing to help build a racer for a young boy currently battling cancer who is not expected to live very long...

So how is it that in the midst of what appears to be the final showdown for James, we can contemplate the soapbox derby, still four months away? Back in November of 1999, we found ourselves in a similar situation when our friends at the Make-A-Wish Foundation introduced us to Chris and Martin Kratt, the stars of the kids' TV show "Zoboomafoo." We were invited to travel to Montreal the following March to spend a day on the set with them. But at that time we never expected James to live that long, and the invitation seemed unrealistic. James, however, eagerly planned for the event. "And you know what?" (favorite expression of James, by the way)—"He made it!" (favorite expression of Dr. Baruchel). We had the time of our life and returned home with the kind of memories you treasure forever. So maybe we can do a bit of foolish dreaming today. James has startled us during this latest crisis by his fierce determination to keep fighting. We can do nothing less than help him with his fight and keep his dreams alive.

I thought this week that James really was not going to get better and that my job was to help him understand that we have tried everything and it's now time to let go and die. What I didn't understand was that James already knew I thought that, and he didn't want me to help him prepare to die, and he didn't want my sympathy; he just wanted me to stand by him and fight the enemy.

It's been a great day for James (favorite expression of Syd). He walked up the hill to the soccer game tonight. He watched his team win. He did a terrific interview with CFTO TV and gave Dana one of his best hugs.

He went to Dairy Queen. We read some more of Tolkien's *The Hobbit* together. And he loves the joke book he got today. "Hey Dad, what did the cat have for breakfast?...Mice Krispies!"

Clearly, it's the pumpkin hour. I'd better sign off. Syd

I will be in trouble with my mother-in-law if I don't bring the following to your attention: James will be on the 6 p.m. "CFTO News," channel 9, tomorrow, May 31, and possibly the noon hour slot as well. The interviewer, Dana Levenson, and her cameraman, Brian, did a terrific job. If you are one of our regular James email readers in Sweden, Germany, England, Wales, Australia, Holland, Brazil, USA, Saudi Arabia, Israel, or even British Columbia, then I am sorry, you may not be able to tune in.   Syd

In haste: We leave for Toronto immediately for a dose of radiation to James' head. It has become obvious that the tumor in his head is growing rapidly, and as a consequence lots of vomiting, pain in both the front and back of the head, and tingling sensations in his right hand. He is cheerful and alert. We appreciate your prayers.   Syd

The image I choose to keep from today's kaleidoscope of events is that of James, pajama clad, tired and fragile yet safe, secure, and happy, cuddled up on the lap of his friend Dr. Baruchel. An image to chase away the many dreadful images of the last few days. Together they were looking at the latest CT scans of the tumor growing in James' head and discussing the plan for radiation. The day had started poorly, with head pain, with James vomiting at 6 a.m., then 6:30, and again, and then again, with veins bulging out on the top and side of his head as a consequence of the tumor pushing on an artery in his brain. Then there was the tingling sensation in his right hand, another ominous sign. A quick email to Sick Kids, a flurry of phone calls, and we were on our way. Thirty-six hours earlier we had removed James' pain patch, thinking that five days of chemo might have done some good, and were rudely shaken by the speed and ferocity of the returning pain. At Princess Margaret Hospital James had an unscheduled consult with his friend the radiation doctor, then got fitted up with a custom head mask (no fun; they mold hot plastic to your face and later use it to keep your head locked in position for the radiation), and then he had the first of five rounds of radiation to his head. We go back again tomorrow, Saturday, Sunday, and Monday. For eighteen months we have been concerned about a lesion in the back of James' skull, and we have tried to keep it at bay, hoping it would not cross the blood brain barrier where most chemos don't work. But that has happened, and so to back up the radiation we will use an oral version of VP 16 as soon as James' platelet count has recovered. Needless to say, we talked about many other ideas for treatment, but none offered greater hope, small as it is.

Back to that image: Dr. Baruchel and James. Two people hurting, two people desperately fighting the enemy, two people with a deep understanding of what is important in life, two people who make very hard decisions. But what gets me is the huge crowd of medical people represented by that image, who dare to work with James as he faces life-threatening illness, who get real close to a dying child so as to best help him. There's Janet, and John, and Sandi, Heather and Rita, Freda, Rosie, Ray, Norma, Rafael, Mary Anne, Carolyn, Posy, Susan, Vince, Mary Catherine, Karen, Graham—I'm just scratching the surface. People seem to think that the Birrells are going through a terrible tragedy, but Pam and I are reminded daily that every step of this road is lined with people who love and care deeply for us. The cancer experience is one that shows you all that is best in God's creation, if you choose to look. So I'm going to bed early tonight with today's image, and I'm going to look forward to four more radiation trips to Toronto in the next four days, four more chances to rub shoulders with some of these remarkably compassionate people, and four more chances to visit the Bowmanville Zoo, or Cooper's Crane Rental, or the car crusher place, or the Toronto subway, or whatever other fun thing strikes our fancy.

Oh, I forgot to tell you the most important part of Dr. Baruchel's new treatment plan, and that's the business of the soapbox derby. It turns out that he knows all about soapbox derbies, and he made racers for his own children, but they're called something else in French. Anyway, he takes the matter of cancer patients having specific goals in the future very seriously and has instructed James to get to work on designing and building a racer with our new friend James (soon to be known as *Big James*) for the September derby in Peterborough. Surviving cancer is more than strictly medical. Pam can tell you that.   Syd

There is a great sadness as we move into this next phase of James' illness. We used to attack pain by attacking the cancer. Cancer gets beat up; pain goes away. We still are fighting the cancer with radiation and chemo, but now the disease progresses, the pain lingers, and some heavy duty narcotics are necessary. Yesterday the head pain was "just half out of ten, nor even one out of ten!" and the right arm was a dull ache, all very satisfactory as far as James was concerned. It is fair to say that pain control is going very well. But it is hard to accept that we are now unable to stop the progress of the neuroblastoma. We have known intellectually for twenty months that recurrent neuroblastoma is terminal, but we have lived with a wild hope that James would beat the odds.

Wild hope I think we will keep. With wild hope you can continue to defy the limitations of terminal cancer. James' week at summer camp is just four weeks away. The soapbox derby is eight weeks after that. And although the last few days have been exhausting, yet another mini marathon, everyone in our family has new memories to cherish. Pam tells me of waking up one morning to see James' grinning face inches away on the pillow, waiting for her to wake up, of the big hug that followed and the enormous relief of starting the day with a happy and pain-free James. Each of the recent Toronto trips has been an opportunity to bring along Rebecca or Ben or both, so I suppose you could say that we've had five family outings to Toronto, something we might only do twice a year under normal circumstances. The Bowmanville Zoo has been added to our list of fun things to do on the way to the big city. I think feeding and petting the deer rate highly. Rebecca was blown away by the peacocks displaying their colors. And at Sick Kids, Rebecca pushes James along in his wheelchair very competently, and it is priceless watching Ben push, barely tall enough to see over but so proud to be allowed to help. You can have great fun racing through the tunnel that connects HSC with Princess Margaret. The Sunday TV interview was very exciting. In the end they only wanted James and I for the interview, so I had to pay Ben—who wanted to be on TV—five dollars not to be on TV, and then another five dollars to James— who did not want to be on TV again—to be on TV. James was disgusted that he needed to put on makeup, though he had a great chat with Lloyd Robertson in the makeup room afterwards as they wiped it all off.

Something I can't help noticing these days is that the richness of human experience gets better and better. The worse things get, the better life gets. Every day I have many notable interactions with the people looking after us, and in normal times I would have labeled any single one of those interactions as exceptionally memorable. Now we are connecting many times a day with people who give so deeply and meaningfully to us. The emails and letters we receive are stunning for their depth of compassion and the encouragement they bring. For me the most moving moments are the occasions of the big hugs James gives so lovingly to those who are helping us. The weak and frail-looking boy gets out of his wheelchair, arms outstretched, and hugs with such strength and love and happiness. Nothing more need be said.   Syd and family

Two hours of panic, a flurry of phone calls, a quick dash to Emerg, some X rays, blood work—what terrible new manifestation of end-time neuroblastoma is this—and then our medical friends give us the good news:

Yes, James' stomach is indeed distended; and yes, the pediatrician has never seen an X ray that shows a large intestine quite so plugged up; but no, there is no evidence of a perforated bowel, and neither is there evidence that the constipation has been caused by cancer tumors. Take a laxative. A big sigh of relief; Pam and I totter off home, with James happily in tow. Sorry, not a very exciting medical problem, but I think it illustrates how close to the edge we live. A distended stomach when you are fighting widespread disease can mean everything or nothing, and things are further complicated by the pain patch James is now wearing, which masks pain that otherwise might sooner alert you to developing problems.

This week has been a subdued one for James. He is pale, weak, and very thin. Climbing stairs is generally too much for him, and usually the wheelchair is necessary for out-of-house trips. He has been very tired (chemo? radiation? disease? pain patch?) and is usually unable to participate in much beyond videos and reading *The Hobbit* together. Then suddenly he feels well, so we zip off to the airport to build a bit more of the soapbox derby racer, or go for an afternoon cruise on the houseboat with Uncle Tony, or even do a sleepover with Rebecca and Ben at Peggy Three's place. Earlier today James traveled to Toronto Airport with Ben and me to pick up my sister Diana, who has come to visit and help for a few days, but even sitting in the car became an effort after a while, so he flopped sideways onto some pillows, contentedly watching out for interesting trucks. As Ben pointed out, "James and I just can't go to sleep on the 401 'cause of all the trucks!" I thought at first Ben meant the trucks were too noisy, but then I realized it was the thrill of seeing all those exciting big trucks that banished sleep.

I suppose much of this sounds a bit gloomy. It is very hard to watch two of your children growing and thriving, physically robust and full of energy, while your third child lies in the grip of a deadly disease, exhausted, silent, and distant. But then there are still plenty of times when the old James comes back to life, full of things to say, anxious to get outside and join the other kids playing. And James continues to have firm ideas about things: "I am not going to talk to any more newspaper or TV reporters for *two weeks*!" So we will keep going with our "wild hope." Good night.   Syd

SUBJECT: THIS AND THAT
SENT: JUNE 19, 2001 11:52 PM

Last week Dr. Baruchel gave us orders to go to the cottage, so we did, with a fair bit of apprehension, I freely admit. Just got back. Had a fabulous time. The last seventy-two hours was one of those episodes in the life of James where we watch with disbelief as he moves from a tired, frail, weak, and pale-looking boy, where you are weighed down with the reality of terminal cancer, to a lively, excited, busy fellow fully enjoying summertime at the cottage, and it feels like cancer is ancient history. James played at the beach; he canoed; he sailed; he even went tubing. "I'm having so much fun that I have forgotten all the bad times, even the time of the Great Pain."

He stayed up late playing cards and established himself as the undisputed champion of crazy eights in the Birrell family. Ben, James, and Rebecca are always ready for a noisy, unorthodox game of Monopoly, and play it they did. Though just five years old, Ben has shown a keen interest in the finer points of Monopoly and is the first to mortgage property so he can get on with buying houses and hotels. The children tend to play long games because just when someone should be going bankrupt, big-hearted Ben slips them a bit of money from the bank. But one of the more intriguing sights of the weekend was seeing James sit down with Nanny and in about thirty seconds—hey presto—he had learned to knit. As we drove home, I glanced in the rearview mirror and captured a new image for posterity, that of a seven-year-old boy with a ball of pink wool, happily knitting. (Parental boasting moment: Nanny says she has never seen anyone learn how to knit so fast.)

I want to mention the soapbox derby racer that seems to have become something of a leitmotif, Wagnerian style, as James gets on with the daily battle with cancer. As you know, James has set his sights on the September soapbox derby race, unrealistic as some might say that is, and he has determined not only to participate but to win. Whenever we can, which is usually every day, we slip down to the Peterborough Airport and meet with our friend Big James in the hangar where he works. There we have been building the racer. During the planning stage, Little James was too sick to travel, so the preliminary sketches were made from the hospital bed at our house, in between bouts of vomiting.

There the TGV shape was adopted as the profile for the racer (the super-fast 300 km/hr French passenger train).

James arrived at the next session in a wheelchair, and we sketched out a full-size profile of the racer on a large piece of cardboard. Having agreed on the final shape, James officially signed the pattern and took a copy home to paint.

A day later, surrounded by bits of airplanes in various states of repair, James managed to stand up and transfer the shape to some plywood. Next visit saw the body of the racer beginning to take its form, and James carefully spread the wood glue before we clamped and screwed.

Working with aviation people means precision, so Big James made up metal templates for Little James to mark all the screw holes. Any of you medical folk who work with him know that precision sits very well with James, and it better be 3 cc of heparin and not 2.9, and make sure there are no bubbles in my IV line! Today's visit saw the nose of the racer take shape (no wheelchair in sight this time), and it was an opportunity for James to use the bandsaw. James looks forward to these daily visits, and somehow I feel there's a lot more to this project than meets the eye.

On another tack altogether, Sick Kids has announced the first two $25,000 awards of the James Birrell Fund for Neuroblastoma, and it has brought great comfort to our family to know that we have made a contribution to research in this field. We have made many new friends through our work on fund-raising. The *National Post* will carry an article tomorrow (Wednesday) on the fund. Actually, the fund is heading nicely for the six-figure mark, so stand by for further announcements. Rebecca is hoping that the JBFN will help find a cure in time for James, and I join her in that "wild hope." I wish I could share with you all the wonderful stories surrounding the JBFN, from the two young boys and their Kool-Aid stand that raised $50, to the high school car wash that raised $1,400, to the hundreds of families that each gave $100 and the service groups and the corporations, not to mention those who have given thousands.

Rebecca turned nine today, so we partied, and Granny joined us, because it's her birthday too today. And I'm thinking, is Rebecca really nine years old already? Where have those years gone? Four and a half years ago we first began to talk tentatively about cancer at the kitchen table, Pam having just been diagnosed. Now, cancer has been staring Rebecca in the face for half her life. At the beginning Pam and I were so afraid that cancer would destroy our family. But here we are; the story is not over yet; we have experienced friendship that you would not believe; we have been privileged to learn about hope, faith, and love; and I carry untold memories of rich family times. Have four and a half years of cancer robbed Rebecca or enriched her? Is it harder to have cancer or to watch someone you love fight it? Unanswerable questions for the moment, so I will leave them in the question box for another day. But somehow I don't think I need a sleeping pill tonight. Good night!   Syd

SUBJECT: DOWN AND UP
SENT: JUNE 22, 2001 5:44 AM

Wednesday turned out to be one of those classic, mixed-up, pendulum days for the Birrells, where your emotions move from one extreme to the other as the day progresses. Having had five days of steadily improving health for James, it was terrible to come to the breakfast table and hear Pam say in the perfectly calm and matter-of-fact voice she reserves for bad news, "James is complaining of pain in his right shoulder." Goodness knows how many times we have been to this place, but it's always brutal.

Maybe we are better now at remaining outwardly calm, but we dread these moments. It forces us to acknowledge once again that we are in a palliative situation. So, pain in the right shoulder. Plus he can't turn his head to the right. James is crying. Pain in one of the same places as the last recurrence. "Just where does it hurt, James? Is your head hurting too?" So, the disease is likely on the move again. Have we got a fresh pain patch? How about a Dilaudid pill? Phone Janet at Sick Kids. No, send an email. Here we go again. A poor start to the day.

And then Dr. Beamish dropped by to see James. After a lot of prodding and poking of the spine and shoulder area, a pronouncement is made: looks like a pulled muscle. Momentary elation. Off we go to the massage therapist. Yes, he can feel the trapezius muscle; yes, thirty minutes later James can move his head freely again. Euphoria. Always when we hoped for a non-cancer explanation in the past, it was cancer. This time we assumed a cancer explanation, and it's not. Too good to be true? No time to think about it—it's now a great day. *National Post* has a good article on the James Fund; CBC is on the phone for an interview; 2,000 new "House in Heaven" CDs have arrived; a pile of fabulous emails is appearing on the screen; Purolator arrives with a beautiful framed print of the recent *Toronto Star* article on James, courtesy of our friends at the HSC Foundation; and to cap it all, the transport truck is due any minute.

Explanation: a couple of weeks ago I received an email from an employee at Kriska, a major trucking company, in which Laura introduced herself, explained how she'd read about our family in the paper and visited the www.Jamesbirrell.ca Web site and how she'd read my email in which I mentioned James' and Ben's intoxication with trucks on the 401. Would we like a ride in one of their big trucks? Well, we weren't going to turn down that offer. And so at 4:15 p.m., half the neighborhood kids joined our three on the sidewalk, all leaping crazily up and down, to take in seventy-eight feet of transport truck as it pulled up outside our house. Even the moms came to watch. We all swarmed aboard, first in the trailer, which feels big enough to be a bowling alley, and then in the cab with its dozens of switches and gauges, with its bunk beds and room enough for a party. Soon it was time for the ride, and there were some very sad and envious children watching as we left, as this part was just for the Birrells. The truck had a very loud air horn, which we used when going by our friends' houses to great effect.

I always felt that big trucks were kind of a menace, but sitting up so high in the cab with an enormous trailer behind us, trying to maneuver through downtown Peterborough, I changed my tune and decided that it's all those cars that are the menace. We decided to surprise Big James down at the airport and at the same time show Pam and Rebecca the progress on the racer. Our arrival proved to be very satisfactory, Big James stepping out of the office to investigate the unannounced big red truck, air horn sounding, and

Little James leaning out the cab window, waving furiously along with the other seven of us. We had a great inspection session of the racer under construction, and then off we went home. And as we drove back, I couldn't help asking myself, why did it take forty-eight years for me to get round to riding in one of these monsters? Thanks, Laura and Curt! We had a blast!

James and Ben in the Kriska transport truck

So there you are, another day in the life of the Birrell family, the usual mix of fun and terror, surrounded by supportive friends, wondering when and where the next blow will fall, each day filled with memories to cherish.   Syd

Over the weekend James began to experience pain in his right forearm.

The usual pain meds were not adequate. The other worry was the poor results from last Thursday's blood work, which suggested that James' bone marrow was in big trouble. If the bone marrow problem is because of repeated chemos, that's bad, because it means we can't use chemo as effectively as we would like. Or if the bone marrow problem is due to cancer taking over the bone marrow, then that is an even bigger problem. James seemed to be going downhill on the weekend, the happy times overshadowed by times of pain and lethargy. We started making plans for a trip to Sick Kids on Monday morning, with a view to radiation for James aching arm, which we assumed was due to cancer on the move.

This morning began with blood work, done at home in Peterborough. To try and redeem the day, it was decided that Ben would come with James and I and that we would catch the GO Train in Oshawa to add some spice and fun. Meanwhile I had left a message for Carlo, our photographer friend from the *National Post*, who was holidaying nearby and who has been working on a "photo essay" of our family. That means he hangs around with us for several days as we do whatever we do, taking lots of pictures and generally keeping in the background. He said, "Sure, I'll come," and that made four of us boys, setting off at 9:30 this morning for Toronto. James was still in a lot of pain, so Carlo had heated up a beanbag for him to put on his arm, and that seemed to help. Ben and James both went to sleep as we traveled the 115, but right on cue as soon as we hit the 401, they both spontaneously woke up and began counting trucks. James seemed to be perking up.

We got to thinking that we might have some time before the GO Train left the station, and right next door is Cooper's Cranes. So we used the car phone to call ahead, and the nice lady in the office at Cooper's Cranes said, "Sure, drop in." By the time we got there (259 trucks later, according to James), they were ready for us. This was no classroom tour; it was a hands-on adventure. First we got to check out the largest hydraulic crane in Ontario. Very impressive. Brian the operator hauled the boys up to the cab and started the motor. The cab is very high tech, with as many push buttons as the Apollo command module, and the crane can reach up 510 feet and has a maximum lift of 650 tons. (*Reader's Digest/National Geographic* style, I should now say, "That's as much as 500 automobiles," or, "That's as heavy as 12,784,429 Beanie Babies," but I digress.) Both the boys got to rotate the crane, extend the boom, and raise and lower the hook. Then we moved on to the oldest crane in the yard, nicknamed "Snort," and cranked it up for a test drive. Very noisy. By then the responsible adult part of me realized that we needed to leave right away to catch the train, but the boy part of me won. So we stayed for another twenty minutes, missed the train, and tried out a rough-terrain crane with enormous wheels. Again the boys had a blast learning how to operate the controls. A very satisfying start to the day, and James was definitely feeling a lot better. The look of pain that had been in his face all weekend was gone. The look on Carlo's face was interesting.

Having missed the train, it was necessary to continue by road, which allowed the boys to get into some real serious truck counting. Carlo offered to buy them a special treat if they counted 1,000 trucks. No problem. James counted a thousand trucks.

"What will ya give us for 2,000 trucks?" asked James.

"Two treats!" replied Carlo.

Apparently we passed a little over 2,500 trucks by the time we reached Sick Kids parking lot, where James decided the wheelchair was not required, "'cause last time we came Dr. Baruchel told me I don't need to use a wheelchair!" James' arm pain had now dropped to "level two" from a high yesterday of "eleven out of ten," and I was feeling apprehensive about taking Dr. Baruchel's time to check out a boy who was now in much better shape than sixteen hours earlier. Sure enough, after seeing James, Dr. B decided to hold back on radiation, which was just fine with us. And at the same time the morning's blood results came through, indicating a marked improvement, and it was decided that James was ready to start the VP16 chemo again.

By now it was lunchtime and "Two treats time!" The first treat was waiting for us outside the front door of Sick Kids. During our consult with Dr. Baruchel, Carlo had been at work, and his friend Roberta the medic had arrived in a beautiful, shiny ambulance. I guess it's no wonder that Ben once described cancer as "a lot of fun," because here we were, another dream come true for the boys, a chance to have a guided tour of an ambulance, turn on the flashing lights, and check out all the equipment.

Lunch followed, and Carlo made a valiant attempt to teach the boys how to use chopsticks. No. Perhaps another time they will understand why two sticks are better than one fork. Then it was treat two time, and I am ashamed to say I got suckered into a couple of very expensive toys from the gift shop.

And now we had some unexpected free time, as radiation was not happening. So we went off to see long-lost Esther, a friend from the past, where James and Ben had a terrific time with her two large and friendly dogs with their long, wet tongues. Once again I experience the guilt of saying no to our children's deepest desire—that we get a dog. Now at this stage, the day was by all events going much better than anticipated, except for one thing: we hadn't had our train ride. Carlo seemed to have caught the spirit of cramming in as much fun as we could, so it wasn't really surprising when he suggested that we remedy this deficiency by taking the subway and then the light railway train out to McCowan station while he drove our van over to meet us there. We liked the idea, so off we went, Esther joining us for the ride. As always, our thanks to the TTC for providing wonderful entertainment for a mere $5.50. All too soon we reached the end of the line and joined Carlo in the van.

We then had a brief but exciting time at the Bowmanville Zoo feeding and petting the deer, some more photo ops for Carlo, and it was home to see Pam and eat our lamb burgers for supper. A game of croquet with his friend Cam down the street, another chapter of *The Lord of the Rings*, and off to bed. A good day. Perhaps James really will be able to attend Camp Oochigeas next week. More on that later.   Syd

Two train boys

SUBJECT: ROUGH SHAPE
SENT: JUNE 26, 2001 5:20 PM

And now, just twenty-four hours later, James is in rough shape. All the fun of yesterday was forgotten as he struggled downstairs this morning to the family room sofa, there to remain for much of the day. In addition to the pain in his right arm, James' left hip ("where the left femur joins to my body") is hurting. We had already brought the pain patch up to the current full dose and, in addition, were popping the Dilaudid pills for break-through pain, but still the pain was there. So for most of the day he lay watching TV and reading. Later in the afternoon we took a trip to the airport to work on the racer, and although mentally that was a good thing, it proved a huge challenge for James

163

physically. He shuffled along ever so slowly, using a cane as a crutch, and making conversation was clearly a big effort.

Later I carried him up to bed, and after a chapter of *The Lord of the Rings* with Rebecca, he fell asleep, a hot beanbag cradled to his aching arm and his breathing quite labored. Yesterday James resumed chemo, so we can attribute the lethargy to that as well as to the increased pain meds. The pain, one can only assume, is active disease, and at this stage many treatment options are no longer available, when weighed in the risk-versus-benefit scales.

Camp Ooch, the amazing camp for cancer kids that James has been eagerly looking forward to attending this Sunday for a week, is now looking very unlikely. Thank you for your ongoing prayers.   Syd

SUBJECT: IF, WHEN
SENT: JUNE 29, 2001 5:15 AM

I am glad to say that James is feeling a little better as the week draws to a close. Perhaps the pain meds are kicking in, or perhaps the chemo is having some effect, or both. For James, the fight this week is quite specific: it's his right arm and it's his left femur/hip. The one left him learning to eat cereal with his left hand, and the other left him unable to walk. Every few minutes of his waking hours, his beanbag went back to the microwave to be reheated—a job that Carlo became very good at—and then he would cradle it to one or the other spot, the warmth seeming to bring some comfort. At James' request the hospital bed arrived back in our family room. Something of a sign of defeat, but it meant he could lie more comfortably near the center of action, which in our crazy work-out-of-the-home situation is the kitchen/family room. By Wednesday afternoon he was well enough for an outing with his wheelchair, so we took up Marlis on her offer of a dinner for our family on her back porch, a lovely spot that flows into her backyard, an enclosed courtyard with high brick walls that reminds Pam and I of our pre-kids visits to Italy a million years ago. Actually, Marlis' place is a bed and breakfast in downtown Peterborough, but just like Italy, once you're past the front door you are in a different world. The rear courtyard is full of little statues of cherubs peeking out from behind the shrubs and flowers, and there is even a brick firepit where the children lit a fire. We ate a terrific summer meal, with delicious salads, corn on the cob, hot dogs, and cake, and our friend Ron turned up with fresh strawberries and cream. Then, while Pam and James curled up in the hammock, Ben ran through the sprinkler and watered the garden with Rebecca. On the way home we stopped at the waterfront and threw pennies into the new fountain, and then, to the great excitement of some of us, the evening freight train suddenly appeared on the bridge across the river, three locomotives pulling hard, perfectly completing our outing.

Thursday saw some more small gains, with James back periodically walking, very slowly and with a cane but definitely walking. First there was blood work to be done, and I am glad to say the port-a-cath worked well today after several iffy episodes over the last few weeks. Then we managed an outing to work on the racer, a bit of a landmark day there because the visit saw the completion of the woodwork phase of the project. Next we will move to wheels, brakes, and steering.

And then James went off to school for an hour, his arrival causing quite a sensation with his classmates, who all began talking to him at once and who all wanted to push the wheelchair. It was a great achievement to make it to the last day of school.

For Pam and I, the day was the usual flurry of medical arrangements, constantly trying to keep at least the main phone line open in case Dr. Baruchel phoned. The blood work results showed a transfusion of red blood cells was going to be necessary, and, because the pain had lightened, we put radiation of James' sore arm and leg on the back burner and set in motion plans for the transfusion this morning. But that meant a trip in to oncology to do a cross and type, a necessary but irksome chore that precedes a red blood transfusion. Then a visit to Ravi-Inder for a cranial saecro session, always a treat for James, and what do you know, another day has passed without doing a stroke of work, so it seems. Time to carry James upstairs for a bath, and of course, the evening ritual of reading *The Lord of the Rings*. I printed up some Hildebrandt artwork of the Tolkien saga from the Internet, which has thrilled Rebecca and James as we get deeper into the story. Lately James' room remains unused, with James sleeping in our bed with Pam, which leaves me wandering the hallways trying to decide where to sleep. Rebecca always has trouble going to sleep and always wants someone to sleep with her, so that's where I've ended up this week, contrary to the rules of Dr. Ferber, the infant-sleep expert.

So James is pretty cheerful, and we hope (wildly, once again) that he can attend at least part of Camp Ooch, starting on Sunday. It is heartbreaking to see him trying to get in shape to go. His immediate battle is the two places that hurt. I hear him say, "I'm exercising my right arm so it'll be ready for camp!" as he pumps it up and down. "And I do believe my left femur where it attaches to the pelvis is getting better." As we go through this long, drawn-out fight, it seems to me that "if" becomes each day more a matter of "when." But we will take our cue from James, who has never got it wrong yet, and as they say, it ain't over till it's over. An hour ago I was sleepless, pondering bone marrow fatigue and low absolute neuts and James' empty bedroom. Now, after a bit of time at the computer, I can move on. A memorable dinner with family and friends is a wonderful thing to ponder as I head to bed.   Syd

SUBJECT: BEN'S QUESTION
SENT: JULY 3, 2001 1:06 AM

On Friday James got up early and headed off for a blood transfusion at the old St. Jo's Hospital. It being the first day of the school holidays, Rebecca and Ben got to go too, and Pam had all sorts of crafts for them to do during the five hours that it takes for the blood to drip through. So it was a cheerful and noisy scene that greeted Carlo when he arrived a little later to take some more photos. I went home to catch up on some work. Then word arrived that James' health was too precarious for him to attend Camp Ooch. I was disappointed; Pam was relieved; and James was silent. A dream shattered. We altered our plans for the weekend and went off to our cottage, where James promptly got better. His pain went away; he stopped using his cane; he was full of good humor; he ate well; he played busily with his brother and sister; there was lots of excavating in the sand at the beach and a highly competitive Monopoly game. And beckoning in the backyard was fifteen tons of topsoil in a big pile, just delivered, waiting to be spread. That's where James and Ben played for a good six hours today, helping me load the wheelbarrow and spread it over the tile bed and around the foundations.

James seemed to have boundless energy. I guess it was Ben who summed it all up, in the honest but shocking words of a five year old, when he said almost indignantly, "Mommy, is James going to die or not? It's very confusing. He has pain, and then it's gone." Yes, Ben, you have rather hit the nail on the head, and both your mom and I apologize for underestimating your grasp of the situation. We too are confused. Just when you think it's over, you see improvement. Just when you think you are winning, the pain comes back.

This is only half an email. It's quite unfinished, but my head is nodding, and I'll try and pick up the treads—I mean threads—tomorrow.   Syd

SUBJECT: JAMES RUNNING
SENT: JULY 4, 2001 8:31 PM

Often I share bad news in these emails, so it is with pleasure that I tell you that James has now had five days without pain, five days of increasing vigor. In fact, when we traveled to the Cobourg train station to meet Uncle Rodney yesterday, James ran across the platform to greet him. I think it has been many weeks since I've seen James run. As Ben says, "It's very confusing!" Pam and I have been trying not to read too much into this turn of events, because we all know how fast things can change. We are thrilled to be given more time. And James is thrilled that tomorrow we will travel up to Lake Rosseau, where he will experience the fun and challenge of Camp Ooch after all. Maybe for a day, maybe for two days, maybe for a week—who knows? Everything is completely unplannable these days anyway. Because of his uncertain health, Pam and I have been asked to hover nearby, which will be no great hardship as we will be staying at Windermere House while Rebecca and Ben visit grandparents. This will be the first getaway for Pam and me in many months, and we are childishly excited. All in all, it's been a great week.

I should mention that today was a bit of a landmark day in the progress of the soapbox racer. James' friend Cameron joined us at the airport with Uncle Rodney to install the wheels under the guidance of Allan. Now the project has jumped from a nice piece of woodwork on a bench to something that moves. The boys both took turns sitting in it and gliding across the floor. No brakes or steering yet, but what a ride with those high-tech wheels with their fancy ball bearings, hardly any rolling resistance at all. There are times when the project seems quite futile, with James barely able to turn a screwdriver while slumped in his wheelchair; then there are days like today, where he marches in, tells me he doesn't need my help, and gets to work. The second Sunday in September is not quite so unattainable as it seemed last week, encumbered as it was with pain.

In closing I want to say how much your return emails have meant to Pam and I. Every day the encouragement we need to keep going arrives. We print them up, take them to bed or post them on a cupboard, and gain strength as we ponder your words. From the depth of your hearts we find food for our own souls. Our sincere thanks.   Pam and Syd

It was cold, gray, and windy when James, Pam, and I arrived at the village of Rosseau on Thursday and found our way to Camp Oochigeas. James was carsick, and both Pam and I were suffering from the parental-anxiety thing of dropping your supposedly dying child off for camp for the first time. Just six days earlier, James had been asked not to attend camp because of his worsening condition and out-of-control pain, which in our mixed-up little world seemed to suggest that death was imminent. Actually small, silly little things can easily push your emotions into the next stage of the roller coaster when your child has cancer, such as five traffic lights in a row all turning red just as you get to them, or losing your car keys again, or a letter arriving from the government regarding your income tax return. Mixed in with the "drop off kid at camp" syndrome was our elation that James had made it after all. Last fall Pam and James read about Camp Ooch in *Maclean's* magazine, with stories and pictures of children with cancer doing all kinds of incredible things that children with cancer shouldn't be doing. James was really impressed by a photo of a child who had lost a leg to cancer who was climbing a rock wall. James said with great conviction, "I'm going to that camp next summer." Pam and I were both emotionally confused.

So, to pick up the story once more, not forgetting the cold, gray, and windy bit, we arrived, went to the "med shed" to check in James' extensive collection of medications, and met some of the amazing staff of Oochigeas.

It wasn't long before someone said, "This is not the boy that was described to us by Sick Kids six days ago," and it was agreed that James was certainly well enough to spend the night. Pam had packed two bags for James, the two-day short-stay bag, and then the seven-day bag, the long-shot bag, in case by some miracle James kept getting better. While walking over to his dorm, Junior Boys 1 (JB1), we met James' five roommates, clearly a lively, mischievous bunch, all about seven years old, and we could see James fitting right in. A few more quick conversations with the camp doctor and nurse about stuff that I guess all anxious parents dropping their kids off at camp talk about—platelet transfusions, blood work, hearing aids, pain patches, Do Not Resuscitate procedures, and so on—and it was time to say good-bye to James. This is a camp where cancer kids step out from under the umbrella of fiercely protective parents and do the unimaginable. Off we went, the strangest sensation, letting go of one little boy in whom we have invested so much, someone else for the first time in three and a half years taking on the horrendous responsibility of caring for a child living with cancer. It was a teary moment.

Earlier we had been asked to stay close by in case James suddenly deteriorated, so, armed with beepers, we checked into Windermere House. Ben was staying with Nanny, and Rebecca was with Granny, so it was just Pam and me, in a luxurious resort, no kids, no schedule, no phone calls. And at the front desk we were blown away when the receptionist said, "Your first night has been paid for by an anonymous friend." (Many thanks!) I hardly need tell you that two nights on our own was a slice of heaven after the relentless pace of the last twenty months since James' relapse. Of course we phoned Camp Ooch the next morning to hear "James has had his platelet transfusion, and this morning he played baseball, hit the ball, and ran the bases. He's fitting right in and having a great time and wants to stay longer." Very good. Hard to believe this is the boy who was in a wheelchair ten days ago. If anyone is having a problem, it's clearly not James but us. We rented movies, read books, enjoyed the fabulous food, went for walks, didn't use sleeping pills, and felt guilty about thinking about James all the time and not Ben and Rebecca. On Saturday morning, we called again. "James had a great time at the dance last night!" There was no doubt about it; James was going to stay for the week. Open suitcase two. So Pam and I returned to Peterborough, much refreshed by our stay at Windermere House. Back in Peterborough I accidentally ran the car over the beeper. It gave one last wailing series of beeps; the display went black; and it died; so that gave me an excuse to phone the camp twice in a day. "You are not going to believe this, but James has climbed three-quarters of the way up the rock wall! We just can't believe this kid. He's amazing."

As Ben pointed out the other day, it's very confusing. Delightfully confusing, because I don't believe we can explain this return to health just by thinking "successful pain control." I don't know that any of us know what to think any more. But today it's not cold, gray, or windy. It's sunny, and we are just very happy.   Syd

Just after 9 p.m. we had a call from Camp Ooch to say that James today was experiencing rapidly worsening knee, leg, and arm pain and that regretfully it was time for him to be admitted to hospital to get a grip on the pain control. Despite all this, he had a great day and is smiling and happy. I'm afraid that is more than can be said for Pam and I. So as I write, James is saying good-bye to all his new friends; pictures have been taken; and he is packing his bags. Dave, James' counselor at camp, along with nurse Kerri, is kindly driving him to the hospital in Peterborough, where we will meet around midnight. There is no question that camp has been a terrific time for James and somehow it was meant to be. I suspect that five days at camp has been life-changing for James and has prepared him better for what now lies ahead. By all accounts he has thrown himself wholeheartedly into camp life and has made a deep impression on everyone there while he was at it. For some reason the course of his disease was reversed for a short while, and he made the most of it. Can't think of much else to say just now, except James has done what he set out to do and has done it well.   Syd

Tomorrow the *National Post* will run a "photo essay" on James and his fight with cancer. The photos have been chosen from the three thousand or so that were taken over a period of several weeks by their photographer Carlo Allegri, who has become a great friend of the family in the process.

Carlo recently won the Canadian Photo Journalist of the Year Award. The photo spread will be found in the center two pages of the Arts and Life section of the July 11th edition.   Syd

SUBJECT: LIFE'S MINOR CATASTROPHES
SENT: JULY 12, 2001 11:26 PM

I am remiss in not letting you know that after a brief stay in the Peterborough Regional Health Centre on Monday night, James returned home pumped full of some fresh platelets, and we got to work on controlling the recent bout of pain. This has involved increasing the dose of the Duragesic pain patch, popping the Dilaudud break-through pain pills, and applying warm beanbags to his leg. James is able to walk in a limited fashion but mostly uses the wheelchair. There's been a lot of lying in bed reading or watching TV this week, along with his favorite Magic School Bus and Arthur computer games. It's been a dis-couraging few days, cheered by some delightful and exciting anecdotes from his time at Camp Oochigeas when he feels up to talking about it. James is very pleased that he made it to camp, stayed as long as he did, climbed the rock wall, rode on the "Wasp" (the five-seater inflatable that they sit on while being towed behind the ski boat), played baseball, made a bunch of new friends, and a lot of other neat stuff that he is hinting at (usually this includes the famous James wink) but saving full disclosure for another day.

For Pam and I, it has been an exhausting week, with a lot of time spent chasing up medical details when we really wanted to spend time with Rebecca, James, and Ben. On the mundane side of things, this week we lost our camera with its undeveloped film; I inadvertently ran over the beeper with the car; our home care hours have been cut; some kids rifled through our car during the night and stole the garage door opener; and the public trustee has been giving me grief on my handling of my brother's estate. Then, on the plus side, we were very pleased with the *National Post* photo spread; Rebecca did well at soccer; Peg bought us a new garage door opener; some friends dropped by and cheered us up; and we found our camera with its undeveloped film. If James stabilizes, we hope to spend some time at our cottage this weekend. Good night!   Syd

SUBJECT: POTATO LAUNCH
SENT: JULY 18, 2001 1:39 AM

For a week following James' return from camp we had a difficult time, with increasing pain, loss of weight, vomiting, and loss of mobility. A transfusion of platelets and red blood cells was necessary at the week's end. Even our weekend visit with Nanny to the cottage failed to work its magic, with James spending most of his time in bed, cradling his aching left arm with a hot water bottle. The plus side to all this was that it gave us lots of opportunity to read Tolkien together, and we have now moved into the second book of *The Lord of the Rings*. At times all three children would cuddle up in bed for the readings, but then, during the exciting bits, Rebecca would be unable to contain her exuberance and would start jiggling and bouncing, which bothered James in his pain and nausea. Once again Pam, Nanny, and I found ourselves in the place where you feel that this really is the beginning of the end; it's worse than previous downspins; we are losing the battle. Yet James and I got to have some pretty intimate chats, and despite the pain, he said, "I am happy on the inside!"

Monday arrived, and James woke with a sore neck. Jolt. Can't help leaping to dark conclusions about that piece of information. Later on, blood work showed that chemo could be started again, so James took his first dose of 30 mg of VP 16, and the next morning he was a new man. Pain way down. Good-bye to the wheelchair. Dave, his counselor from Camp Ooch, arrived, armed with lots of photos, and our spirits soared. A quick phone call, and we were on our way to the Airtech hangar to show Dave the racer.

Installing the brake system was the order for the day, and it all came together nicely. Just last Friday Dr. Baruchel reminded us that the soapbox derby race is coming up fast, and it looks like we are on schedule, just the paint job to be done now. But there was added interest at Airtech yesterday, in the form of a potato gun, so everyone downed their tools and followed Big James and Little James outside for the ceremony. The potato gun is a piece of plumbing pipe about three feet long, open at one end and connected to a closed chamber with a threaded cleanout plug at the other. A couple of igniter wires complete this simple but elegant device. You ram a raw potato down the pipe, open the cleanout and squirt in some flammable spray, close it up quick, aim, and fire. Bang! and one potato hurls through the air. Very satisfying. But Airtech is an innovative company, always looking for ways to do better, so for the next launch they add pure oxygen to the chamber first. Big bang! Potato leaves too fast for the human eye to see. Cannot see impact point. Hmmmm. Little James wants to mount the potato gun on his soapbox racer.

So, like the oxygen-enhanced launch with its disappearing potato, life these days seems to consist of big bangs, and we cannot see where we are going. But the news is good today, and we thank our friends for helping make our lives so rich.   Syd

SUBJECT: A GREAT DAY
SENT: JULY 20, 2001 4:18 AM

This is day three of James' recent turn-around for the better, and it began with the VON nurse knocking on the door at 8:15 a.m. for blood work. As we woke up James, the idea that this might be a good day for an adventure took root in my mind. We hadn't been on a train for a while, so I felt a desire to call VIA Rail and discuss the matter. As usual, the nice person at VIA complicated things by insisting on a destination, but we got through that and found that a train would leave from Cobourg at 10:36 traveling east, though the cost would be excessive as we weren't booking five days in advance. That was a start, so I mentioned the concept to Pam, who doesn't surface very quickly in the morning and was unreceptive. But now it was 9 a.m., James' blood samples had been drawn, and it was time to deliver them to the lab at the hospital, so off I went. By the time I returned at 9:25, the idea was gaining acceptance, but time too was moving on, and we needed forty minutes to get to Cobourg.

I called the office of the VP for Customer Service at VIA headquarters in Montreal, wondering if they might be able to help us with the five days in advance rule. When you are battling late-stage neuroblastoma, making plans five hours in advance is difficult, let alone five days.

The VP's assistant quickly got a hold of the situation, took down the details of the train time, and then James began barfing, so that was that. Time out.

A quick reassessment. James ate a couple of Gravol pills and agreed to travel as far as Cobourg and see how he was feeling. Then we remembered that Cobourg has a fabulous beach, so we threw in some bathing suits. Then we remembered that Peggy Two's new father lives in Kingston, so we called him up and got his address.

9:56 a.m. We jumped in the van and zipped. Discovered my watch had been reset by Ben and was five minutes slow. Now actually 10:02. Zipped a little faster. Well, we pulled into Cobourg station just in time for the 10:36 train; James gave the thumbs up; we parked illegally, went to the ticket wicket, and found that we were expected. Our names were there on the computer screen, spelled correctly. Tickets to Kingston, returning 12:31. Very nice. Now, getting on a train at a small station is a cheerful and virtually instantaneous event, in stark contrast to the tedious process of catching a plane at some mega airport, and we were all excited, even Pam. The conductor seemed to know about us too, chatted with the children, brought them gifts, and made sure we had everything we needed.

Rebecca reminded me that I owed her a Daddy/daughter overnight sleepover on a train sometime. Children never forget a parental promise, no matter how rash. An hour of train travel passed very quickly and pleasantly, lots of interesting scenery, and before we knew it we were pulling into Kingston. Another small station event, enhanced by James, who paused as he stepped off the train to give the conductor a terrific James hug, to the obvious pleasure of the crowd waiting to board the train.

A short explanation is now necessary. Our wonderful friend Peggy Two, the only child of her adoptive parents who died ten years ago, was recently advised by the bureaucracy that handles these matters that her birth father was still alive. Likewise, her birth father Alex was advised that he had a daughter, dating back to his premarital days, contrary to information supplied many years earlier that the baby had died at birth.

The long and short of this is that Peggy Two now has eight brothers and sisters, and it's an ongoing story, a very happy one, and we were delighted to drop by Alex and Colleen's home in Kingston to say hello.

We were just settling in when we realized that the return train was leaving shortly. Sure enough, as we approached the train tracks the bells began ringing, the gate descended, and the train arrived, leaving us in the traffic jam on the wrong side of the tracks. Then the gates lifted and we started moving ahead, only to see the gates drop again for a freight train. A long one—107 cars, James informs us calmly when the gate finally lifts once again. We tear into the station, tooting the horn freely, waving at the engineer to hold the train, and somehow we make it just in time. Cobourg, here we come.

Ninety minutes later we were reunited with our van, had lunch at the station, and popped down to the Cobourg beach. First we played minigolf, where James managed a hole-in-one, and then we went swimming in the refreshing waters of Lake Ontario. James decided to build sandcastles while Ben and Rebecca went crashing into the surf. I don't know if I've ever seen Ben and Rebecca have more fun, leaping out of the water as the waves rolled in, shrieking and laughing. Had another idea, made a phone call, and soon our good friends Clare and Lois joined us from their nearby apartment to share the memories in the making. There's a colorful ice cream place called Harbourside Delights nearby, so before leaving for home we sat for a bit, eating ice cream, watching the world go by. I noticed that a large coast guard vessel stood beckoning just across the street, but Pam thought we'd had enough spontaneous adventures for one day and suggested that if we went home now she would cook a leg of lamb for a late supper. Deal.

On the way home we noted that the Cobourg to Peterborough travel time is really fifty minutes, not forty, something we will remember next time we plan a train day. Rebecca piped up, "This was a wonderful day!"

And then James said, "This was one of the best days of my life!" And as an afterthought, "We were so excited that we didn't even phone to get my blood counts!"

All too true. Later in the evening, after enjoying Pam's gourmet lamb dinner, after some road hockey, after a visit from Peggy Two, we sat basking in all the good things that had happened that day. We found an old photo album full of pictures of Rebecca and James when they were very young, and all five of us sat on the bed laughing and talking while we flipped the pages. Then the children began giving out hugs.

Rebecca and James give each other very tender and meaningful hugs these days. A week ago James was in too much pain to give or take hugs, but now it seems he is making up for lost time—lots of hugs, no holds barred. *Perhaps he knows it is time to say good-bye, I brood; perhaps he is going to die in his sleep tonight...then again, perhaps these are silly thoughts. Get a grip; don't be so serious, Syd!* Time to figure out an equitable sleeping arrangement, and it ended up with Pam and James in our bed, Ben in a sleeping bag at their feet, and Rebecca and I together in the guest room. There we read some more of C. S. Lewis's *Magician's Nephew*, the part about the creation of Narnia, and Rebecca surprised me by her grasp of the theology of it all. A great end to a great day, for which we all give thanks to our Creator.   Syd

SUBJECT: THE COUSINS ARE HERE!
SENT: JULY 26, 2001 4:23 AM

After a weekend full of pain and vomiting, James began to improve on Monday. Perhaps the arrival of his three cousins and his aunt and uncle from Burnaby, B.C., for a week's stay had something of a therapeutic effect (delirious excitement?), for there was no denying that by Tuesday morning he was well enough for an adventure. Thanks to the publicity James has been receiving lately, the folk at the Bowmanville Zoo had become aware of us and extended an open invitation to come for a V.I.P. tour. So I got in touch, and off we went, all ten of us in two vans. It was the most incredible day.

We got to do and see all the neat things in a zoo that are normally off limits to the public. Caroline, the zoo's vice president, was there to look after us for the day, along with Michael, the zoologist, who introduced us to the animals and answered all our questions. We started by admiring Sandy, a forty-four-year-old monkey, who is a lot more vigorous and agile than any other forty-four year old, any species, that I know of. Then we fed bananas to the lemurs, with their soft little hands and long, raccoon-like tails. The goats and sheep were next, greedily butting each other out of the way to reach the treats the children were offering. Next up were the lions, and here there was quite a poignant moment. One of the lions, Bongo, the star of many movies requiring a lion on the set, was sitting quietly and majestically near the fence. Bongo is dying of cancer but, like James, is still enjoying life, and the two of them, lion and boy, sat gazing at each other for some time. As we left the area, James said, "I was just wishing Bongo well, and I could hear him wishing me well, too!" The day held many more exciting moments. There was the black jaguar, the elephant rides, the hands-on visit with the python, to name but a few, and we were blown away by the kindness and thoughtfulness of our Bowmanville Zoo friends. It was a great start to the week's visit of the cousins.

Later that evening at bedtime, Ben was flipping through a very battered copy of the *Book Of Common Prayer* that he has adopted, and he asked Uncle Jamie to read Evening Prayer. And then he wandered over to find me and asked, "Daddy, is James going to die?"

As I took a deep breath and wondered just where to begin, Rebecca interrupted us. "My tummy is sore! I need you!"

And so I have more time to prepare an answer. I suppose the place to start is to say that we are all going to die, it's just a case of when, and go from there.

Wednesday proved to be another stimulating day. We began by heading over to the Peterborough Regional Health Centre, where a ceremony had been arranged at short notice so that James could give a check for $10,000 towards the oncology unit of the new hospital. This is the money to date from the sale of the "House In Heaven" CD that my Peterborough Singers put together. Time for a plug: If you would like one, let me know—we also have a few left that Tom Hanks has autographed. Or see the James Web site, at www.jamesbirrell.ca. Anyway, it was a cheerful, noisy ceremony, with six cousins making faces for the press while the parents attempted to keep order. Afterwards, Rebecca, Pam, Anne, Joanna, and Jessica decided to have exclusive girl time and go shopping, an appalling idea for a fine summer day, so James, Ben, Jared, Jamie and I did a boy thing and headed to the airport to work on the soapbox racer. After all the boys had a test ride, Allan helped us recess the screws and sand down the rough edges. Soon it will be time to do the paint job.

The evening brought us pleasure of a different sort, as twenty-four of Pam's family joined us for a cruise with my brother Tony on his houseboat. We keep the boat at the downtown Peterborough marina, where huge, free, open-air concerts are held twice a week throughout the summer. We took in a bit of the concert, a Glen Miller band, while we floated a little way offshore, then went off looking for expensive yachts to terrorize—this being one of the delights having a forty-foot houseboat—had our dessert and coffee, and then sat up on the roof to take in the fireworks display that always follows the concerts. There's nothing quite like watching the fireworks display on a dark night from the middle of the lake, the sound effects rivaling the sights in the sky over your head, and nothing quite like having James still with us, surrounded by family, hollering his head off with excitement as the rockets rise and burst overhead. We are so conscious of every day being a gift.   Syd

SUBJECT: TWELVE GOOD DAYS
SENT: AUGUST 5, 2001 8:35 AM

For twelve days, since the arrival of the cousins from B.C., James has been slowly but steadily improving. No wheelchair, very little pain, appetite back, some nausea, lots of activity, and we've even been able to reduce the pain patch by 20 percent. Today he will have completed a twenty-one-day course of oral chemo, and the plan is to start chemo again in a week. It would be nice to offer an explanation for this improvement, but Pam and I have got to the point where we have given up trying to get our heads around the ups and downs of this disease. We are thrilled that James is doing so well yet terrified of the next crash. Meanwhile, we had a memorable week with the cousins, full of fun and adventures and family time, and when I asked Rebecca what was best, she said, "Everything!"— and I guess that's pretty well how we all feel. Rebecca, by the way, is off to camp for a week, starting today. James has been making regular visits to Airtech, and with the help of Alan and Big James, the soapbox derby racer is now structurally complete, leaving just the paint job. The derby is on Saturday, September 8th, and will be held at the east end of Hunter Street, on the nice, steep hill that comes down from the Liftlocks.

The only blip on the James health scene happened last Thursday during a platelet transfusion. The last bag was dripping in when I noticed some blotches on his head, followed moments later by the appearance of hives. A reaction to the blood product, and, as in most severe allergic reactions, it happened very quickly. His lips swelled grotesquely; his voice became hoarse; and I can still see James frantically pushing his fingers into his ears, trying to open the ear canals that had swollen shut so that he couldn't hear. The good news is that the antidote was promptly administered, and it worked. A couple of hours later, James was playing cards with Pam and was pretty pleased about having had an ambulance ride over to the other hospital. From now on, we will use blood products of the single donor variety, to cut down his exposure to other people's antibodies. The episode left both Pam and I emotionally exhausted, and we were very pleased to find ourselves at the cottage the next day, soaking up the heat wave in a very leisurely kind of way. Lots of time for reading, and we are down to the final few chapters of the last book of *The Lord of the Rings*. James is finding it very exciting.

My apologies for keeping you waiting for news.   Syd

*Rebecca, James and Ben on the ladder
to the kids' loft at the cottage*

SUBJECT: SETBACK
SENT: AUGUST 12, 2001 4:50 PM

Without any warning, James' twenty-day run of good health ended Thursday, Aug 9th, at 6:30 a.m., when he awoke crying with leg and arm pain. We upped the pain patch dose from 25 to 75 mcg/hr, popped some Dilaudid break-through pain pills, and after consulting Sick Kids, we restarted chemo. By today, Sunday, at 125 mcg/hr, he was no longer able to stand, and picking him up to carry him causes him considerable pain. The boy who was amazing us all earlier in the week with his boundless energy and activity is now either in bed or in his wheelchair. Today was a day of reading, videos, and computer games. Needless to say, our lives are on hold once again. One of the challenges is knowing how to keep Rebecca and Ben from feeling excluded from our family as we care for James.   Syd

SUBJECT: OZ
SENT: AUGUST 24, 2001 1:20 AM

Last night our family hopped in the van for the hour's drive to Stirling to see the children's theater, now an annual summer event for us, and we thoroughly enjoyed *The Wizard of Oz*. Actually, it seemed like two shows, because watching my children watch the show was equally entertaining. Rebecca beamed with pleasure and admiration when the beautiful good witch danced on; James was enthralled when the scarecrow suddenly came alive; and Ben quivered with excitement on my lap when the wicked witch suddenly appeared. James was in fine form, despite the need of the blood transfusion scheduled for later this morning. It is always good to hear Pam laugh, though I took the precaution of sitting several seats away, children in between, because people do tend to turn around and look to see who it is that is enjoying the show so boisterously. The drive home was an unexpected bonus, for the children chattered on about the story and added to the pleasure of the evening. All the way home a crescent moon led the way, low on the horizon in the west, wisps of clouds adding a veil of mystery, and we half expected to see the wicked witch outlined in the sky. Later at home, we helped James up the stairs and then did this nightly Birrell thing of "who is sleeping where," Ben fortunately abstaining this time and going to his own bed, and it ended up Pam with Rebecca and James with me in the guest room. As we cuddled up, I noticed the bump under his pajama top, remembered that his port-a-cath was still accessed so as to be ready for the transfusion, and wondered, if it were me trying to go to sleep with a needle device poked through my skin and taped up with the tubes and lines on my tummy, whether I would be complaining. So I asked James, and he said, "No problem, ya just hafta remember not to roll too much this way." And then, a little more tentatively, I asked how he puts up with all the other indignities of living with cancer, and he said, "I've made my choice. I'm always gonna be choosing to live." And that choice is hard work.

I needed to hear those words of James and the challenge of them, as of late Pam and I have found ourselves tired and discouraged by this endless war. At this stage in the progress of the disease, there is both sadness and exhaustion, and a sapping of the will to plan, to move ahead, to think positively. One is always looking for a pattern of James' ups and downs, and there really isn't one, except that every marvelous recovery is accompanied by fear of the next crash, which then arrives with its usual awful ferocity. And then we are given one more chance, and he slowly improves, slowly regaining what was lost—or is it not quite as much this time? But the last two days have been good ones, very good ones. Yesterday even included a trip in our ancient micro motorboat to climb on the rocks and jump over the rapids at the end of our cottage lake. At a certain stage of the upward spells, I stop taking sleeping pills and get back to my middle-of-the-night email writing and dare to make long-term plans (like going to see Dr. Baruchel next Wednesday—very long-term planning at the moment, but I think all of us will go, by train, and we must have a Toronto family adventure while we are at it). James talked of choice, and, as you have always known but I have only started to figure out, writing these emails is very therapeutic for me, especially when James hands me the punch line of the sermon on a plate with his "I'm always gonna be choosing to live." Tonight's therapy is completed, and I am off to bed.   Syd

SUBJECT: TEST RUN
SENT: AUGUST 28, 2001 4:15 PM

Raw fear. Big James at the bottom of the hill, me at the top. Little James snug, confident, and unafraid in the Orange Rocket, eager to start the first test run of his soapbox racer. Nice, quiet, freshly paved country road; check for traffic; all clear; time to let go. I hesitate, still clutching the racer, scared to let Little James take his fate in his own hands. Later, Big James tells me he was scared too and that all parents feel the same way when they watch their child zoom down the hill for the first time. Then I get reckless and let go. The racer quickly accelerates down the hill, and I experience the novel feeling of having no control over my son's life. He's on his own, and if he's going to crash there's nothing I can do about it. I quickly jump in the car and follow him down the hill.

But James is fine, and it is clear that neither chemo nor narcotic pain patches nor brain tumor nor anything else is affecting his judgment, for he steers true and straight and pulls up beautifully next to Big James at the bottom of the hill. Three more practice runs, each a little faster, and we reach thirty-five km/h. We are "Go" for the soapbox derby. Three months ago I would hardly have thought this moment possible.

Which brings me to the date and time: Saturday, Sept 8th, Hunter Street East, just a block west of the Liftlocks. James is competing in the hobby class, and the first heat is at 10 a.m. Then the other classes have their first heat. After that, the second round of heats for the hobby class is held. And then the other classes have their heat two. Get it? Many heats later, the final heat of the hobby class takes place, perhaps at 3 p.m. And we are not making any predictions on how far James will proceed! There will be many worthy young contestants out there. In addition to the soapbox derby, there are all sorts of kid activities taking place to fill the gaps. It's a great series of family events. See you there! Syd and company

SUBJECT: BACK TO SCHOOL
SENT: SEPTEMBER 5, 2001 12:38 AM

And there you have it. The first day of school, and three Birrell children—not two—bounced out of bed, gobbled breakfast, and then posed for the obligatory photo that their dad always inflicts to mark the occasion. Time for blood work, hurry, hurry, and then, eagerly and cheerfully, the children went to school. One was going to grade one for the very first time, wearing some new back-to-school clothes and sporting a cool new haircut, and his mother celebrated while his father cried privately for a bit, none of which bothered this boy because he has learned to handle much harder things in his five years. One had chosen a very pretty new red dress to wear and just couldn't wait to see all her friends again and isn't it wonderful that the summer holidays are over at last. And one put aside the pain in his arm, and the fatigue, and the uncertainty of wondering whether his body would let him down, and said to his dad, "I can carry my own backpack!" and confidently marched into the playground to greet his friends. He just wants to be like all the other kids. Deep down, his parents hadn't really expected him to ever go to school again, and so some of his back-to-school shopping had been last minute. Three very excited and happy children.

I remember so well the words "He made it!" that Dr. Baruchel used to describe James' return from some earlier medical catastrophe, and today it seemed once more the right thing to say. Yes, James must put a great deal of physical effort into getting dressed, or climbing a staircase, or tying his shoes, while his younger brother bounces around the planet with infinite energy, bursting with good health. But there he was, back at school, first day of grade three, and in response to one of the questions on today's homework, "What is your goal this year?," James wrote "Get to grade four." Last week we had our first visit to Sick Kids in some time, and it was a delight to see Janet and Dr. Baruchel again. All five of us went (actually six, because Nanny came too), because cancer really is a family affair, and besides, in case you haven't noticed, we like to add adventure to our medical appointments wherever possible. So, afterwards we went on the ferry to Toronto Island Airport for a private tour of the Air Ambulance Helicopter place and got to inspect one of the helicopters as it sat undergoing maintenance. We sat in the pilot's seat, inspected the twin jet engines, poked the titanium driveshafts, and even got to climb into the "Hell Hole," the confined space in the tail. Fascinating. And then, observing that it costs an exorbitant amount of money to go up the CN Tower to the viewing area, we cunningly had dinner in the revolving restaurant, because that gets you into the viewing area for free, which makes you feel good until you get the bill. Anyway, it was a great outing. Especially the part where you walk on the glass floor, looking straight down one thousand feet to the ground. It helps you forget about that bill.

But I forgot to finish the medical part. Clearly Dr. Baruchel was delighted, though puzzled, to see James in such good shape. How to explain the improvement in James' health is the mystery, and in lieu of a better explanation, we wondered if we perhaps we have stumbled on a concoction of drugs that is producing the anti-angiogenic effects that we sought in the mouse medicine of ten months ago. Or is it a different medicine, the kind where you stay alive because on September 8th you are going to compete in the soapbox derby and nothing is going to stop you from achieving that goal. Meanwhile, our forever quest for a new and better treatment, the elusive magic bullet, is put aside in favor of the old edict, "If it ain't bust, don't fix it." Whatever James is taking now is working, so don't mess with it. Although there is no suggestion that we have found a cure, it seems that for now the disease is being controlled, for how long is anyone's guess.

So, a difficult summer has ended, filled with despair and hope, weariness and then exuberance, questions with no answers. And a host of wonderful memories. And the words "He made it!" ringing in my ears.   Syd

James had a terrific day at the races. His words at the end of the first run pretty well summed up the emotions in all our hearts. 'I did it! I did it!' Against all odds our James has lived to fulfill his lifelong dream of racing in the Soapbox Derby. Ended with a magnificent wipeout crash from which he emerged safe, happy, and in fourth place. His best time was the fastest of the day. In haste, nursing my shattered nerves but absolutely elated.   Syd

Today I had hoped to write you an account of the soapbox derby, but instead I fear I must tell you that James is lying in our bed at home in terrible pain, sobbing hysterically. A whopping increase in pain medications has yet to achieve anything, and if there is no improvement today, he will likely be admitted tomorrow to the Peterborough hospital for pain management. We would appreciate your prayers.   Syd

James appears to be responding well to the increase in pain medications. The turning point came yesterday afternoon, with the arrival via special courier from Toronto of the freshly edited film footage taken on the day of the race. James began to laugh again as we watched his last race, the "spin crash" one, and then rewound slowly so that we saw the crashed car emerge from the crowd, spin, and zoom backwards up the hill and into the starting ramp. Very funny. "Do it again, Dad!" In that things like soapbox races wonderfully motivate a sick child to live, I felt that last Saturday's race was a landmark in James' life, and I wanted to share the moment with you. However, the demands of James' care just now don't allow me time to write an email that would do justice to the story. I asked Big James if he could help, and here is the story in his words. I warn you that it may bring tears. It did for me.   Syd

THE WORDS OF BIG JAMES:

I have been oblivious to most of James' seven years of life. The tragic news of his fight with neuroblastoma did not catch my eye. The car wash rallies registered only vaguely on my radar screen. If Carole mentioned James, his story was one of many.

That changed when Carole described this young boy's dream to build and race a soapbox racer. This was a dream I could understand and identify with. This was a dream I could help become, if not a reality, at least a promise of reality. This boy spoke to me before I even met him.

To meet James is to love him. His remarkable intelligence is apparent immediately, even through the haze of medication or between bouts of vomiting. At James' age I was building Mecano elevators and following my grandfather around fixing refrigerators, so perhaps I responded particularly strongly to this kindred spirit. What may be even more remarkable than his intelligence, however, is the grace with which he bears his burden. He simply does not complain about his lot. He accepts adversity but not defeat. We whose lives are so much simpler are humbled by the object lesson in living that James provides.

JAMES BIRRELL

James and James

Awareness comes slowly though, and I didn't appreciate what I had been handed when Syd gave me his binder of emails on my first visit. As I read through it over the next few days, I joined the many followers of the Birrell family saga. I doubt that Syd could have could have imagined where these emails would lead when he started them, nor the profound effect they have on their readers. Confronted with Syd's position, I would find it so easy to retire into my own private misery.

As we began to design the soapbox racer that became James' TGV Orange Rocket, we realized that getting James out of the house to work on the racer would give James a reason to get out of bed. Our first attempts to schedule visits quickly revealed that James' life had a schedule of its own. We came to see that there was actually nothing in our day more important than a half-hour visit from James, and we could easily accommodate him any time he was up to a visit.

From day one, James had settled on the idea of a racer patterned after the famous TGV train. The initial concept sketches were transferred to cardboard at full scale and signed off by James to finalize the design. Each day that James came to visit, we tackled a small part of the project, and each day that James was absent, the project stood idle. Whether confined to his wheelchair or struggling with a cane or bounding with seemingly limitless energy and perfect health, James always lent his hand to some part of the day's efforts. My daughter's soapbox racer stood always at the ready for a bit of driving practice. Sometimes when James was not feeling very well, the example of Ben taking a test drive was enough to rouse James' energy. Sibling rivalry appears at times to be a positive force.

Eventually, the TGV woodwork was finished, and it was time to install the axles, brakes, and steering. Steering cables needed tensioning; wheels needed alignment; brakes needed adjusting. Painting could wait for a few test drives. Often Ben and Rebecca would join the visit, and occa-

sionally friends and relatives. On driving days, anyone small enough to fit could try a push down the gentle slope at the hangar.

Applying the paint and decals brought out the true elegance of James' design. This racer was sleek, beautiful, and functional. All that remained was a test on a real hill. Real hills require real drivers, and only James was qualified to drive the TGV on a real hill. The practice hill on Whittington Drive had been freshly paved, has little traffic, and has a good, long slope. Whereas the real race would provide twenty seconds at high speed, Whittington Drive provides a smooth and gradual acceleration over a fifty-second run.

With Syd in close pursuit in the Subaru and me at the bottom of the hill warding off any traffic from below, our hill provided relative safety from traffic while also providing very unforgiving ditches on both sides. A child's first run down such a hill is a very special thing for a grown-up to observe—as thrilling as it is terrifying.

We had built a car capable of winning. We had not built a car that was easy to drive. At high speed the car became directionally unstable and required continuous attention to maintain course. As ballast was added, this tendency was accentuated. Worse, the thin tires, while providing low rolling resistance, offered virtually no cornering capability. The driver must be smooth, and his concentration must be total. Enter James, compromised by pain and/or medication.

While we had started this project with only a small hope of actually reaching race day, we found race day actually within our grasp. And we found ourselves confronted with a cost benefit analysis that said: at risk—James' life; benefit—quality of life. Every run down the practice hill was tense. As we increased the ballast toward race weight, the tension rose. Some days James drove arrow straight. Some days we could not discern if James was chasing shadows or simply minimizing his pain and driving just well enough to stay on the road.

James showed a marked preference for the right lane, while we would have preferred him to take the center of the road to provide the largest margin of safety relative to those ditches. On one occasion, James' approach proved wiser when to our horror a truck pulled onto the road and the two vehicles passed each other in opposite directions and opposite lanes. Two days before race day, we had our last two practice runs. On the last run, we were on the receiving end of a verbal tirade by an irate trucker who did not appreciate our use of a public road. We had, however, satisfied ourselves that James could drive the car safely at race weight, although full race speed would have to wait for race day.

The afternoon before race day, we changed all the wheel bearings and packed up the car. The race would be run on brand new bearings, carefully cleaned and lubricated with a secret formula that had served my son and daughter well in previous years. Having done our homework, we parted

knowing we had done all we could to prepare.
Immediately, though, I began thinking of things I
hadn't previously considered. Wouldn't the car be
easier to drive if we had a better directional refer-
ence for James? Okay, that I can build and install on
race day. Wouldn't the car be more directionally
*stable and easier to drive and **safer** if the wheels had*
two bearings? That change would be tough, and Syd
reminded me that both my kids had driven on single
bearing wheels (yes, but my son's car was as notori-
ously difficult to drive as it was fast, and my
daughter crashed twice). Mercifully, I didn't dream
about soapbox racing that night.

There had been a threat of rain on race day, but the
weather was perfect. Syd and I had arranged to meet
for weigh-in at 9:30. It didn't surprise me that he
was early and beat me there. Weigh-in was
uneventful, as we had carefully ballasted the car
exactly ten pounds below the maximum to allow
James to have a big breakfast (and because we were
simply unwilling to push our luck any higher). The
aiming reference was installed by James, and he
seemed delighted by the addition.

Qualifying against Car 104 was extremely fortu-
nate, as 104 was the second fastest car in the class.
James, with Car 103, won both heats, the second by
only .005 seconds. This was great racing, and James
was clearly the driver to beat. As eliminations
began, a peculiar rule placed James in Lane 1 for
every race. Lane 1 may have been a bit faster, but it
had an obstacle fifty yards from the finish that made

it much harder to drive. As eliminations continued, James' continued success had him jumping from wagon to racer without a rest. On his eighth run, the pace of action took its toll. James steered beautifully, but a slight overcorrection toward the end forced him to take the short side around the obstacle and then to steer hard to avoid the timing light. The narrow tires were not up to the cornering, and the car spun out, passed through the finish line backwards, and struck a curb. Disaster was narrowly averted, as both the finish-line worker and the other car were only barely missed. The car was damaged and James shaken but not stirred. He finished the day elated, in fourth place.

The race, you might say, was not all it could have been. I would argue, it was more. James had put on a terrific show but had not stolen the show. He had done so as just another seven-year-old boy, despite the intense attention focused on him. He showed an absolute obliviousness to any real or perceived pressure and simply had fun. He presented himself honestly to the world as an absolutely charming and delightful young boy. His fellow racers and their families responded in kind, and the day had the wonderful feeling of kids simply having fun.

Thank you, James, for sharing your dream with us. Thank you, Syd, Pam, Rebecca, and Ben, for sharing James with us.

Your friend,

Big James

How do you write news of one little boy and his family in the wake of this week's hideous terrorism? Our family's struggle seems very insignificant next to such tragedy. Perhaps I can add a little good news at the end of a week of bad news by saying that James is better; he went happily off to school today; he is free of pain, somewhat bruised from his soapbox derby "spin crash," as he calls it, and we are shortly leaving for the cottage.   Syd

I wake from some mellow dream, and then, with that all-too-familiar jolt, sleep instantly vanishes, and I remember that James is fighting cancer. I remember that four and a half hours ago James was still awake when Pam and I returned home from a postconcert party; I remember his cheerful, "Hi, Dad!," and his delight at being awake at midnight to welcome us home. Then, "Hey, Mom, wanna see my Lego Technic battle cars I made? They're really cool! Dr. Squire gave them to me." But then, apologetically, he adds, "My shoulder is hurting a bit." Would a warm beanbag help? "Sure!" I remember that the last two days have been sacrificed on the altar of nuclear medicine—that powerful tool of diagnostic imaging, the MIBG scan—and that there is no escaping reality. Cancer throughout his body, hardly a bone that does not show lesions, left scapula has a particularly large lesion, signifi-

201

cantly more disease than the MIBG scan of last January. None of this is a surprise, given the nature of recurrent neuroblastoma. The surprise is James and his indomitable spirit, his love of life, his excitement. How does a boy so sick manage to race in the soapbox derby? "Hey, Mom! When we went to Dr. Squire's lab today, they were showing us the chromosomes, and the neuroblastoma ones were red, and they were breaking off and growing on other chromosomes!" Yes, as is our custom, we combined the chore of a trip to Sick Kids with an adventure and had a fascinating visit to the lab of Dr. Jeremy Squire while we were in Toronto. Dr. Squire is one of the award winners of the James Birrell Fund for Neuroblastoma, the JBFN as we call it, and he and his assistants were eager to show us the direction that their research into neuroblastoma was going. Rebecca had come too, as it seemed the benefit of seeing some cutting-edge science outweighed missing a day of school. "Mom, the good chromosomes have a couple of red dots at each end, but the cancer ones don't have them, so that makes the ends sticky, and then they stick onto other chromosomes."

There we were, peeking into the intriguing world of mutant genes and chromosomes and at the same time looking at the evidence of the devastation caused in James' body by those rogue cells. The MIBG scan has reminded us just how tenuous is James' hold on life. Once again we review goals, reassess priorities, and wonder how it is that James is still with us. "I think I'll go to bed now." The desire to haul James into bed with us for the night is enormous, to snuggle up and hold him close while we can. But James happily heads off to his own bed, the warm beanbag on his sore shoulder.   Syd

Last Sunday turned out to be one of those gut-wrenching, panic-stricken days that we know so well. James quite abruptly developed a numbness in one leg, between the ankle and the knee, and fell to pieces emotionally as a result. I was playing the organ for Sunday morning church service at the time, Pam in the choir nearby, when it became apparent to us that James, sitting with his buddies in the junior choir, was in trouble. We left church early, trying hard not to believe that cancer somewhere in James' brain or spinal cord was causing the loss of sensation, and fearing that paralysis was just around the corner. We got on the phone, and as we described the symptoms to Dr. Beamish, always the man to bring hope into a dark situation, it seemed that perhaps we were dealing instead with a pinched nerve in James' knee and that twenty-four hours would see the problem disappear. And sure enough, by Monday morning it had disappeared. Here endeth the bad part.

So, Monday after school, we were able to proceed with our plans for a trip to Ottawa, all five of us, and leave behind the ugliness of Sunday's misadventure. Perhaps you remember an email from a year ago about a lost shipment of a radioactive isotope necessary for a diagnostic scan—the MIBG—that James had been booked for. Air Canada lost it, and I made a fuss, and it all turned out quite nicely, and along the way we made some new friends at the manufacturer of the drug, MDS Nordion. We kept in touch, and it seemed that even a well-run, highly innovative company can benefit from contact with the people who end up using their product, especially if it's a boy called James. We were pleased to give MDS Nordion permission to use James' photo and story in some of their marketing, and we were delighted when MDS made a donation to the James Fund. And now we were on our way to Ottawa, to make an appearance at the company's quarterly employee meeting. MDS Nordion had kindly booked us in for two nights at the Marriot Hotel, close to the parliament buildings and all kinds of other neat places, so that we could have a holiday while we were there. The three-hour drive was uneventful, apart from Rebecca losing her shoe in Perth, and instead of listening to the Chipmunks CD till the parents went crazy, I told the children about Bach's Goldberg Variations, and how the count suffered from insomnia, and how old Bach wrote the music for the count, and how the count was so grateful he gave Bach a bag of gold, and before they could protest, I started the music. Believe it or not, the children now ask for the Goldberg Variations every time we get into the car. As a professional musician, I am much encouraged. I am digressing. The Marriot, although very ritzy and fancy, has a number of features to encourage families to come and stay, such as juice and cookies delivered to your room at bedtime, and such as super-bouncy beds for jumping up and down on, as well as a great swimming pool, a huge kids' playroom, and minigolf on the roof. The children had their first exposure to billiards and pool, though they insisted on using the cues backwards, hitting the balls with the fat end.

Tuesday we planned as an educational day, ostensibly to make up for missing school, so after the obligatory game of minigolf at 7 a.m., and after driving by the houses of Parliament and saying hello to our member of Parliament, Peter Adams, we checked out the Museum of Civilization, which I must say was superb, especially the children's section. Could have spent the whole day there, but instead we cruised down Sussex Drive past the prime minister's house to the Aviation Museum for another fascinating display. The children were very interested in the Avro Arrow display, and then James zeroed in on the Hawker Harrier jump jet. Lots of fun, and very educational. We went out for supper at the fish market, where even Ben went exotic and ate shrimp. Later, at bedtime, I couldn't help reflecting yet again at the contrast between the difficult moments our family faces and then the great times we share when the going is good.

Wednesday was our date with MDS Nordion, so we smartened up and headed out to the Corel Centre. We were the final number for the morning and found ourselves seated at the front of a large conference hall, surrounded by MDS Nordion employees listening to various company presentations. Ben made himself at home on the floor and got busy with his coloring book, while James settled in to Jules Verne's *Twenty Thousand Leagues Under the Sea* and Rebecca reread *The Lion, Witch and Wardrobe*. I suppose our children have got used to the unusual being the norm, and for half an hour they read and played while 600 folk did their business around them. Then it was our turn. Pam took the microphone first to tell the story of the lost shipment, and then I spoke about the James Fund and of our hope to find a cure for neuroblastoma. Feeling the need to relate the work of these highly motivated, intelligent, and energetic people back to their ultimate customer, I closed by reading the email about Ben and James as they sat playing together at the cottage some time ago, pulling out James' hair in great chunks, making up funny new words in the process.

Rebecca was next: "Thank you for inviting us to Ottawa. We had a great time!"

And James: "Thank you for donating money to my fund and helping kids like me fight cancer!"

A company barbecue back at the company headquarters followed, everything laid out on the front lawn, where we were able to make many new friends while Rebecca, James, and Ben took turns riding in James' wheelchair up and down the grassy slopes, laughing hysterically, James clearly not in need of a wheelchair today. Then it was time for the Goldberg Variations, a brief stop in Perth to pick up Rebecca's missing shoe, and home sweet home. Thanks, MDS Nordion!   Syd and family

SUBJECT: CHEMO STOPS
SENT: OCTOBER 9, 2001 7:29 PM

I wish we could pass on lots of good news all the time, but the reality is otherwise. The weekend at the cottage was a wonderful break, but today's blood work wrenched us back into the battle. James' white blood count and absolute neutrophil counts were low, putting him in neutropenia territory, which means he is particularly susceptible to infections, and that places us on the "go straight to hospital without delay" should he develop a fever. More significantly, James must stop his daily chemo till and if his white count recovers. Past experience shows us that even a few days off chemo results in the disease moving into high gear. We know from the MIBG scan of three weeks ago that James is a very sick boy. So it looks as if we are in for a rough time.

None of which is overly obvious if you were to visit James today. Although fragile and tired, he is still up and about, very cheerful, uncomplaining, and full of plans for the future. He is busy reading *Robinson Crusoe* for the second time and looking forward to his buddy Cam's birthday party. Once again Pam and I are not quite sure how to plan anything, whether to back off on our commitments or move ahead in a guarded fashion. More could be said, but Ben is wanting to show me his moon rocket. Will keep in touch. Syd

SUBJECT: AN UNEXPECTED EVENT
SENT: OCTOBER 11, 2001 3:35 AM

This has been an extremely difficult week for us as we face the fact that James' time with us may be running out. The idea is not new to us; you just hope that it's still a long way off. This week, it doesn't seem like being a long way off. On the medical front, it was decided to restart chemo and see what happens. James has been up and about, pretty well pain free, and enjoying life quite nicely in his inimitable way despite his limited energy. He has been grappling with a loose tooth for days, and yesterday the project came to fulfillment. On our return from choir practice last night, he proudly bore a platter on which the tooth was being displayed. Having made the point, he went off to his bedroom to make the appropriate arrangements for a visit from the tooth fairy. Pam and I exchanged meaningful glances, hoping that we wouldn't have to cook up yet again one of those stories about the tooth fairy being too busy in Africa or that we had wrapped it up in the wrong kind of paper, or whatever.

Finding ourselves in a situation where one feels that life can't get much worse, and therefore one more complication will make no difference, Pam and I picked up the threads of a long-standing family debate, reviewed our parental position, and decided that it was time to concede. We placed a call to our friend Mary the vet and said, "Have you got a dog, house-trained, nonallergenic, doesn't bark, and loves children?"

Mary and her team got to work, and a couple of hours later we got a call. "We've found a twelve-week-old miniature poodle, white, male, in Arthur, Ontario." Where's that? About three hours away, apparently.

I phoned the place, and the helpful owner said, "I've got someone going your way later tonight. Do you want him?"

So, in typical "Why wait?" Birrell fashion, late last night the cutest little puppy arrived (yes, I know, they are all cute at that age). It has been the single-most asked for wish of all our children, so you can imagine their complete and utter delight. "I've always been wishing to get a dog!" said James. Then he phoned Uncle Jamie in Vancouver. "Hi, this is James. We just got a dog!" I guess Uncle Jamie then said, "I thought your parents didn't want a dog," because the next thing James said was, "Actually, they really did want a pet!"

Rebecca discovered that the puppy gives the best snuggles, licks, and kisses imaginable, and then went off to make dog toys out of old socks. Ben's comment to Pam and me: "You two always wanted another baby. And here it is!" Where did he get that idea from? And for the first time in ages, Pam looked really happy. It seems that Bigsby, or Pippin, or whatever his name is going to be, is the distraction we needed. And we have the satisfaction of knowing we won't have to deal later with the thought "James always wanted to have a dog." Perhaps he will help us all through the difficult times ahead.

I forgot to mention the strangest thing: James eventually went off to bed, only to come tearing back to say that the tooth fairy had already been! "She must'a snuck in while we were playing with the puppy!" Odd.   Syd

Bigsby bringing smiles

SUBJECT: JAMES AND BIGSBY
SENT: OCTOBER 12, 2001 8:42 AM

By way of a postscript to the business of our new dog, I've decided to forward the following note that I sent to my cousin Nick Bigsby who lives in England with his family. James has perked up considerably since the puppy arrived.

Dear Nick,

In an attempt to keep a good name alive in Canada, and more importantly in my family, we have named our new dog Bigsby. Surely we now have the only dog in the world named Bigsby. Looking at old photos of our mutual grandfather, which, along with a few stories passed on by Mum, is all I've got to go on as we never got to meet, I am struck by his look of quiet determination. So there you are. I hope you are not offended, and I am now relieved of forever standing at the door shouting "Snowball!" or "Adventure!" the two leading names submitted by my children. The first might be misinterpreted as an invitation for someone to toss one, and as for the second, I just couldn't face the thought of folk wondering for the next fifteen years why that man insists in calling for an adventure in the same way you might hail a taxi. Bigsby is a very nice little miniature poodle, whitish, and has instantly made himself at home, particularly in the matter of the back hall carpet. Although I can still see no flaw in our long-standing argument against having a dog, the timing of his arrival just seems to be right. He has brought great joy to the children, and even Ben, right into the lunchtime playground gang at school, wants to come home for lunch these days to play with the Bigsby. Rebecca has perfected the under-the-chin cuddle, and as for James, Bigsby has got him running all over the house playing ball. Last night Big James, of soapbox derby fame, came over, and after a week of feeling pretty negative about James' health, I had to admit that Little James, at 10 p.m., tearing happily and energetically around the kitchen with Bigsby, was looking pretty good. Bigsby has been very good for all of us here.

Best wishes to you, Syd.

CHAPTER 4
LAST DAYS

SUBJECT: JAMES HAS HAIR AGAIN
SENT: OCTOBER 17, 2001 2:09 AM

On Monday, the fax machine growled out a piece of paper that we found devastating. The results of the morning's blood work were arriving, and they were not good figures. Why those results should upset us I don't know, because the road James is traveling is clear enough. The daily chemo that James has been taking has done a good job of slowing the progress of the disease, but we know that the cumulative toxicity will eventually become a problem, and after an early warning last week, it was no surprise to find the white blood cell count dangerously low. The treatment is now a threat to his life. But going without treatment is a threat to his life. So we moped around, cried a bit, and skipped the evening chemo ritual. James' condition: pale, lethargic, various aches and pains, some large mouth ulcers. I had a chat with Rebecca and said, "You probably noticed Mom and I are very worried about James today," to which she replied, "Yes. I can always tell when that happens because you and Mom start talking strange and acting worried."

213

But then in the evening James began to get perky. Pam had decided that she needed a sleepover with James in the guest room, but the moment she entered the bedroom he leapt out from under the covers and shouted, "Boo!" Then he began jumping around in the bed like a wild man. And following an excellent night's sleep, he woke early, beat Rebecca down to breakfast, and looked like a boy waiting for an adventure. The Cobourg railway station popped into mind. Now, Ben has become a very conscientious grade one student and didn't want to miss school, but I offered to phone his teacher, and that clinched the deal. With Mrs. O'Toole's blessing, we were on our way.

We have a bit of a ritual for the Cobourg station, where the boys feel quite at home. The nice lady in the ticket office always finds time to shoot the breeze with us, and we discovered that VIA Rail is doing quite well lately, especially since Sept 11th, and that first class between Montreal and Toronto is always fully booked these days. Hot news: the passenger trains are getting new locomotives in a couple of weeks, and a lot of new coaches from England will be in service soon. Best of all, we heard that soon you will be able to catch a train to Toronto late morning and return mid afternoon, an adventure opportunity if ever there was one. She gave us some cardboard train cutouts to assemble, so we did that in the van, windows open a crack, the better to hear while waiting for the first train. Soon enough we heard a train coming, and James amazed me by leaping out of the van and running down the platform to watch. It was a long freight train. Lots of double-decker container cars. But bonus: just as it arrived, a fast nonstop passenger train flashed through, a very satisfying experience. A bit of a lull followed as we waited for the 10:36 to Montreal and

Ottawa, so we ate colored-sprinkle doughnuts, and then Ben found out that without using a quarter, if carefully manipulated, one of the machines that is supposed to dole out a handful of candy will give you one piece at a time.

Well, the 10:36 arrived just three minutes late, and as usual the boys took up positions adjacent to the train's washrooms, looked for the plumbing pipes, and waited. This time, we struck gold. Liquid cascaded down onto the tracks. From the washbasin waste pipe, I hasten to add, but still very gratifying. The train pulled out; we watched a bit of shunting; and then it was time to return to Peterborough, get Ben to school, and get James some rest. Because of the low white blood cell count, James needs to avoid high-germ places like school. So instead, James showing no signs of flagging, we went off to the airport to find Big James and work on the soapbox derby racer, which is undergoing repairs necessary after his crash in the race. Airtech was just buzzing with activity—a helicopter being transformed into an air ambulance, workmen finishing off the new building—but everyone found time to say hello to James. We made up a nice metal plate to strengthen the place that holds the rear axle. (Hello, Dr. Baruchel—only eleven months till the next soapbox derby.) Then we discovered that the solid steel rear axle was bent—must have been quite an impact when the racer hit that curb. A very nice visit, all the more so as I watched James running after Big James, full of energy, just loving the action.

Now for a dilemma, because today was his good friend Cameron's birthday party, at Kid Spot—children's delight, bedlam, extreme noise, the bane of all parents, surely a place where he would be exposed to dozens of sick children and get inadvertently roughed up on the inflatable slides and all the other inflatable climbing and jumping thingies. But James desperately wanted to go. Another risk-versus-benefit decision. We went. James was all over the place, doing things I thought were beyond him, played air hockey with gusto—no neurological problems with that boy. It was a great party.

Ready for bed? No way. Back home there was lots of playtime with Bigsby to catch up on. "Ya don't have to help me up the stairs!"

And then, a very notable event. "James, you hairy man," said Pam, "you need a shampoo!" It's true. James' hair has returned, a very respectable-looking buzz cut, and his first shampoo in six months was in order. I ended up being the bath parent, and as I tried to remember James' protocol for shampoos, I reflected for the millionth time on the impossibility of getting your head around the ups and downs of this disease. Why should a piece of paper out of the fax machine make you so sad while shampooing your son's hair makes you so happy? I weary of hearing the expression "one day at a time," but it does seem to be true. And from James: "I'm always forgetting about the bad times when I'm having fun. I can't even remember them any more."   Syd

SUBJECT: UP AND DOWN AGAIN
SENT: OCTOBER 19, 2001 2:30 PM

When you stop taking chemo, the side effects stop too, and you start to feel pretty good. So James, who had to stop chemo last Monday because of low blood counts, has had a

216

great week, with energy levels we haven't seen for months, tearing around like a wild man, happy as can be, gaining strength by the hour. The James that we long to see. We went down to Airtech and straightened out the rear axle that had been bent in the soapbox derby crash. The gauge was registering over 5000 pounds pressure when it finally bent straight. Must have taken quite a hit in the crash. Then on Thursday he asked if he could rejoin the junior choir at church and take part in this Sunday's performance of "Joseph," which Pam and I are putting on. So he joined the other kids for the dress rehearsal, put on his costume, sang his heart out, and even decided that it was time to bare his head in public, for the first time since losing his hair, and show off his new hairdo. What a treat to see James unleashed, running around like any other seven-year-old boy.

But if you stop chemo, you also stop fighting the disease, and at bedtime Thursday night he pleasantly remarked, "For some reason, my left leg is hurting." So we stayed outwardly calm, had a parents-and-son meeting, and decided to take a Dilaudid pain pill, apply a hot beanbag, and hope it was just too much activity too soon. That's what we always hope when the pain comes. But at 4:30 a.m. he awoke, crying with the leg pain. "I just can't stand the pain in my leg!" So we restarted the chemo there and then, took some more pain pills, and tried to go back to sleep. A few hours later, the nurse arrived for the scheduled blood work, and by lunch the results came in and showed that although his counts were up since Monday, they were barely adequate to be restarting chemo. On the positive side, at least the pain was now under control. And James managed to carve out a reasonable day, joining me to repair a church organ nearby and then royally entertaining a visiting two year old with the Brio train set. Then of course there were plenty of entertaining moments with irrepressible Bigsby, the puppy who cheers us up many times a day. It's very nice to have a wagging tail and lots of wet kisses.   Syd

It is always a shock to see how fast James goes downhill when the disease is on the move. Last week we saw James briefly liberated from both chemo and disease. It was wonderful to see him as he might have been, or perhaps I should say how he will be in the next life, a boy of endless enthusiasm, thrilled to be alive, full of hope and love. But as of Thursday last week, James was once again in trouble. Today he is unable to walk or stand and has widespread pain throughout his body. The pain patches are generally doing a good job, and when the break-through pain comes, we add some Dilaudid pills. The warm beanbag is a great comfort. His spirits are good, and he is doing a lot of reading. On Saturday we did a wheelchair trip to Home Depot, and James asked if he could choose a treat. That translated into a nice, shiny Robertson No. 1 screwdriver, so I bought it for him, and later I cut up some pine into short lengths, which he then assembled into a pencil box using his new screwdriver.

Back to the medical. We have exhausted the treatment options that we consider to be humane at this stage of recurrent neuroblastoma. In October of 1999, James relapsed, and the verdict was, "We can probably give you one year, but not two." Notwithstanding, we have managed

218

two very good years. Over the last eight months or so, we have been making a relentless shift from hoping for a cure to buying time, always emphasizing quality of life. Several treatments have worked wonders for James for a while, but ultimately they have failed. Our efforts with the James Fund have been very rewarding, and as James said to me last night, "With all this experimenting, they'll get it figured out, and then all the kids in Canada with neuroblastoma will be able to survive." For now, James is continuing the low-dose chemo that he restarted last Friday, as we think it helps with pain control, but that will have to stop if his blood counts drop too far. So, this time it looks as if there won't be one more amazing James bounce back but that we really are approaching the end. Timetable unknown.

Pam and I find ourselves very sad and weary, and we wonder how all the parents who have faced this kind of situation find the strength to keep going. James helps. This morning he said to the visiting nurse, "When I'm real sick and going through a lot of suffering, and one of my parents is sleeping in the same bed with me, I like to hold their hand in the night to make them feel better." Another reason to stay at home as long as possible.

Trying to figure out how to help Rebecca and Ben through the days ahead is another challenge. When James is so fragile, one has an overwhelming desire be with him, cuddle him, and comfort him. Maybe one day they will read these emails and understand that the last five years have been as much about them as the two cancer fighters, Pam and James. This hasn't been an easy email to write, and maybe not an easy one to read either, but your encouragement over the months and years has been wonderful. Thank you.   Syd and family

Rebecca, Ben and Bigsby

Over the last ten days, we have struggled with some difficult decisions on how aggressive to be with regard to James' treatment. Pam and I needed no convincing when, after visiting, one of the medical team said, "He's not going to get better this time." So we have had some days where the best we could do was to carry him downstairs in the morning, up the pain patch dose, keep reheating the beanbags for him to place on the worst bone-pain spots, and then cuddle up to read a distracting book. And meanwhile, the regular blood work would tell us the story of what's happening in his bone marrow. The blood counts drop, leaving him very prone to infection or whatever, and we have to stop the chemo. The counts get better, but the pain increases. Then a few days later the counts rise. We start chemo again, at a lower dose, and the cycle repeats itself. One decision: if he develops a fever during the low-count phase, then we will not rush to hospital for hookup to intravenous antibiotic within the hour, which has been the rule to date when James is immunosuppresssed. Another decision: Bigsby, the exuberant dog currently on antibiotics for a bowel parasite and busy soiling carpets around our house and generally posing a health threat, Bigsby the morale booster who dashes madly around lifting our spirits and who provides great comfort to James and all the rest of us, Bigsby the bundle of fun, gets to stay.

A decision of another sort was made last weekend. Although planning for a Halloween still five days away— an eternity considering James' present state of health— seemed a little ambitious, we did it anyway. As James wasn't walking, a couple of creative moms came up with the idea of a wheelchair costume. And as Halloween approached, James started feeling better. In fact, he started walking again; the pain vanished; and he didn't really need a wheelchair costume. So last night Rebecca looked stunning dressed as a shooting star; Ben was adorable as a mouse; and James stole the show, grinning away, his wheelchair magnificently transformed into a front-end loader complete with a movable bucket, lights on the roof, danger sign on the back, and the envy of all the other kids on the street. Even nicer than all of this, we got to do the annual ceremony of taking the children's photo on the staircase before they left to go trick-or-treating. "We have to do it! It's a tradition!" said Rebecca as Ben scowled. We did it, and hooray! Against the odds, there's yet another Halloween for James.

Halloween!

And today James is eight years old. Over half his life has been taken up with battling cancer. I had an interesting email conversation with a friend, and I confess that the gist of it was the thought that were it possible to wave the magic wand and undo James' birth on November 1st, 1993, would I say, sure, erase it all, and then we wouldn't have to go through this mess. Of course the answer is, No Way! We will take the good with the bad. It is not better that James had never been born. On Saturday we are planning a family and friends' birthday party, and we hope that he remains as perky as he has been for the last few days. A final word from James: "All of us want to go to heaven, but not without each other."   Syd

Do I start with the good times or the bad times? For the roller-coaster ride continues, life being completely unpredictable from one moment to the next. On Saturday James had his birthday party, a day where the pain was enough to warrant the wheelchair but not enough to curtail his activity. The highlight was a magic show right at home in our living room, a very thoughtful gift from our VON nurse and her husband, who is a magician, and a very fine one at that. Not knowing what shape James was going to be in, we had not invited a host of noisy boys to the party, so it was just his good friend Cameron along with Rebecca and Ben. Peggy One and Peggy Two and family were both there, and Uncle Jeff and Auntie Wendy. Big James and Carole came to keep the magician on his toes. The show was full of rabbits and doves appearing out of hats and other unexpected places and fully involved the children. It was one of those happy occasions where as an adult you get to enjoy not only the show itself but also the sight of four children absolutely enthralled by what they are seeing. It was barely possible to restrain Ben, who was leaping up and down, engaging in a constant banter with the magician. "I know how you're doing that!" But then, just when it seemed the trick was a dud, hey presto! and the rabbit, or your wedding ring, or the playing card was somewhere inexplicable. For Ben it was all quite straightforward, because when you couldn't explain it any more, well, as Ben told me solemnly later, "That's when it's magic." And it sure looked that way when Pam's jack of hearts turned up and

Rebecca found herself levitating, with a bit of hypnotism thrown in to boot. A memorable birthday party, all the more so as just five days earlier we were scrambling for a viable alternative to James' request that we have the party at Kids' Spot, one of those noisy, out-of-control, nightmare-for-parents birthday places.

Birthday magic!

Sunday was another day of surprise, because suddenly James was better, pain free, walking and climbing staircases. Aha! we thought, four days back on chemo and we have control of pain once again. So we were able to visit our friends the Ciscos and check out their immaculate collection of Volkswagon Beetles. We went for rides in various Beetles, dating back to 1957, complete with that compartment behind the rear seat that was so much fun to ride around in when I was a kid. A good day.

But Monday the pain returned with a vengeance, and it was only with lots of tears that I carried James downstairs for what turned out to be a tough day. Lots of pain pills, increase the pain patch. Tuesday was even harder, and we felt it was time to set the wheels in motion for overnight nursing care at home. A kind friend had arranged a limo ride to Casa Loma where *The Lord of the Rings* movie props were being exhibited. But James was in far too much pain to travel; in fact, even the one visit to the bathroom proved to be an ordeal that left us all in tears. There were more tears when the limo arrived. We had decided to do the trip anyway for the sake of the other children, who would have been bitterly disappointed if we had cancelled. So it ended up being a party of seven people and not nine, with Pam staying with James at home. Big James had bought the tickets for the show, and his family made up the remainder of the party. It turned out to be a fabulous trip. Barry the limo driver was wonderful; the ride down was a bundle of fun; and the exhibit was magical. The whole thing had the feeling of being a dream. Although the gift shop had completely sold out of *The Lord of the Rings* memorabilia, the manager found a spectacular poster hidden away that she gave to me when I explained the situation. Best of all, when we got home James seemed to have turned a corner, pain under control, and he even stood up for a moment to prove that he was better. He was thrilled with the poster, which turned out to be a scene that we had just read about in the book that morning.

So there you go. Although the challenge is greater with each passing day, we keep having family times that we can treasure forever. Thanks to all those who have been sending over soups and suppers, which has helped immeasurably, and thanks to those who have provided us with all these wonderful, morale-boosting adventures.   Syd

SUBJECT: "I'VE BEEN HAVING A REALLY GOOD DAY!"
SENT: NOVEMBER 13, 2001 11:53 AM

"I got a new tumor right here in my jaw. It's pushing against my tooth, and I'm just going for a shot of radiation!" So James cheerfully related the latest development to a pleasant stranger in the elevator at Princess Margaret Hospital. Let me backtrack. On the weekend, James' dentist took an X ray that showed something displacing James' teeth in his lower jaw. We know that there are many cancer sites throughout James' body, but this one had the potential to make quite a negative impact on his quality of life, so it seemed sensible to try and stop its growth. By Monday morning, Pam, James, and I were on our way to Toronto (one detour to brighten the day on our way was the Toys R Us store) to see our friend Dr. Baruchel, and by early afternoon we had taken the tunnel from Sick Kids over to PMH to see Dr. Laperriere, the radiation doctor who has been looking after James' radiation needs for the last four years. In pretty short order we visited the simulator, where they drew lines on James' face with a blue marker to line up for the radiation, and then it was off to the radiation room for a four-minute blast of 800 rads to the tumor site. James, from the age of three, has always been very good about lying perfectly still for these kinds of medical procedures, and he kept up the tradition.

At this point we felt that the day could do with some fun stuff, and I remembered that we had a standing invitation

226

to visit Dr. Squire's research lab upstairs on the ninth floor of PMH. We phoned ahead and had a fascinating time doing experiments with dry ice, dropping lumps of the stuff into water and watching clouds of vapor emerge and flow down to the floor. I think Dr. Squire and his assistants also had a lot of fun. And then, it being the height of the rush hour, and not wanting to face the 401 traffic, we went for supper at Rosie's house, our home away from home when we need to stay over in Toronto. Dropping in at Rosie's after a busy day at the hospital is always therapeutic, and today was no exception. It was interesting to see James playing with her two children in a far more spirited manner than we had seen yet that day. Sometimes I think we forget that James spends an awful lot of time with adults at the expense of plain old kid time. I know that what he really wants to do is forget the pain and be able to run around like crazy with his brother and sister and his friends.

So how is James? He is facing widespread disease throughout his body, far too many cancer sites to count. He is facing the cumulative toxicity of years of treatment. His bone marrow is very compromised from both disease and treatment, leaving him in poor shape when it comes to production of blood cells. To mask the pain, he receives big doses of narcotics, which leave him sleepy, irritable, and a little irrational. Some days he can walk a little. On Saturday night, he joined the rest of us at the theater to see his friend Cam performing in *Music Man*. Sunday evening was our family movie night, and we watched *Richie Rich*. The previous two days have been wheelchair days, and today is a stay-in-bed day, with lots of hurting when we sit him up to change his clothes, so it's a good day for continuing our second read of *The Lord of the Rings*. We now have nursing help in our home four nights a week, which gives Pam and I uninterrupted sleep. James doesn't like this arrangement, preferring to sleep with Mom or Dad, and neither do Pam and I, but we realize we can't be good caregivers as the load increases unless we can rest. There are always daily decisions to make about James' treatment, decisions that are now more complicated as we have to choose and judge what interventions are improving quality of life versus prolonging suffering. When you see James in pain, you tend to forget that usually it's under control in a day or two. Yesterday evening when I popped the question, James said, "I've been having a really good day!" A good comment to leave with you as I end this update.   Syd

SUBJECT: BRIEF UPDATE FOR HARRY POTTER DAY
SENT: NOVEMBER 16, 2001 2:26 PM

As this week draws to a close, it's a pleasure to be able to report that James is in better shape, that the tumor in his mouth is shrinking following Monday's radiation treatment, and that yesterday he was once again walking. Today the Harry Potter movie made its debut, and I want to relate the Birrell angle. You need to know some background: Rebecca's best friend is also a Rebecca, Rebecca Ballarin, to be precise. Our Rebecca and our Ben have no interest in the *Harry Potter* stories—they are too scary! But James has been eagerly reading the chronicles on his own, and so has Rebecca Ballarin. Both have been very excited ever since hearing that the movie would soon be coming out. For the last three weeks, Rebecca Ballarin has been earnestly praying every night at bedtime that James would be well enough to go to the movie and that she would be able to go with him and sit next to him. That prayer was nicely answered today, and you could not have found two happier children than James and Rebecca Ballarin.   Syd

I am listening to a very chipper boy chatting happily on the phone to his Aunt Diana while Rebecca is playing a new computer game called Roller Coaster (how appropriate) and is hooting with laughter. A few moments ago Ben and I had a wild time inventing new gymnastic moves up in the bedroom, and earlier in the day Pam and I had a six-hour visit to the cottage to celebrate her birthday.

Restart—that was two days ago, got interrupted—let's try again.

Life these days is full of difficult questions for us. If at the end of each day we can describe scenes like the ones above, we feel that maybe we are dealing with the questions adequately. A distinct change in our attitude has come about in the last weeks as it becomes clear that we are no longer able to control James' disease. Instead, the primary focus has moved to pain control. Now we fear prolonged suffering more than death. We have been greatly helped by many parents who have lost their children to recurrent neuroblastoma and have shared their stories with us. (I note also a fierce determination amongst these parents to find a cure for this monster disease, so that other children will never have to face what their children did. The James Fund, by the

229

way, is going very well. Second round of research grants will be awarded early January.)

Pain control has its own learning curve. Sometimes it can take a day or two to get fully back on top of the pain. Because the cancer is in countless spots throughout his body, we never know where the pain will next hit. A persistent pain hot spot can be radiated, assuming James is well enough to travel to Toronto. We did radiation to the tumor growing in his jaw, but a more recent growth on the back of his head we have decided to observe for the time being, as it is not painful and there are bigger crises to deal with. Our main tool to date has been the family of fentanyl pain patches. You stick on a Band-Aid kind of thing, and the narcotic is slowly absorbed through the skin. Two or three days later, you peel it off and put on a new one. In May we started with a dose of 25 mg, and now we are at ten times that level, 250 mg, which actually means three patches. The great advantage of fentanyl is the freedom it gives you to carry on with life, unattached to an IV pump. Of course we regularly use Dilaudid for break-through pain, along with the usual Vioxx and Decadron and Zofran and Gravol and I can't remember what else. Oddly enough, morphine is not a drug that suits James.

Many questions relate to medical intervention. Always we ask ourselves what we will be returning James to if we proceed with radiation, or transfusions, or whatever other novel treatment might be on the horizon. Options that might have passed the risk-versus-benefit equation in the past may no longer be valid.

Other questions involve what to tell all three children. The answer is, usually, everything, as they figure it out anyway.

Last night James was in great shape, and so Ben said, "James, you were dying yesterday, but today you are not dying!" and they got the Hot Wheels track out and had a blast. I think that Ben feels that James gets more than his fair share of his parents' time. Not so Rebecca. Often Rebecca will say when we pick her up from school, "Is James walking today?" When James is well, Rebecca leaps at the chance to do things with him, so last night it was crazy eights. Later on, they had a noisy time on the bed together, reading books. James, on his second reading of *The Lord of the Rings*, identifies with the character of Frodo, who is weighed down with the burden of the Ring and often fighting the pain of the old knife wound inflicted by one of the evil nazgul. James' top request is that I read *The Lord of the Rings* with him, *Harry Potter* being a close second, followed by the Lego magazine, containing beautiful pictures of horrendously expensive Lego electric trains that James constantly hints he would enjoy.

So life at the Birrells remains a strange mix of appalling and unthinkable things, with lots of very happy moments, never any idea what a new day might bring, never enough time to say thank you to the host of folk helping us out. Every day, unexpected acts of kindness come our way. Every day, too, there is a new medical panic, another call to Sick Kids for a dose of hand holding. I am trying to keep up a semblance of working, keeping the bills paid being a constant underlying worry. Planning anything seems almost laughable at times, yet somehow the adventures keep happening, and at bedtime you can say, "That was a good day."   Syd

Yesterday was another great day for James. I will carry with me many mini-memories from yesterday, but the one that stands out is a simple bedtime anecdote. We had had a bit of a post-concert party, my Peterborough Singers having just delivered the goods in their usual superb fashion. About midnight, James was upstairs in bed reading, or so I thought—until I walked into the bedroom to be surprised by an exuberant "Boo!" from James as he flung back the covers under which he had been hiding, patiently waiting for my arrival. It was a "Boo!" that I will always remember, a 100 percent "Boo!" musical, and full of humor and mischief, and full of the love of life that James represents. Perhaps not very loud in terms of decibels, but off the scale when it comes to touching a dad's heart. A "Boo!" that was followed by lots of laughter and a tickle fight, and then Pam arrived with crazy Bigsby, all licks and kisses, and then Rebecca too climbed aboard for a late-night romp on the bed.

Now the sad part of the email begins, because today was one of the few days in James' life in which there was no happiness detectable. He awoke crying and in considerable pain, shattering the afterglow of the previous day. As I carried him, wailing with pain, downstairs, the whole tired process of going through a another medical crisis at the Birrell household began to unfold.

Where is it hurting, James? Pam grabs some pills and a drink. Rebecca puts a beanbag in the microwave and then brings it in to put on James' sore leg and then another for his foot. "Can I have a warm beanbag for my head?" Pillow under the knee; here, take these pills James; breathe deeply; let go of the pain. I cuddle up with James and stroke his head; is that a new bump to add to the others growing on his head? Do we add another pain patch? Ten minutes into all of this I become aware that Ben has been hiding behind the sofa, sucking his thumb and cuddling his blankie. It soon becomes apparent that Dilaudid is not enough, so we add Ativan, and James begins to drift in and out of a drugged doze, little whimpers and cries emerging every now and then. I try to find Ben and hug him. Peggy Two arrives, and for the first time ever she cannot comfort James. Only Mum or Dad this time. But it's time for church; I'm the organist and the choir is waiting; Pam assures me that I can go, she can handle things; so I leave, all the while wanting desperately to stay and try to comfort James and Rebecca and Ben.

I wish I could say that the day improved, but the evening brought greater trials. In a moment of wakefulness, James asks me to carry him upstairs to bed, which turns out to be excruciating for him and leaves all of us crying. A mistake; we shouldn't have moved him; forty seconds of agony; seems like forty hours; can't get the sound of him crying out of my mind. Rebecca leaps up, follows, cuddles up, weeping, and tries to comfort him. Later I thank her for helping so well and share with her the Scripture "weep with those who weep" (Romans 12:15). More pills; knock him out; add another pain patch; Pam beckons. "Was this lump here on the side of his face here before?" How fast the cancer is growing now. How does he keep going with a body riddled with cancer? Pam gets James calmed down, as only a mother can. I finally get to Ben, in his pajamas, clutching his Anglican *Book of Common Prayer*, where he has found the page for evening prayer. "Will you read this to me, Dad?" Soon enough we reach the third collect, "Lighten our darkness, we beseech Thee, O Lord…" I am comforted by my child. Rebecca invites me up to her room, and we decide that when we have terrible images of James' suffering in our heads, we must think of moments of great happiness that James has experienced. I remember his triumphant "Boo!" of twenty hours earlier and take courage, tears notwithstanding.   Syd

SUBJECT: PRAYING FOR A QUICK END
SENT: NOVEMBER 28, 2001 3:24 AM

Three days have passed since James began what seems to be the final and most terrible round of his illness. New evidence of the rapid progression of the disease is seen daily. Pain control is now administered through a device called a Cadd pump, which delivers continuous doses of Dilaudid subcutaneously through a small needle in his leg. Pain patches are now a thing of the past. James is fairly comfortable while resting, but a movement such as lifting him from bed to sofa causes him frightful pain, leaving him crying hysterically. Visitors are a sore trial for him. Conversation is a big effort. It is no longer possible to hug him, and the gentle stroking of his head with your hand now hurts because of the numerous tumors growing there. The hearing is going in one ear; occasionally he has double vision; and he is losing the sensation in his behind. It is very difficult to comfort him and, to be frank, he is in very poor spirits. Anyone who has lost a child to this monster of a disease will recognize these symptoms all too well. We have reached the point where we pray for a quick end to his suffering.

While he is awake he asks for *The Lord of the Rings* to be read to him. When he is sleeping, we try to comfort each other and give time to Rebecca and Ben. Bigsby the puppy is a great fellow to have around in these dark days, and his cheerfulness is a welcome tonic. Yesterday I took Rebecca to the coffee shop for breakfast and later built a huge Brio train track with Ben. Rebecca wants to be close to James and help him, while Ben is angry that James' illness means I have less time for him. With a strange blend of tranquility and resignation, Pam and I have been planning the funeral and the memorial service that will follow a week or so later. And now I feel an overwhelming desire to return to James' bedside, to touch him and to think many things.   Syd

SUBJECT: CAM COMES OVER
SENT: NOVEMBER 30, 2001 8:02 PM

A package arrived from Lego Canada. I confess that I felt James was beyond ever playing with Lego again, and I put it aside while James continued to sleep. But when he awoke and it was time to take the morning pills, I showed him the parcel and he said, "Let's open it!" Do I detect a perkiness in his voice? Inside was a top-of-the-line Lego, the Harry Potter Hogwort Express Train set. But James had just received this same set for his birthday and had assembled it at once. "I can give it to my best friend Cam!" We found some nice wrapping paper, did the gift wrap thing, and then I called Cam's mom and set up a visit.

Cameron has been James' friend for eons. He is also eight years old, and in better days he and James could often be found playing road hockey or hanging out in the backyard with their younger brothers. Cam has an exceptional under-standing of what James faces in his fight with cancer, and like most of us he has believed that James has his ups and downs and that ultimately he will get better. But now, things are different.

As he leaves to visit James, his mother says, "Remember, Cam, any time you have with James—"

But Cam interrupts, "Is precious! This might be the last time I see my best friend James' beautiful face."

With a child's directness, Cam walks in and says, "Hi James. What's wrong with your eye?" I explain about the one tumor that is pushing on James' right eye.

"Hey, Cam, I got something for you!" says James, pulling back the covers and revealing the package.

Off comes the gift wrap. "Wow! James, you shouldn't have! This is incredible!"

There's nothing quite like spending an evening with a friend working on a project, so the two get down to work, James lying in bed building the engine while Cam assembles the passenger coach nearby. Later, as Cam leaves, I draw him aside and tell him that if he wants to, it would be all right to take the engine apart and have the fun of putting it together himself.

The next day I hear from Cam's mom and pick up the story. In no uncertain terms, Cam announces that James made the Hogwort Express engine for him and no one is to touch it! "James made it for me!" Then, "If I had one wish in the whole world, it would be to make James better." And even more poignantly, "I would rather give my own life for James so he could live. I can't imagine a world without James."

And we can't imagine a world without friends. I suppose an official chart report on James today would include reference to the fact that good pain control has been achieved, that he is eating and drinking well, that with the help of two adults he is able to manage a transfer to his wheelchair. What might be missing is mention of the unnumbered host of friends like Cameron who carry the load with us. We are very grateful and much comforted.   Syd

SUBJECT: LONDON BRIDGE
SENT: DECEMBER 1, 2001 9:37 PM

The quest this week has been to snatch some good quality of life for James in the face of his miserable physical condition. Bag of bones, very limited movement, right eye quite disfigured, many cancerous bumps growing on his head, nausea, jaw sore, ear feeling weird, new pain every day. Some important work was done earlier in the week in the pain management area, but I think an equally important achievement was one of communication. I can't remember the words we spoke, but James and I talked openly about his imminent death, and there followed a great sense of relief on James' part that we can now talk freely on the subject. I cried a fair bit with James as we lay side by side on his bed trying to find the right words for each other, but the sharing brought great comfort. We talked about how hard James had tried to beat his cancer and how his body is finally losing the battle, but we also talked about how cancer cannot kill the soul. "Cancer gets you ready to go to heaven," James said. He knows he's dying; we know he's dying; he knows we know he's dying; and out of all this it is much easier for James to get through the pain when it happens. None of us need to pretend anything.

Perhaps you can now understand how it is possible to say that James has lived well for the last few days. We had been cautioned that James would probably manage only two hours a day of waking time because of the high level of pain medication. But today was another twelve-hour day, and though it began awkwardly with a round of vomiting, things soon improved, and Mrs. M, James' favorite Sunday school teacher, arrived with stories and crafts, which gave him great pleasure. Then his pen pal from grade two arrived for a chat. The midday snooze ended abruptly with a new pain, this time in the left arm, but we watched a Thomas the Tank Engine video that brought solace. "Ya can't let cancer ruin your day." We did plenty of reading of *The Lord of the Rings* today and found many passages that begged a detour into James' world of pain, death, adventure, and friendship. Only 212 pages to go. Then Pam walked in with the old 1971 version of the LOTR on video and cuddled up to watch it with James. By the way, we have all been invited to attend the Toronto premiere of the new *Lord of the Rings* movie and meet the actors on December 14th. James has been counting off the days for weeks, and we still hold out the ridiculous hope that somehow we will make it.

Rebecca and Ben had disappeared earlier in the evening with Peggy Three to see the Santa Claus parade, and I wondered how to make it up to James for not being able to go. Ben has been begging us to buy one of those ghastly, tacky plastic Santas that light up and you stick up outside your house and hope your neighbors don't think too poorly of you, and that got me thinking that a string of Christmas lights might be fun for James. At the store I found that you could buy the plain version or the kind that were programmable, so I bought the latter. I am glad I did, because here was another example of James, sick as he is, taking control of what he can, and he spent a good hour demonstrating to all of us sixteen different ways of making 340 colored light bulbs flash in sequence or otherwise.

When we have no overnight nursing care, I sleep with James in the family room on the sofa next to his hospital bed. Actually, it is hard not to do this when the nurse is here, so don't feel sorry for me. Tonight Rebecca joined us for the sleepover, so there was that sense of adventure for all of us as we made the preparations. Rebecca is always ready to help James, and lots of nice things were said between them. At 11 p.m. I said good night and turned off the light, only to hear a minute later James mischievously singing "London Bridge is Falling Down." A week ago I thought "Boo!" was to be my last memory of the old cheerful James. Wrong again.   Syd

Subject: Day Eight
Sent: December 3, 2001 12:58 am

Amidst the great sorrow of our last days with James has been much beauty and peace. Today was day eight of what we know deep in our hearts is the final run. How strange it is to be past the time where a new symptom galvanized us into adrenaline-charged action, where you fought tooth and nail for another reprieve. Now we have even dropped regular blood work, for we can no longer reasonably act on the information so gained. Medical people, don't laugh, but here is a sample of Pam and Syd talk: "James is complaining of a swollen foot." "*Yes. At this stage that can be a sign of liver failure.*" "Do you think his stomach is looking a little distended today?" "*Yes.*" "Probably the liver." Maybe liver failure would be the best thing, all things considered. We will talk it over with the doctor tomorrow. Of far more importance now is how we redeem each hour. The rest of the family is now sleeping, and I can ponder what day eight has brought us.

We are trying to balance things for Rebecca and Ben so that they spend time with James while keeping up on the fun stuff. We have a rule in our house that cancer must not stop the fun. You are allowed to smile when you are sad. This afternoon they went off to see the Snow White pantomime in Stirling and returned full of excitement, Ben telling me, "We all shouted Boo! really loud and long and ugly every time the wicked witch came on!" While they were gone, Pam and I took turns lying with James, sharing secret things, savoring the gentlest of cuddles, banking memories for the future.

Our family room, the place where James now lies in his hospital bed, has a new feel to it. Several hundred little Christmas lights strung around the walls and bookcase certainly change the atmosphere, in a very nice way. Stuck on the brick wall is a picture James painted four years ago while in hospital just after diagnosis. It's a picture of a tree, lots of branches, lots of green, and it has always brought me reassurance, though I don't know why. A mounted photo of a Royal Hudson locomotive sits underneath a magnificent *Lord of the Rings* poster showing the nine companions passing down the river between two massive statues into a blaze of light, the kingdom beckoning. The initial concept sketch of the soapbox derby racer still remains where it was temporarily taped to the bookcase six months ago. Lately the toys have been disappearing—as James can no longer play with them—to be replaced by get-well cards and gifts.

A mattress now lies on the floor for Rebecca. "I am very comforted by being able to sleep with James." She gives him the tenderest of hugs at bedtime and says, "I hope you're feeling better in the morning." "I love you, Becca," he responds. I am very proud of Rebecca, who moves through the tragedy of James' illness with beauty and maturity.

We discuss the inhumanity of hospital beds, which are not big enough to allow someone to sleep in the same bed with their sick child when they need you most. Of course James is now too fragile to contemplate a move to another bed. How Pam and I treasured the overnights in bed with James upstairs, where he would fall asleep clutching your hand and then later in the night reach out to find your hand once again. This, in case you have forgotten, is to comfort us, as James pointed out in times gone past.

So far the things that I feared most for James as he lays dying have been kept at bay. The pain level is acceptable to James. The disfigurement factor I feel better about ever since my friend John reminded me that it's the disfigurement inside a person's soul that matters, not the external appearance. The disease has not stolen his sight yet and neither has it clouded his mind. He can still eat. He is awake ten or twelve hours a day, far more than predicted, and his waking hours are happy and full of family and friends. James is accepting of his situation, and we can talk about death and eternal life. And, inexplicably, an unexpected peace has settled on our house. How I pray we can hold this course. Lots of tears and lumps in the throat, but no more rushing off to work, no more evenings away from home, no more dashing off to hospitals. When I told James last Thursday after choir practice that I would not be returning to work, he smiled at me, grasped my hand, and said, "Thanks, Dad."

The day included 160 pages of the *The Lord of the Rings*; the book could almost be a manual of what to discuss with your dying child. Tonight Pam, Rebecca and James played cards, "Go Fish," with James missing not a thing. Ben joined James and I to watch a documentary on submarines, and later at bedtime Ben told me the best things he used to do with James, like going to the Cobourg station to watch trains, or making Water World in the sand at the beach at our cottage, or jumping off the bunk beds at the cottage. Ben being a noisy, busy, rough-and-tumble five year old, it is hard to find ways for him to spend time with a very fragile James.

So, it now being 12:40 a.m., I will join James and Rebecca for some sleep, not knowing if James might die during the night and at the same time not fearing that eventuality either. The danger of late-night emails is that they become very honest. Our journey continues, as unpredictable as ever, and I hope the peace stays with us.   Syd

SUBJECT: PRECIOUS GIFT
SENT: DECEMBER 4, 2001 11:39 PM

"Dad, I've been thinkin' that every day is like a very precious gift. You gotta use each day."

For an hour I have been attempting to find some profound words to frame this quote from bedtime last night. Instead, I pray that I, who perhaps will have many more days to live on this world than James, will accept the challenge.   Syd

SUBJECT: THE LORD OF THE RINGS
SENT: DECEMBER 8, 2001 3:00 PM

Several times I asked, "Do you want to go home now?" but James always responded with, "No, I want to stay." Once again our family was experiencing one of those make-believe events, a James' trademark it seems. We were seated in a local movie theater watching the yet to be released movie *The Lord of the Rings*, an unbelievably spectacular movie if ever there was one. Some friends had quietly made the impossible happen, a private screening for James and friends, knowing that James likely would not be able to make it to the premiere in Toronto on December 14th. Just how they managed to make it happen I cannot guess, and we are at a loss to know how to say thank you adequately. James has been eagerly looking forward to seeing the movie, having read the trilogy twice. He has found much comfort in the story, and I have too, I might add. Yesterday James was in pretty good shape, so we had a family meeting to decide whether we might invite the press to attend and help us with the cause of the James Fund, and the vote was a yes. But had we known how much James was to deteriorate overnight, we would have kept things under wraps. James awoke crying with pain at 4:30 a.m., and the need for a fairly massive increase in pain meds became very clear over the next few hours.

However, James remained determined to see the movie he has longed to see, so with much help we lifted James, sheets and all, into the reclining wheelchair, carefully wheeled him out the door and up the ramp into the minivan, and ever so delicately drove over to the theater. Was it right to predict that this was to be his last outing? We all had no doubt of that. We arrived and ran the gauntlet of the photographers and joined many friends and family for three hours of what will undoubtedly be judged an epic film. But how much more memorable for all of us who sat watching with James and also sometimes watching James himself, as time after time we saw James in Frodo, or the other way around, and felt the tears on our cheeks.

What did James think of it all? I don't know, and maybe now he will never be able to tell us in so many words, for James has gone a long way downhill today. But he wanted to stay till the end, and when I asked him if he liked it, he made a big effort and said, "Yes!" And as soon as we got home, he asked me to begin reading the book to him again. Dr. Beamish arrived and reset the Cadd pump to a higher dose, and James has been asleep ever since.

Another day of powerful emotions. Pam told me how happy she was that James made it to the movie. Ben, very excited, went off this afternoon to celebrate his sixth birthday. Both he and Rebecca were thrilled by the movie, very proud not to be frightened by the scary bits. Two children full of life, and one other clinging to life right to the end.   Syd

Yesterday, as James continued down the cruel path that is neuroblastoma, Rebecca and Ben slipped into the family room where James lies in his hospital bed, and they began playing quietly. A few nights ago I had dragged the sofa over so as to be able to sleep as close to James as possible, so there was a newly created space in the corner of the room, and there Ben and Rebecca began to build a house. I didn't notice at first what they were up to, as I was reading to James, *The Lord of the Rings* as always, and supplying him with warm beanbags, or a drink, or a some food, or a pill, or adjusting the pillows. But I was aware of their happy presence, suitably quiet because there are new rules now for the family room: don't disturb James or upset him with noise, no fast movement or loud laughing or jumping up and down on the sofa or all the fun things all three kids used to do in this room. They had taken the foam mattress we keep for hospital-floor sleeping and folded it into an arch to make the roof of their house. Then they made a nest of pillows, with many of the colorful little blankets that have come James' way during his illness spread out on the floor. Perhaps they were playing video store, for dozens of videos were carefully laid out on the floor. My token involvement was to offer them a mailbox, which they eagerly accepted and began filling with Christmas cards. As happens frequently these days, I felt a stab of guilt as once again I was too busy with James and his minute-by-minute care to play with them. But later I felt very happy that they had found a way to be close by their brother, to be a part of his dying while they continue to live.

It's around 5 a.m., and Pam just walked in. "How are you doing?"

"Just wondering if James is still alive."

We cuddle up on the sofa and watch. "Look, he just moved." We hold each other. Yesterday James stopped holding us. Now his hand reaches out, not for our hands—which he pushes impatiently aside—but to tightly grasp the metal bars of the hospital bed. Physical touch has become uncomfortable for him. Pam and I struggle to comprehend a role where as parents it seems we can no longer comfort our child.

Earlier in the day were some better moments; in fact, he told me, "That was the best movie I ever saw."

"I love you, James"

"I love you too, Dad."

Then he was hungry, but had to stop eating after a mouthful and started crying because his jaw hurt too much. "I'll try applesauce." We're out of applesauce. "I'll try some Rice Krispies." No good; still hurts. "I'll try tortellini." No good. "Jello?" Yes, a couple of teaspoons. Later in the day comes a new indignity. His lower belly is rock hard, and he cannot pee. A flurry of phone calls and the nurse arrives and installs a catheter. A little of the old James is still there, for he wants to see the device, check the drain holes, and understand how the little balloon will be blown up with 3 cc's of saline to keep it in place inside his bladder.

It's bedtime, and Rebecca is crying, sobbing, as she hears what she does not want to hear. "James is not going to get better this time. He is dying. We hope he doesn't have to suffer much longer." Nanny takes her up to bed, and soon she is asleep. My sister Diana had flown in from B.C., and Pam, she, and I take turns to sit with James as he dozes. Are we comforting him, or are we just comforting ourselves by being there? In the dim light we see new bumps on his forehead. His right eye looks very ugly, a great bruise spreading downwards and the white of the eye now mostly blood-red. Little bulges near the hinge of his jaw. His body emaciated.

I think a lot about the need to find a cure for this disease, and I think of the other parents who have trod this same terrible path and the doctors and nurses who are there to help, at great emotional cost to themselves. I think of the parents and children who have yet to face this monster. I think of some words that Pam penned nine months ago when we launched the James Fund: "The fifty Canadian children a year who are diagnosed with neuroblastoma are too young and too ill to advocate and fund-raise for themselves to find a cure for this disease. I am the mother of one of them. The time has come for those of us who are able to make a huge effort and help cure neuroblastoma." And that is why we did the press thing. A ton of wonderful emails have arrived since the press coverage of James' *Lord of the Rings* outing. The www.JamesBirrell.ca site has been inundated with lovely messages. Several researchers have gotten in touch. Perhaps meaning can come out of James' present suffering if we can stop this disease from ravaging other children. The Ring is indeed very heavy as James walks through Mordor.   Syd

James, as always, continues to hold on to life with great determination. Each day the disfigurement grows, as a great bruise engulfs his right eye and right side of his face. New tumors appear daily as bumps under his skin. A couple of days ago, a catheter became necessary, another indignity, minor as things go, yet in typical James' fashion he first wanted to check out the device, see how it worked, confirm that the nurse had the right amount of saline in the syringe, and then direct the insertion. The Cadd pump now delivers the pain medication Dilaudid at a dose ten times what we began with sixteen days ago, and on the whole it is proving very effective when he is at rest. But when some movement of the body or legs is required or if you touch him in the wrong place (many of those), it hurts, a lot. A kiss from Pam on his face yesterday left him crying in pain. We are discovering that our role as comforters is just to be close by but not touching. A hard role. No more cuddling, except for the final one.

But to pick up on the "holding on to life with great determination" part: though he is on huge doses of a narcotic and ought to be asleep most of the time, James has chosen to stay awake. Thirteen hours yesterday. The medical professionals are mystified. Time enough to listen to many pages of *The Lord of the Rings*, third time through now. Time to start a new Lego, 570 pieces, once again no sign of cognitive deficits here. TVO Kids brings smiles as he watches "Arthur," "Zoboomafoo," "The Big Bang," "Brilliant Creatures" and "Art Attack." A nice mix of nature, science, creativity, and kid life. "Dad, did you know that there's this one lizard that squirts blood out of its eye at its enemies?" Thank you, "Brilliant Creatures," for coming up with that one.

We are all mystified that James is still awake and alert at a point where one expects otherwise. James' primary nurse calls from Toronto to see how we are doing; we talk a bit, and she wonders why James is holding on. "Is there something he still needs to do?" So later I talk with James and ask the question.

Without hesitation he responds, "I want to be a teenager and have a really great Super Soaker water fight!" I ponder this one for a moment, wondering where you can buy water guns in December, surveying our family room, thinking maybe we could drape the place with plastic, have a water gun extravaganza...We talk a bit more about the *Lord of the Rings* movie. "It's the best movie I ever saw." We talk about Frodo, who deserved a long and happy life after fulfilling his mission, but it wasn't to be; the wounds were incurable, and he left instead for the Havens. Just like James. He nods his head. I whisper to James that if he is ready to go to his house in heaven, then he has our permission to go. We don't want to lose him, and we will be very sad when he dies and miss him very much, but he doesn't have to keep suffering just for us.

I had thought that arranging the *Lord of the Rings* screening was something we were doing for James. Yet it has become a great therapy for many of us. On Sunday night, as Rebecca cried and sobbed as she grappled with James' imminent death, Pam spoke with her and said, "A lot of people think James is like Frodo, but I think that our whole family is like Frodo because we are all carrying the weight of the Ring, and that the family and friends who are helping us are like the rest of the nine companions, the Fellowship, who walk with him. The Fellowship cannot carry the Ring, but they valiantly stand by the Ring bearer, protecting and helping in any way that they can." Rebecca understands, she is comforted, she slips downstairs to say, "Good night, James! I hope you are feeling better in the morning!"

And amidst all of this, Ben had his birthday. Now he is six. We gather round James' bed, light the candles on the cupcakes, and sing happy birthday. "Make a wish before you blow them out!" He starts to tell me his wish, then changes his mind and says, "I wish all my wishes would come true!"

James pipes in, "Ben, can I help put together your Rescue Heroes fire truck?"

Ben was just ten months old when cancer first struck our family and Pam withdrew from motherhood for seven months of aggressive treatment, leaving him to be cuddled by countless babysitters. In his short life, he has seen much pain and grief and yet seen the best of love, compassion, and friendship. Not to mention the adventures. Good luck, Ben, twenty years from now, as you bring up a family and wonder what "normal" family life is supposed to be. I hear in my mind some little voices saying, "Why can't we have adventures like you and Uncle James and Auntie Rebecca used to have?" Nanny is sitting close by, flipping through the photo albums as I write, as we choose some of the best to be enlarged for the inevitable memorial service. So many memories, every page filled with smiling faces, another spectacular adventure, another once-in-a-lifetime moment.

Thank you, once again, to you, the Fellowship, who stand by as the burden grows greater every day.   Syd and family

Dr. Beamish visited this morning, and it would seem fairly certain that James is experiencing secondary renal (kidney) failure. His right kidney was removed during surgery three years ago. The pain in his back left side, plus the fact that very little urine is coming out despite fresh catheters and lots of flushing, suggests that tumors are pressing on the ureter, blocking the flow. Probably he will slip into unconsciousness, and in two or three days he will die. Renal failure at this point is considered a good way to go. Pam and I wanted you to know this latest news. James is comfortable, very bright when awake, and we have good pain control following yesterday's boost from 20 to 30 mg an hour of Dilaudid. After much thought, and at the urging of Dr. Beamish, I will go ahead and take Rebecca to the *Lord of the Rings* premiere in Toronto tonight. As you know, the private (family and close friends) funeral will take place within two days of his death. It looks as though the memorial service might be on Saturday, December 29th, 2 p.m.   Syd and Pam

This will be a mixed-up email, because the interruptions are many and frequent and because James' condition rapidly changes.

Yesterday the Super Soakers started arriving, and soon the end of James' bed was piled with giant water guns. James awoke, grinned, and uttered a quiet, "Hi, Dad," and then,

"Wow!" as he saw the arsenal. But then we were unable to go further, and draping the room with plastic for a water fight became an idea best forgotten. Pain under control, but James too weak for much more than watching a movie with Pam. He enjoyed *Land before Time 8*, sharing all kinds of astute comments with Pam. I walked past with a dirty furnace filter. "What's that, Dad? How does it work?" His mind buzzes along, never missing a beat.

The day was filled with new memories, some shocking and others beautiful. In the morning James sleeps in, and every unexplained noise causes me to leap to my feet and move to the family room to gee if the noise was James. Usually it was Bigsby, moaning or growling in some exciting dog dream, or perhaps it was the creak of a door being closed.

I will treasure the half hour during which he allowed me to hold his hand as we watched the kids TV show "Art Attack." I reach out tentatively from the sofa and lay my hand on one of the pillows surrounding and padding him. Usually these days he pushes you away, as any touch adds to his discomfort, but this time I am lucky. He reaches out to find my hand, his fingers wrapping firmly around three of mine, unexpectedly strong for one so ill. While he watches and gets on with the show, I go in a different direction and seek to fix the details of this hand-holding session in my memory, the gentle strength of his grip, the warmth of his small hand, the way his child's hand fits into my adult hand.

We spend a lot of time reading in the evening. Lots of stories from our battered *Children's Bible*. It's beautifully illustrated, and as I hold up a picture James says, "I like that one." We read of Jesus calming the storm, Jesus calling the children to him, Jesus calling the disciples, the miracle of the water into wine. Somehow I don't have the courage to hold up the pictures of Jesus performing miraculous healings for James to choose, and I pass by the healing of Jairus's daughter, but we read the crucifixion and the resurrection accounts.

The growing medical concern of the day is the urine output. The catheter appears blocked. We flush with saline; it works for a while; it stops; we put in a new catheter; no improvement. We understand the implications all too well. There are no emergencies any more. Dr. Beamish arrives this morning, and it seems clear that James is in secondary renal failure. His right kidney was removed with the tumor three years ago. As always, Sick Kids phones to check that all is as well as can be. Our friends there have been a great comfort to us.

So here we are at last, the final stretch. Two or three days? This morning was rough. He awoke in much pain, rejecting all our efforts to comfort him. "I can't stand it when you put your hand on my head!" We administer this pain med and that one, add a warm beanbag here, another there, and he begins to calm down and asks us to read to him. "More Bible stories, please." He sleeps. The rest of us slip out of the room and have a big cry in the kitchen.

James has awoken, and I end this note abruptly.   Syd

SUBJECT: THROUGH THE BLIZZARD
SENT: DECEMBER 15, 2001 12:33 PM

Good news now becomes bad news today. James has always had a way of defying the doctor's predictions, and this morning his kidney started producing again, which means an early end to his ordeal is no longer imminent. If this offered James any quality-of-life time, we would be grateful, but just now he is beyond comfort. The pain is sort of under control, thanks to the high doses of Dilaudid, but the drug, or maybe the disease, leaves him twitching, jerking, and thrashing, unable to find rest, and is clearly exhausting him. Any attempt to hold his hand or stroke his head or any physical contact is promptly rejected. By lunchtime today, even the offer of reading a book to him is turned down. The most exotic Lego set would not be given a glance. The long-expected double vision problem arrived today, so TV or a video is not an option. A challenge for the caregivers as we hover at his bedside feeling completely inadequate. The awful thought is that the next logical step will be that he won't even want us to sit quietly by his bedside. The fact that today is the Birrell Christmas, that family are shortly due to arrive, and that there are gifts waiting under the tree to be opened is meaningless. But for the sake of the other children we move ahead with the special dinner and the opening of the presents.

And along those lines, after much thought, we went ahead with our plans to take Rebecca to the premiere of the *Lord of the Rings* movie in Toronto yesterday. Pam stayed with James, supported by a number of friends, and off we went through the blizzard, Rebecca and her friend Heather both dressed to the nines in their best party dresses. We were treated royally, met at the door and escorted to our reserved seats, and then afterwards we moved on to the Royal Ontario Museum for a very glitzy party. "Amazing, awesome, extraordinary, wonderful!" says Rebecca. The girls were thrilled, and so were Auntie Diana and my friend John and I. We adults found an odd feeling lurking in our minds as we waited for the film to begin. It was hard to resist the urge to stand up and say to the expectant crowds, "We've already seen it; it's a great film; this is the second time for us; we had a private screening for our James a week ago!" It was after 2:30 a.m. when we finally arrived back home in Peterborough.

I will try to keep a daily update going for all of you who care so much and who hold us in your prayers. Knowing that James has changed so many lives means a lot to us.   Syd

SUBJECT: I LOVE YOU!
SENT: DECEMBER 16, 2001 4:33 AM

5:30 a.m.

"I love you, James."

And his strong little voice responds, "I love you too, Dad."

There he is, lying permanently on his right side, ever so skinny, constantly making little movements in an attempt to find a more comfortable position. There is a medical moment. Another blocked catheter. Always ready to assume command of medical procedures, James pulls out the old one. We carefully put in a new one and inflate it. A minute later it pops out, the balloon deflated. "Blip!" we say, using the new expletive Uncle Rodney has taught our children after we had reproved him for using stronger words. We try another catheter; this time we succeed and the flow resumes. "I'm thirsty!" James declares, and he guzzles down 100 ml of his latest drink, "make it half fruit punch, half ginger ale, three ice cubes." He firmly grasps the juice container with his left hand, but the right hand now has lost fine motor control and flops vaguely over to help and misses, so I gently hold his fingers. I think how clever that right hand used to be, James having amazed us for years with his incredible dexterity, his ability to work with tiny screws that defeated us adults. We wonder how he can be so alert, given the thirteen Ativan knockout pills of the last sixteen hours and the mega doses of Dilaudid.

The Birrell Christmas was a cheerful and noisy affair, Nanny all the while with James in the family room, and we enjoyed the roast beef dinner that Winston's restaurant had generously given us. "Can we open the presents yet?" pipes in Ben at regular intervals. So as we eat, Ben, long since finished his supper, chooses his noisiest toy and plays on the floor with his birthday Super Heroes fire truck. Somehow Bigsby has managed to slip into the dining room, no doubt recognizing the peculiar racket this toy makes, and the two of them face off, Bigsby waiting expectantly with his head cocked, tail wagging, while Ben prepares to fire the plastic water missiles. It's become a ritual. "Fire!" shouts Ben, and the missiles shoot across the room, which is the cue for Bigsby to snatch one and run. The great chase begins, under the dining room table, under the piano, past the Christmas tree, between our legs. There is terrific excitement as at last the presents are opened. And all the while James lies twenty feet away in another room, still fighting his great battle, too sick to show the slightest interest in his presents. His gifts remain unopened. We will figure that mini problem out some other day. I slip in to see him and ask if he would like me to read Psalm 23. His left eye flickers open for a moment and I see a little smile, so I read. A good psalm, one of the best, none the worse for centuries of use.   Syd

James had a peaceful night. He is now mostly asleep, or perhaps unconscious, except for brief moments awake to have a drink. Beside me at the computer as I write is a photo of Ben, taken two days ago, as he gives James the juice bottle. Young Ben, reaching out to his older brother. I hope one day Ben will remember that there were good times too.   Syd

Rebecca and Auntie Diana and I returned from Handel's *Messiah* in a wonderful post-concert state of euphoria. James had been quiet and comfortable all day. Pam had urged me to go, to conduct the performance for James and for her, and so I did. It was so good to hear the choir, to hear the soloists. The old words took on new meaning for all of us, musicians and audience alike, as we all thought of James, right from the moment the tenor began singing the opening phrase, "Comfort Ye." How was it possible to have performed this work so many times before and missed so much of the message? What a gift it was to me.

All was instantly shattered as we walked in the front door. "How is James?" we ask as we enter.

"Not good for the last hour." But I have no need to ask as I hear his crying and whimpering. The pain has returned with a vengeance, and James has been dragged back into consciousness. Boluses of Dilaudid pain med every twenty minutes, Ativan pill every twenty minutes, still no relief.

"I need a drink!" he says frequently, and we guide the juice bottle to his lips, and he noisily sucks it down. Surely the meds will soon sedate him. But two hours pass with no improvement, James surrounded by Pam and Peggy and Auntie Diana and the nurse. Rebecca creeps in, desperately wanting to help, her concert flowers forgotten. Again we are in that terrible place where we can do nothing to comfort him. This afternoon Pam's stomach ulcer returned, and she is in the same pain that she faced during her chemotherapy four and a half years ago, and we all know she must rest. Peggy Two stays with James while the rest of us reluctantly go to bed, all but Rebecca tanked up with sleeping pills.

It's 3:30 a.m. now, and I have been back to James' bedside. The nurse shakes her head in disbelief, for despite the massive doses of drugs, James is still not comfortable. He is breathing in deep gasps, the pain not quite as bad, but still appalling to watch. I must get back to him. Does he hear what we say? Every now and then he babbles incoherently, and then for a bit he talks lucidly. Auntie Peggy clasps his hand between hers and talks of angels, and heaven, and many things. Please may he be there soon.

His best friend Cam came over at suppertime. How hard it is for an eight year old to see his friend dying. "I brought you a gift, James. It's the *Lord of the Rings* CD...I've come to say good-bye to you, James. I'm going to miss you very much...Good-bye, James!...I can't seem to concentrate in school just now. I am always thinking about you...I love you, James." Thank you, Cameron; you have said it all, and we will always remember your tears.   Syd

James just died.   Syd

Birrell, James Anthony, eight years old, left for his House in Heaven, on Tuesday, December 18th, 2001.

James is the cherished son of Sydney and Pamela Birrell, beloved brother of Rebecca and Benjamin, and grandson of Bruce and Primrose Birrell, and Peggy and the late Ralph Braund. James will be sadly missed by many aunts, uncles, cousins, and friends. A memorial service to celebrate his life will be held at Murray St. Baptist Church on Saturday December 29th, 2 PM, children especially welcome. The Birrells send heartfelt thanks to their friends, family, and the compassionate army of medical supporters. In lieu of flowers, the family asks that donations be made to the James Birrell Neuroblastoma Research Fund or Camp Oochigeas, a cancer camp for children.

"James, a boy who showed us we could sing when we thought we could only cry."

Ever since my son was diagnosed with cancer, some words have found a resonance in my head, words that surface unexpectedly, and I have not been able to put them from me, words cried out loud three thousand or so years ago by a father who has just lost his son, words that I had hoped would never take personal meaning for me. King David's son, Absalom, leading a rebellion against his father, is killed, and when news reaches the king, he cries, "O my son Absalom! My son, my son Absalom! If only I had died instead of you—O Absalom, my son, my son!" (2 Samuel 18:33, NIV). Would the same day come for me, the father of a child with cancer? Four happy years passed.

O my son James! O James, my son…today the words are no longer resonating in my head, but instead they are gripping my heart. They have become intensely personal.

James died. Plans that had long been talked about became reality for our family. The last forty hours have been filled with tears, but they have been very beautiful hours. Pam and I didn't know whether it was right to share these very personal times with you, but then your emails kept arriving, hundreds and hundreds, each written from the depth of your own hearts, full of compassion. I had always thought that JJD email, James just died, would be the last. But JJD was followed by dozens of new requests to be added to the James Update mailing list. "Why?" I wondered; the story is over. But perhaps you can take encouragement if I tell you a bit more about the beauty of these hours. Maybe there will be therapy for me to pen the story.

For some time now we have felt as if we were running a marathon. But they kept changing the finish line, adding a mile or two, and James kept fighting; death did not come. On Monday, Peggy Two had been sitting with James all night as he struggled to breathe, and I had joined her, along with our overnight nurse. At one point we had been speaking briefly of some other people in another situation, and I had spoken words that related to that situation, not ours. I had ended by saying, "We should just let him go home."

James gasped one last breath as I spoke, and then, seeming to have heard what I had said, he stopped breathing. "It's as though he heard what you just said!" said Peggy.

I ran upstairs to wake Pam, and then together we went slowly and gently to James. No more running now. The nurse, having checked for pulse, stepped aside. And we hugged him and hugged him and cried and cried and said, "James, O James…" The children and Auntie Diana joined us; Nanny arrived; and we all hugged him. We told him how brave he was, how well he had done, how much we loved him, how much we will miss him. Yes, we had said those things many times before, but this time it was for us. But Ben did not cry.

The plans we had planned for weeks and months, so hard at the time, now began to unfold, and how glad we were that we had wrestled with these matters ahead of time. (The JJD email, by the way, was not planned.) A phone call or two set everything in motion. The priest arrived, but we call him John. Ben produced his prayer book, gave it to John, and we prayed. From that point on everything seemed to happen the way we needed it to happen for the Birrell family's needs. Peace at last.

A big bowl of warm water was brought in with lots of washcloths, and we bathed James. At last we could touch him again without howls of pain; at last we could wash away the hurts from his battered body. With great satisfaction, I beat the nurse to it and removed the SC needle and the catheter, once necessary intrusions but no longer welcome now. The simple pleasure of a mother washing her child was a marvelous thing. Rebecca brushed his hair, while Ben mostly watched. The children kept the right to choose what to participate in and what to miss. When James was clean and dry, John blessed some oil and we gently rubbed it all over his body. How shockingly skinny he is! Another time of healing. Pam had chosen happy, casual clothes, green, James' favorite color, and we dressed him. I got to lift him in my arms as the soiled sheets were replaced by his Thomas the Tank Engine duvet. Put his trademark train hat on his head. As we laid him back down, we now saw a beautiful boy, all the lines of pain in his face gone, happy and peaceful. You made it, James!

Now we had a family discussion about what special objects might be laid on the bed next to James and later put with him in his coffin. Rebecca brought a picture she had painted for him and a Beanie Baby. Ben went and got James' favorite Brio engine, "Big Boy." Ever practical, he said, "But I'm going to take the batteries out first, 'cause they will have different batteries in heaven and James won't need these ones." Cam's CD gift from the night before was added. The gold spoon promised to each grandchild if they are good was retrieved from Nanny's condo and placed in his hand. Ben decided to keep James' little stuffed dog, while Rebecca kept the small cushion that James used to ease the pain in his legs. As all this happened, we found ourselves surprised at how comfortable we all found ourselves as we touched James, sat on the bed with him, walked (ran, in the case of Ben) in and out of the room.

The morning moves on, and close friends and family begin to arrive. Uncle Jeff takes over the job of policing the incoming phone calls, while cousin Amy prints off the emails that pour in. Others make tea, coffee, lunch, and answer the front door. The phone rings incessantly; I have to slip out to do a press conference; guests need to be welcomed; but again and again I slip back to the family room to touch James, to cuddle up to his still warm body, to shed some more tears, to whisper a few more good-byes, to memorize the physical feel of his body. I even manage a short nap with James. Pam snuggles up, enjoying the freedom to stroke and cuddle. Family and friends come and sit and touch and cry.

But watching the children is a real eye-opener. I have a delightful image of the two Rebeccas sitting on the bed with James, stroking his hair, chatting away, perfectly at ease. Cam and his little brother Clay arrive, go straight to James, put a hand on his chest and pronounce, "His heart is not beating. He's dead." Then they get on with their good-byes, looking for all the world as if this were a daily occurrence. It is so good for Cam to see James at peace after his difficult visit with James the night before. Never are any of the children inappropriate in their actions. We adults learn much from the children this day.

Later his body becomes quite cool, and now as we touch him our own bodies as well as our minds tell us that James is indeed dead. Around 9 p.m. we gather again with John for the hardest moment of the day, and we all cry buckets, even Ben this time. The coffin is brought into the room and laid on the sofa; we say our last good-byes, and using Ben's prayer book we pray once more. Then, for the last time, I pick up James, and we gently lay him in the coffin. He is quite cold, and in my heart I know it is time to say good-bye. Carefully we place the toys and objects in the coffin. The final kiss, a prayer, and one of the hardest moments of my life follows as the coffin lid is closed.

Four have been chosen as pallbearers, and James leaves his home, borne by four who love him very much. It is a tranquil, starlit night. We all gather outside as the coffin is loaded into the van. How good it is that we do this after dark, free from the gaze of strangers. Ben is in my arms, crying a little. "Look, there is a new star in the sky for James tonight."

Amidst our sorrow is a deep feeling that we have done the right thing for James and his family. We go to bed sad, but with a sense of achievement, for in sixteen hours we have moved from the sheer terror of uncontrollable pain to a place of great peace. Tomorrow, the burial. Many wonderful memories of the day help ease the pain that is seared on our minds from sitting as helpless observers of his final hours. And as I go to bed, I am faced with a choice. Will I dwell on the pain, or will I dwell in that beautiful picture of James resting peacefully with children playing happily round about? I choose the latter.   Syd

SUBJECT: THE FUNERAL
SENT: DECEMBER 22, 2001 3:55 AM

We buried James the day after he died, on a very wet and gray Wednesday afternoon. On the way to the chapel, I tried to make conversation by saying, "It always seems to rain when there is a funeral."

After a pause, Pam said, "Well, I think it's James using his heavenly Super Soaker."

Instantly Rebecca spoke up and said, "No. It's the angels crying."

So we drove on through the rain to a small chapel in the cemetery, where our family and a few close friends were waiting. We had wanted a very private ceremony, mostly for the sake of Rebecca and Ben, and there was not a person there who had not shared significantly in James' life and in the lives of Rebecca and Ben. On the coffin was a beautiful flower arrangement that Rebecca and her best friend Rebecca had spent three happy hours putting together in the back of the flower shop. The concept of flowers for a boy was new to me, but the Rebeccas had it figured out: a colorful, bold splash of many different flowers, with some of James' toys carefully placed within the arrangement. A front-end loader, a Thomas the Tank engine, a Harry Potter card, a space shuttle, and a Frodo action figure. Two ribbons, one reading "Son" and the other "Brother." The Rebeccas had honored James with something unique that money never could have bought.

So this is it, your ultimate nightmare, your child lying six feet away from you in a coffin.

It is Ben's turn to contribute, and John begins the rite by asking Ben if he may borrow his prayer book once more. Ben obliges. The two surviving children are playing their part. John reads, familiar words of Scripture heard many times before, but now they cut so deep into my heart. Then

I hear words I have read out loud to James in our journey through *The Lord of the Rings*. The service of the burial of the dead continues, and I am grateful in a new way for ritual as it carries me through the numbness and despair of losing James. Through the blur, I am aware that the pall-bearers are now lifting James' coffin, sharing for a moment a physical weight of grief, and then the final scene unfolds as the cavalcade moves across town to the cemetery. The grave is very close to the river, and I think how many times we have cruised past this very spot in our houseboat with ten or twenty guests on board for one of our happy dessert, coffee, and fireworks evenings. James often drove the houseboat and steered it very well. We stand around the grave as the final words are spoken, and I feel the bitterness of this final parting. Now all the children are coming forward, each with a flower to place on the coffin, and then others come too with more flowers. Bold Ben chooses to follow the example of the priest, and he takes a handful of dirt and sprinkles it on the coffin. I am compelled to reach down and touch the coffin one last time; then I move to Pamela and hug her, then Rebecca and Ben; then all of us have a big, long, family hug, the four who are left. It is over. Good-bye, James!

SUBJECT: JAMES AND HIS FAMILY
SENT: DECEMBER 23, 2001 4:14 AM

I had always thought of happiness and sadness as being two opposites that you could not experience at the same time. The first days following James' death have made me rethink this position. Rebecca began this process for me at bedtime on

Tuesday, the day of James' death, by saying, "I am very sad, and I am very happy." Why? "I am sad because James has died, and I am happy because his suffering is over and because I get to see all my relatives." It reminds me of another paradox that we learned to live with. For two years since relapse, we did everything we could to help James beat neuroblastoma while at the same time we prepared for his death.

As we ended the burial and turned to leave James' grave, Pam and I decided to make an announcement: "You are all invited back to our house for coffee and dessert." And there followed six hours of visiting, a few tears, but much laughter. You can't let cancer ruin your day, as we always used to say. It was a good party. Our home has been blessed in the last five days by many tears, by much laughter, and by much compassion.

The day after the funeral, we decided to go to the cottage. Two reasons: first, to have some quiet time away, and second, to confront the memories. James' last visit to the cottage had been in October, and I read in our cottage journal that it was a "James-and-Daddy night to replace the one cut short on January 19th when James' pain came back." The cottage has always been our cancer-free zone, a place for family time and lots of fun. Indeed, the memories are powerful, and for a long time I had feared that we would be unable to return to the cottage if James died. So we went, with Uncles Jamie, and Tim, and Nanny, and crazy, wild Bigsby too. I had asked Uncle Jamie to guide us through this challenge, and as we sat warming ourselves in front of the fireplace he said to the children, "Tell me all the memories you have of James at the cottage." And as I reached for a pen and paper, Rebecca and Ben fired away.

"Crafts, swimming, boating, fishing, marbles, the swing, ringing the dinner bell, lighting the wood stove, cooking and baking with Mom, reading, hiking, skating on the lake, going to Peck's Camp, playing with the other cottage kids, fireworks, canoeing, knitting, learning wiring with Dad, plumbing, breakfast in the boathouse, building towers with Buell blocks, playing in the T-room, playing tennis at the Zerkers, catching minnows and frogs, sleepovers in the boathouse, the Titanic tree house, Hot Wheels, the Kids Clubhouse under the stairs, Monopoly, crazy eights (James always won!), euchre, Go Fish,"—Pam interrupts at this point and says, "I don't want to hear you kids ever say you're bored at the cottage again!"—"after-supper candy in the log cabin, jumping off the bunk bed, Water World at the beach, winter campfires, launching rockets on the ice, northern lights, Shakespeare plays, stargazing, skating, cross-country skiing, rock climbing, driving the motorboat, sunsets from the screened in porch..." Great memories. We prayed, thanking God for all the happiness we had found here. Then we talked some more.

"Let's name the new pond we made the James' Pond."

Rebecca pipes in, "Double O Heaven."

I am a little slower than the rest. "I get it: James Bond, 007." Later we go down to James' Pond, and on the way we see lots of fresh deer tracks in the snow, all converging on the pond, to drink I suppose. We light a campfire in our favorite winter campfire spot, and I notice some blackened, half-burned logs left from last winter. I remember the scene and shed more tears. James, Ben, and I, seated on upturned logs, the boys burning pieces of birchbark on the ends of their sticks.

Bigsby has decided that he likes the cottage; in fact, he is deliriously happy in this puppy heaven. We look back and see that his arrival in our home was one of the best moves we made. Our day away proves to be a great success, and now we look forward without fear to our annual New Year's Eve sleepover party at the cottage, something that has become a tradition for us. How are we doing, you ask? Well, as Rebecca says, we are very sad, and we are very happy. All at the same time. Rebecca and Ben are leading us. We are okay. Ask us again in a month, a year, ten years. Your emails, by the way, have been tremendously uplifting. We print them off, each day making a new thick binder to read and take comfort from. The www.JamesBirrell.ca guest book (or perhaps I should say, the second guest book, as the first one is full up) has hundreds more uplifting entries, the new format allowing much longer messages. Perhaps I will see many of you at 2 p.m. on Saturday at the memorial service. Unlike the funeral, this service is one we are looking forward to. I mustn't let out any secrets, but it will be different, just as James loved to be different.   Syd

SUBJECT: JAMES' CHRISTMAS PRESENCE
SENT: DECEMBER 25, 2001 1:34 PM

6:39 a.m. Christmas morning. Ben is the first to wake. He comes to our bedroom and says, "I miss James, Momma." Well said, Ben! Your priorities are right. As a dear friend recently reminded me, presence is more important than presents.

Pamela showed me a piece of paper yesterday. It was James' letter to Santa, written eight weeks ago, dutifully intercepted, and the order placed with Sears.

"Dear Santa, I have been a good boy. Please may I have the Mighty Loader and Mighty Dump Truck and the Alpha-Team Bomb Squad. Thank you very much, Santa. I love you. from James."

In our basement those toys still sit, and we wonder how best to use them. Not a big problem, but another reminder that James is no longer with us.

Perhaps you think that this email is starting off a bit on the gloomy side. Yes, there are lots of tears. But I must tell you that this Christmas Day has been filled with much happiness and laughter, as have the last few days since James' death. We had a grand time emptying the stockings and opening the presents. A boisterous, fun-filled Christmas breakfast with our extended family. "You can't let cancer ruin your day," James would say. So we choose to take the path of life that James chose. We acknowledge the loss, but we choose to move on. Our family has been immeasurably helped by the words of many who have written to us over the last week. Today I am going to keep my words brief, and in closing let me share from the James Web site just some of the many words of comfort we have received. My best wishes to you all.   Syd

> *"James' story is a true Christmas gift for me. What a precious and beautiful boy. May God bless you and your family...today and always. Thank you, James...for rekindling my faith."*

> *"I will be thinking about James and, though he didn't know me, I feel he has changed my life, the way I think, feel, act towards others. Thank you, James, for this gift. It's probably the best one I will receive today."*

"What a difference this child made in so many lives."

"You taught us all a very important lesson, James. We really can understand to appreciate life and wake up and face the day. You have taught us to love life every day and to look for the good in every second. Thanks, James."

"I have just recently learned of your story and in the past twenty-four hours have read each and every entry in your daily updates. I, for one, will never be the same."

"Somehow your story has enabled me to look at my own children in a different light. We tend to get caught up in our daily routines and forget just how precious our children are. You have helped me gain a new perspective. James, may you rest in peace."

"James, thank you for awakening all of our souls."

"I 'met' James through the Toronto Star *a few weeks ago and have been captivated since. I cannot get James and your family out of my mind. I need you to know what an amazing impact you and your family have had on my life...Please know that I for one have forever changed my impression of the true meaning of Christmas, mindful of all those less fortunate and suffering."*

"It is hard to believe that a boy so young could have made such an impact on this world..."

"Take comfort in knowing that my life, along with many others, have been enriched by having known

and loved James. He was an inspiration to us all...an angel sent down to us, to teach how to live and love. I will never forget you, James, for your legacy will live on, deep within my heart."

"We loved you James! What an incredible young boy!"

"We'll miss you, James, but our lives are enriched forever because of you!"

"I have a three-year-old son, and reading about James made me really change my priorities in life. I will always remember him."

"Thank you for sharing James' story with the world. You have given us a wonderful gift. We are all better for knowing the story of James; he is truly an inspiration to us all."

"I am a husband and father of a four year old and a seven month old. When one becomes a father—if you don't already know (I didn't)—you very quickly realize a child is the most precious creation in the world, amazing us in ways we can't anticipate. After reading James' story here, I am astounded. James is a true inspiration. He has obviously touched many more people in his eight years than most could hope to touch in eighty."

"I will go home tonight and try to be a better father so I know that my time with my child, however long he is with me, will not be wasted."

"He is a hero and has helped me to appreciate life to its fullest."

"I have a three-year-old son, and your story reminds me how lucky I am that he is healthy. We need to treasure every day, because we never know what is around the corner."

"I am a social worker. Thank you for sharing James with us. You have inspired us to keep fighting, hoping, and loving."

"I have just learned about James when I read the news of his death in our local paper today. I immediately visited his Web site, and I cannot begin to express how impressed and touched I am by James' beauty and courage."

"Your little man touched my heart. This world was blessed by a child wise beyond his years, who teaches us that 'you can't let cancer ruin your day.'"

"My wife told me of your updates, which I had not heard of previously. I sit at my desk now, trying to write words of comfort to you, yet I find myself unable to put them together...I want to hug my kids at this moment. I know I can draw strength from your letters in the future."

"After hearing the struggle that your son has endured over his short, precious life, I realized what a gift life really is. And that everyone who complains about the little things should really think about just how lucky they are."

"I am in James' class at Armour Heights School and had lots of fun over the past two years that we spent *together. Thanks for the memories; they will be there for the rest of my life."*

"Thank you for sharing your incredible journey. James' struggle to live his life to the fullest has made us look beyond and within our own lives and presence. Your son has touched us deeply, and his spirit lives on."

"James, I never knew you. But your valiant fight and that of your family has touched me very deeply. Thank you for touching my life and for reminding me of what is really important: life, love, and family."

SUBJECT: DAVE OPIOLA'S EULOGY
SENT: DECEMBER 29, 2001 6:49 PM

Tonight Rebecca and Ben are eagerly waiting for me to read them a science book that Ben received as a gift today. I have not spent much time with them over the last couple of days, as preparations for James' memorial service have kept me busy. Much as I would like to tell you all about today's marvelous time of celebration, I choose instead to cuddle up and read the science book. As soon as I can, I will put my thoughts into words. However, I have the text of the eulogy delivered by Dave, James' counselor from Camp Oochigeas, and I want to share that with you now. Watch out! The tears arrived for me right after the first sentence. Here are Dave's words:

A great thing happened to me this July—I met a superhero. Not a fictional character, but a real, live, caped crusader. He was without a doubt slower than a speeding bullet, and he was nowhere near as strong as a locomotive. He couldn't fly, and in fact, this hero had to be carried quite often. He didn't have an S emblazoned on his chest—just a small scar that verified his membership as a card-carrying, bona fide child with cancer. He didn't wear bright-colored tights, but now that I think about it, he did have a distinctive hat that set him apart.

I was introduced to James Birrell's medical history before I met James the boy. It was clear that he was a sick little boy with pain and mobility issues. It was less clear, though, whether James would actually make it to camp, due to his health.

So when I first spotted James at Camp Oochigeas, I was startled by his powers. You see, he was standing, and, before I knew it, he was running. This was no normal run; this was awkward, almost a trot, because one leg just didn't want to co-operate. This was quite impressive for a boy who was supposed to be in a wheelchair.

I was fortunate enough to spend five days with James during his stay at Camp Ooch, and for this I am eternally grateful. I'm thankful that James was well enough to come, but also that Syd and Pam were able to let go of James and let him experience camp.

Camp, for children, is as important in the battle against cancer as some of the treatments. It's an opportunity for the kids to be given permission to be a child again, a regular child.

Camp Oochigeas appears like any other summer camp, with lots of activities, laughter, excitement, early mornings, and loud, rambunctious meals. A visitor may notice the bald heads, the wispy hair, the missing limbs, the scars, the swelling, the port catheters and the fully functional Med Shed staffed by a pediatric oncologist and three oncology nurses. But soon the visitor would see the campers for what they are: children.

And when children like James are allowed to be children, they can teach us some of the great lessons in life. All those things that seem important to adults, well, they're really pretty meaningless until you've accomplished your own personal dreams. And when you believe like a child, dreams can come true.

Neuroblastoma is powerful, but in comparison to James' determination and stamina, it was a pale, weak foe. It was not enough to stymie the dreams of James Birrell.

And that's why we are here today—to remember a boy who dared to dream.

James wanted to go to camp and climb a rock wall. Well, he did both, and he did them well. These would be major accomplishments for any seven year old. The fact that James accomplished these feats while on aggressive treatment for cancer and pain is simply awe-inspiring.

The sight of James on the rock wall is a sight I won't soon forget. And when I need some strength and determination, I'll always have that memory.

As James was being harnessed for the climb, it became obvious that this was going to be an ordeal. James had to rest and nap during the day while he was at camp, and this was going to take a lot of energy. His limited mobility and pain in one leg was another issue. It was tough to get the harness on, simply because he had to bend his bad leg and then he had to support his weight on his bad leg as the good leg was slipped through the harness.

I thought, if we are having trouble on flat ground, what will happen when he's on a small support? And that's when I stopped believing. I began preparing for dealing with a disappointed boy.

But if you know James, you know he's full of surprises. And he surprised everyone that day as he climbed and climbed. He didn't make it to the top, but he made it twenty-four feet off the ground.

His cheering section of little boys, the rock wall staff, his counselors, and his fan club from the Med Shed were impressed.

James, upon being lowered down, announced that he just couldn't make it to the top—this time. Not bad for a boy who had spent the previous morning receiving a blood transfusion—another great Ooch activity.

It was during this blood transfusion that James and I became very close. Being only seven years old, it was obvious that James wanted his mum or dad to be with him as he underwent medical treatments.

But this was camp, and achieving things without your parents is what the experience is all about. I asked James what I could do, and in James fashion, he gave me a detailed list.

I was to let him lean against me and provide a finger for him to squeeze as he was poked with the needle. Then we were going to play crazy eights. And that's exactly how it happened.

Some hours later, the transfusion was over and I had a new little buddy. James would become very reflective during his time in the Med Shed. Out of nowhere, James would say things like, "I've had cancer for a long time." And then he'd promptly display an eight and change the suit.

Another time during blood work, James said to me, "You know, cancer doesn't often hit a family twice. My mum had cancer, too."

He then told me about his mum. I thought to myself, wow, what a kid. He's seven, and he's concerned about his mum while he's in pain and being medically treated.

I was very fortunate, not just in knowing James but in knowing about James from James. I was probably the only person in the world getting updates on Syd, not from Syd. And it was James himself who told me about a soapbox he was building.

As with all dreams, we eventually wake up and the dream ends. James' dream about camp and climbing *a rock wall came to an ugly end one evening at campfire. "I can't take it any more."*

With those words, the evacuation plan was set into motion. I picked up James and carried him over to the gator. The nurses and the oncologist did triage on the banks of Lake Rousseau, and without saying anything, the adults knew what was going to happen.

James, the sentimentalist that he is, tossed his stick off to Nurse Matina and told her to put it into the fire and make a wish. Now, James wasn't the only one with tears in his eyes. The wish was made, and since we're here today, it's obvious that the wish didn't come true.

James only told me one lie. He told me the pain was gone and asked me if he could now stay. As always, it was his body that betrayed him. The tension in his face, the rigidity in his leg, and the irritation of such small things as the hearing aid told a far different story.

James went home, but his memory and spirit stayed to the end of camp. His memory and spirit are still with me today, for it has been said that camp is more about a state of mind than a physical place. James and I, with his family, revisited that place only a few weeks ago via a slide show. It was good to see James smiling again and great to see him eating at the table.

As I told Syd and Pam the day James died, "I'll never forget your little boy." And I never will.

Good-bye, James. Thank you for letting me share your dreams.

David Opiola

SUBJECT: JAMES' MEMORIAL SERVICE
SENT: DECEMBER 30, 2001 3:12 AM

James' funeral service ten days ago was a stark acknowledgement of our grief and loss. In contrast, yesterday's memorial service was a celebration of his life. Much planning, hard work, and imagination went into the service, and I am deeply grateful to the small army who worked so hard to give James a fitting send-off.

The previous evening, with the help of children and adults alike, we had transformed the sanctuary of our church. Hanging by invisible wire at a rakish angle above the choir, James' soapbox derby racer, the Orange Rocket, undeniably caught the eye. Large blowups of photos of James and his family were hung on the walls. The "Big Ball Factory," an impressive six-foot-high structure built by James, stood on the platform, the electric motor sending balls cascading down various ramps and tilting devices. Stretching thirty feet across the platform was a giant Brio wooden train set layout, and at last, the goal of James and Ben for years, we had used every single piece, every single locomotive and coach, of their Brio collection. We never could figure out why Pam objected to a three-room layout at home; it looked pretty exciting to us here. The general effect was quintessential James—a splash of fun, construction on a large scale, let's do something that's never been done before.

The next day, people began arriving for the service two hours ahead of the start. My first indication that we had gotten things right was when I noticed two well-dressed children tentatively hovering just outside the sanctuary. The look on their faces suggested that they were a little frightened, going to their first funeral, perhaps carrying some unintended parental baggage. I brought the children in, and as they saw the train set, the Big Ball Factory, the racer, their eyes opened wide with excitement, and they began to play with the trains. Other children joined them, and as some of James' favorite songs were played on the PA, a crowd of children could soon be seen happily playing at the front of the church.

And so it was when Pam and I and Rebecca and Ben arrived at 2 p.m., it was to see a packed church, with overflow set up across the street in the Armories building, remote video and all. We looked out on a sea of friendly faces, part of that army that had fought for us over the last four years. Our pastor began the service, and as he spoke of James' love of life and his great interest in all that goes on around him, one line sticks with me. "I think James is going to have a couple of extra angels assigned to him, just to answer all those questions about heaven that James is sure to be asking!"

We sang some of James' favorite songs. Dave Opiola spoke, James' counselor from Camp Oochigeas. "A great thing happened to me this July—I met a superhero."

Then James Mewett took the podium. "James was a boy who saw and inspired the best in others. He lived to the fullest, never letting cancer spoil his day."

We heard one of James' favorite Bible stories, David and Goliath. Then all the young children gathered at the front, and Barb sang a beautiful arrangement of "Jesus Loves Me." I chose this for its last verse: "Jesus loves me! He will stay close beside me all the way. If I love him when I die, He will take me home on high."

Then our dear friend Jennifer Reid began the children's story, eighty or so children gathered around her. She drew their attention to the Brio train layout in front of them. "When I was a young child, we took the train a lot…every Friday we caught the train to Cornwall, me and my brothers and my mom…and the best part was when the train got to the station, there was my father waiting for me, and I got to jump into his arms…" There is a lump in my throat as I make the connection. "James used to love riding in trains. And now James just took a special train trip, and when he got to the station, God was waiting for him, waiting for James to jump into God's arms."

The choir sings. "Jesus is building me a House in Heaven." We all join in singing the last verse. The words take on fresh meaning.

This is my Father's world
O, let me ne'er forget
That though the wrong seems oft so strong,
God is the ruler yet.
This is my Father's world
Why should my heart be sad
The Lord is King: let the heavens ring.
God reigns; let the earth be glad.

As the triumphant singing ends my eyes drift down the printed page, and through my tears I find the words of a poem written by my mother. A mother's comfort, isn't that where we all ultimately turn in times of great sorrow? Thank you, Mum.

To James:

When people go to heaven
They shine like stars above
Their good deeds are their haloes,
A crown of joy and love.

The children have their playground
On clouds they play their games,
The brightest star among them
Is our beloved James.

Do you see the Orange Rocket
Straight and true through sun and rain?
And those little puffy clouds you see
Are steam from James' train.

Dear James we'll sorely miss you
But you've bravely borne your pain
And you'll have fun forever
Aboard your heavenly train.

From Granny

Primrose Birrell
December 2001

CHAPTER 5

IS THERE LIFE AFTER DEATH?

SUBJECT: STARTING OVER
SENT: JANUARY 10, 2002 6:47 PM

James had made it to school perhaps four times this fall. I dropped by the school the other day to pick up his things from the classroom. A difficult visit. Definitely a lump-in-the-throat time. There were his light-up shoes, which always attracted attention wherever he went. There was his desk, waiting to be cleared out. The shiny green pencil case and the green pencil sharpener, chosen with excitement last August. His favorite color, green. A few workbooks. Not much writing in them. A happy entry in his journal on September 5th: "In three days it will be the soapbox derby!" James, always looking ahead, living out his dreams. I am so glad he made it to the soapbox derby. One of the most memorable days of his memorable life, a day I will treasure forever.

How are the Birrells? Living without James is hard, as hard as we feared and then some. But living without recurrent neuroblastoma is truly delightful. We have been released from a prison that daily grew more confining and every hour took us farther away from all that is normal. But we are also grieving. I guess the surprise is that you can be happy while you get on with grieving. A good friend related to me that shortly after the death of his own young son he had realized that life was still about choices. You can choose to dwell on pain and death and loss, or you can choose to move ahead and embrace life. So that's what we have been doing. Choosing. One reason I have delayed writing this email is because I felt that our family's present happiness might be misunderstood and construed as mental instability, or a refusal to face reality, or the prelude to an inevitable crash. I think all four Birrells are a little taken aback that we are enjoying life and each other so much and so soon.

"Dad, now you are spending a lot of time with me!" says Ben. That makes me feel good. It used to be that when Ben tentatively asked me if I would play with him, I would have to say something like, "Just let me give James his pain pills," or, "As soon as James' blood work is done." Now I just say, "Sure. What would you like to play?" I am getting to know Ben a lot better now. And by the by, I am learning that Ben is not James and that to look for James in Ben is a bad idea. Ben is a terrific fellow, and the sooner I stop comparing him to James, the better.

So the choices our family has been making lately include surrounding ourselves with positive, cheerful people who can talk of their memories of James without leading us back into the swamp of self-pity and despair. We must have been out to breakfast, lunch, tea, and dinner more times in the last three weeks than in the last six months. Our house has been filled with laughter. I took Ben, Cam (James' friend), and his brother Clay up to the cottage for a day of fun and excitement. Pam has discovered the pleasure and freedom of having lunch with her friends. Pam also discovered that even cleaning the bathrooms is satisfying. I, too, found pleasure in having the time to catch up on mundane jobs that have been piling up for a year or two. On Sunday, Pam came to church (when was the last time she was able to do that?) and sang an impromptu solo. Both Pam and I have kicked the sleeping pill habit. Sleep is harder, and maybe the dreams that were repressed by the pills for so long are now all surfacing, dreams full of strange reruns of James' illness and death. But it is nice to leave behind the lethargy that accompanied the sleeping pills. Rebecca was quite concerned about returning to school after the holidays and came home early on the first day, but since then she has been enjoying school the way she always has. These days we all especially enjoy the early morning, which usually begins with a family cuddle in our bed, Bigsby crazily licking everyone on the face.

We talk about James a lot. We try to dwell on the good times, not just the last terrible weeks. And every now and then, we allow ourselves to include the bad things James did. "James was always too bossy when we played trains," says Ben. This way we avoid bestowing sainthood on James and put down any tendency of setting James up on a pedestal that might invite comparisons with Ben and Rebecca. Rebecca has a very good line she uses when she has had enough James talk: "Could we please change the subject?" and of course we do. The hundreds of cards and emails that you have sent have been wonderfully therapeutic. It helps us process so many extraordinary and powerful events that we have experienced during both James' and Pam's illnesses and that too often were buried by the next medical crisis before we could digest the current one. Your stories help me put to rest the idea that James' uniqueness was in some way just an imaginary product of a dad typing emails. We have been astounded to find out how far James' story has gone and how his courage has inspired so many. There have been times when we review some distant chain of medical events, wondering what would have happened if only we had done this or that, but I am glad to say that we always conclude by recognizing that we did our best; we made good decisions; we have no regrets. One of the great legacies of James we find to be the James Fund, which seems poised to go places we only dared to dream of. It provides us with a perfect way to take James' words, "I will always be fighting cancer," and give them continued meaning.

So the green pencil case is now in Rebecca's possession, and the light-up shoes are in the closet waiting for Ben to grow into them. The lump in the throat is still in my throat. Actually, it can stay for a while, for I am not in a hurry to forget James. But the remembering is now a part of the choice we have made to move ahead. I would never have believed that there would be a life after James worth living, a life that would still have adventure, love, spontaneity, hope. I make no predictions about the next three weeks, three months, or three years. But here we are, three weeks after James' death, enjoying a fresh start, finding that life can still be abundant.   Syd

SUBJECT: JAMES' BEDROOM AND THE GREEN SOFA
SENT: JANUARY 24, 2002 4:24 AM

I guess The Bedroom is always a hard place for parents who lose a child. It's a mini snapshot of the bigger picture; it reminds us harshly that something is missing. I go there a lot. Sometimes I visit during the day, but always at bedtime. Old habits die hard, and a visit last thing at night to each child's room as they sleep has always been important to me. James' bedroom is in the new wing of our funny old house, and since he died Rebecca asks at bedtime that I close the door in the corridor that leads to his room. That's fine. I used to think about The Bedroom before James died, wondering if one day we would seal it up, just as James left it, a shocking reminder of all that is lost. Or would we empty the room, dispose of the toys and clothes, rip out the custom green desk and shelves we put in for James, and create a new, practical room, devoid of any reminders of the past. The bed is particularly hard to see, a visual reminder of the emptiness in our lives. "Now I lay me down to sleep, I pray the Lord my soul to keep. When in the morning light I wake, help me the path of love to take." Then, "I love you, James." "I love you too, Dad!" A good memory to cry about.

What happened instead was we went shopping. Not a deliberate thing, just an impromptu family drive that took in a furniture store. We were vaguely thinking of a dresser for Ben's room at the cottage. Instead, we stumbled across a child's sofa, green, James' green in fact, a cute, friendly piece, and we knew what to do. Now there is no longer a redundant bed in James' bedroom but a green sofa in its place that says to the children, "Come in and play! Make me into a fort, or cuddle up here and read a book." The cousins from Rochester came up last weekend, and it was great to see and hear four children playing happily in James' room. James' room, a happy place for living, instead of The Bedroom, a gravestone in our home. We all like the transformation, and now it's much easier to visit James' room

291

and look at all of James' magnificent Lego models and other creations of his active and brilliant young mind.

The green sofa represents many changes that have been happening in our lives. We seek not to enshrine the past, and neither do we wish to wipe out the past. But let's acknowledge the grief and move on. There are lots of green sofas appearing in our lives these days. Each time a new one arrives, I have a vision of James as he was when he wanted to communicate approval. Many of you would also remember this picture: James, a smile on his face, giving the thumbs-up accompanied by a big conspirator's wink.

I want to tell you a funny story. It's secondhand, because I only found out about it later. Last week Rebecca had what might be called "behavioral problems." Some anger, inappropriately expressed. A talk session with Pam follows as they cuddle in bed. They resolve the problem, and then the tears flow, the two of them crying together in bed. Ben strolls in to check out the commotion, takes in the scene, and says, "What are you guys doing?" And then, after further thought, "Shall I call an ambulance?" Ben, dear Ben, we love you.   Syd

SUBJECT: FINE!
SENT: FEBRUARY 22, 2002 7:01 AM

It used to be that writing a James update often came about because of a crisis of one sort of another. The Birrell family is not experiencing anything remotely definable as a crisis these days, and perhaps that explains why I have been silent for some weeks. Sorry! I know that many of you are anxious to know how we are doing. The short answer is, "Fine!" Not "Fine!" as in wife's response to husband's query as he arrives home after pleasant day of golf while she looks after badly behaved children—one sick with chicken pox—overflowing toilet, and dog repeatedly making mess on floor. Not "Fine!" as in snappy reply to well-meant enquiry from nice people during very trying moment of James' illness. Rather, "Fine!" as in things are going so well that we can't really believe it.

The startling aspect of life after James is just how far from our expectations it all is. Pam and I had expected a choking, dark cloud of grief, a time of relentless sadness, an inability to move on, behavioral problems with Ben and Rebecca, and perhaps the return of Pam's clinical depression. Maybe all that is still to come. So far, no sign of it. About the only accurate prediction was that we would miss James very much. We do, and it hurts intensely. The big surprise is to be experiencing happiness, guilt-free happiness at that. Along with this has been the revelation that for us the course of our grieving is often a matter of choice. You do not have to stare at a photo of James until you cry; you can look away. You do not have to relive his suffering; you can remember instead his joy. You do not have to recall his screams of pain; you can instead delight in his laughter. You do not have to dwell on unfulfilled dreams; instead you can think of the soapbox derby or climbing the rock wall. Then there are times that you welcome sadness and tears, because you want to know that James was worth grieving. And we recognize that the loss of a child is fundamentally wrong; it's not the way life is supposed to be. It is the ultimate tragedy, and no one has the right to tell you otherwise. I guess that every day for the rest of my life, my heart will cry for James.

Speaking of the heart, I find myself looking at people in a different light these days, a kind of protectiveness for those around who seem to be carrying heavy loads. The other day I found myself asking an young immigrant waitress in the doughnut store about her family, and then I slipped her an unjustifiable tip of $20 to spend on her son. And speaking of money, I must tell you that the James Fund has been leaping ahead, $26,000 coming in over the last seven days alone, the total now over $200,000. Thank you. We are determined to push ahead the cause of neuroblastoma research. I keep thinking of more than fifty children diagnosed every year in Canada. One child is dying every week, likely in frightful pain. I will bring a full report on the JBFN soon. The achievement has been remarkable.

Srul Irving Glick arranged a JBFN benefit concert in Toronto last Sunday. We went, and what a thrill it was to see Srul conducting and to hear the choirs singing to a full house of nine hundred people. I was asked to say a word or two, and feeling pretty confident, I began by saying, "I find it very odd that life became immeasurably richer for me after first my wife and then my son was diagnosed with cancer. And strangely enough, that richness continues after my son's death eight weeks ago." Then I made the mistake of looking over at Srul, who was just beaming, grinning from ear to ear, and I lost it. Got pretty choked up. Never mind; so did the choir. It was a great occasion.

Life moves on. We are having lots of family time, now that the all-consuming demands of James' illness are past. It's great to be able to enjoy a family cuddle in bed first thing in the morning, Bigsby snuffling and licking everyone like crazy. It's wonderful to see Ben and Rebecca gain the confidence to ask us to play with them or read a book with them, after months of "Just let me give James his pills" or whatever. Pam has taken on a musical at school, *Jack and the Beanstalk*. Actually, some difficulty was encountered here, because by far the best candidate to audition was one Rebecca Birrell, so after some soul-searching about the director's daughter getting the star role, common sense prevailed and Rebecca got the part. The musical has been renamed *Jackie and the Beanstalk*.

I have been concerned about my relationship with Ben, cancer having kept us apart for much of his six years. I don't feel the closeness that James and I shared. (Yes, I know, never compare one child to another!) Ben and I went to Cobourg to watch trains yesterday, a little hard without James but it seemed to go well. We have made plans for a father-son time at the cottage this weekend. Feedback from Ben is not great as a rule, he being of the undemonstrative school of thought, so I was really pleased to receive the following in an email from a teacher: "When I came to Ben, I said, 'I hear you are taking a holiday.' 'Yep,' he said, 'me and my dad. We are going to the cottage tomorrow night, and we are going to have pasgetti.' He was beaming as he said this, so I decided to tease him a bit. 'Well, I love pasgetti, can I come too?' With eyes sparkling and a grin from ear to ear, Ben denied my intrusion on his weekend holiday."

I guess it's just not cool to let on to your dad that you are looking forward to spending time with him.   Sincerely, Syd

P.S. Must remember to buy pasgetti!

As the three-month mark approached following James' death, it seemed that a family holiday would be a good idea. We had found ourselves incredibly busy in January and February, not in a bad way, for the new cancer-free life we are now living is full of opportunity, of picking up threads old and new, of renewing friendships, and of discovering the joys of normal life, if there is such a thing. What fun it is to be able to phone a friend at a moment's notice and meet for breakfast or lunch or coffee or whatever. How nice it for all four of us to go to church together, to hear Pam singing solos once more, and then to bring home a gang of church-goers for soup and sandwiches. Pam has been able to take on a musical at the children's school, and I have been able to write a bit of music for it. I took a whole day off to go on a school trip with Ben. On the career end of things, it is gratifying to be able to put in an honest day's work, to sit in a board meeting and let the imagination flow, unfettered by the constant worry of James' situation. Nevertheless, it seemed that the time was right to step away from all this excitement for a bit, spend time with the family, and take stock of life, more specifically, life without James.

We took a sixteen-day holiday, our first real holiday in some time and the longest since Pam and I were married. On March 7th we said good-bye to Bigsby, picked up Nanny, and caught a plane to Vancouver, where two of Pam's brothers live. We last stayed with Jamie and Ann and the cousins when we visited them at their previous home in Bermuda, James' gift from the Make-A-Wish organization over three years ago, a magical time if ever there was one.

The three cousins, Joanna, Jared, and Jessica, are closely matched in age to Rebecca, James, and Ben, and the connection has always been very deep, and I guess we were all a bit apprehensive about how things would work out with James missing. Jared and James had always shared so many good times together, not to mention some very difficult times in hospital as well. We need not have worried, for no sooner had we arrived than the party began, and it only got better with the addition of the two other cousins, Luke and Julia. As the adults sat around chatting, the cousins could be heard in the basement hooting and yelling and laughing, occasionally appearing to show off their dress-up creativity or to present an impromptu play. And much later that night, what a reassuring picture to tiptoe into bedrooms to see cousins cuddled up, fast asleep.

Soon the big surprise of this trip began to emerge. Ben. Six years old. Just ten months old when Pam was diagnosed and began her cancer treatment, not to be held again by his mother for many a week. Twenty-one months old when James was diagnosed. Always pushed away from the traditional position of the youngest, that of the center of attention. Summed up in a ghastly scene from early December: a sudden crisis, James screaming in pain as I carried him downstairs, frantic phone calls to the doctor, a flurry of bedside activity, and then the awful discovery of Ben, hiding behind the sofa next to James' bed, clutching his blanket and sucking his thumb. So it was a delight to witness the emergence of the new Ben, the youngest cousin—but not the follower, the smallest cousin—but not the runt. Ben, gaining confidence, asserting himself, happy, noisy, running, inventing new games, mastering old ones, creaming us all at Monopoly, grinning from ear to ear as he cleaned up cards.

Later we spent four days on our own in Victoria, and I treasure my early mornings with Ben, cuddled up together at the hotel window while Rebecca and Pam slept, looking out over the harbor, watching the boats arriving, the seaplanes taking off, the early-morning train departing, and lots of other boy stuff. "Dad, can we go on that train?" No more excuses needed these days. "Sure. Tomorrow?" I have a lot of catching up to do with Ben, and we made a good start. We enjoyed the train ride enormously, even though trains without James is hard. "Dad, I know James would really like this train!" One night Ben showed me his first loose tooth, then paid me the ultimate compliment by letting me pull it out. Our time in Victoria was full of family time, visiting Buchart Gardens, taking tea at the Empress Hotel, visiting Bug World, Miniature World, Crystal Gardens, Underwater Gardens, and about twenty-eight other expensive tourist attractions. We took a horse and buggy ride, Ben, of course, falling asleep. The hotel swimming pool proved to be a big hit. Rebecca loved our meal out at the fancy seafood restaurant, being the gourmet she is. Perhaps one of the best outings was our walk in Goldstream Park, admiring the gigantic trees, breathing in the atmosphere of an ancient rain forest. And we had a memorable evening with our new friends the Hopkins, whom we met on the Internet, their young son having recently battled his way to remission status in his fight with neuroblastoma.

Back in Vancouver, we rounded off our holiday with a great mix of putting our feet up, seeing the sights, having family dinners, and enjoying the odd gourmet restaurant meals without the kids. My sister Diana arrived for a day, as always a great hit with the children, and she was able to confirm our opinion that Ben is a changed person. It snowed, so Jared, Ben, and I made an igloo, probably a first for Vancouver in March. Following yet another fresh fall of snow, we took a trip to Grouse Mountain, where the cousins took their first skiing lessons (even Ben) and I skied too. Spectacular conditions, and quite an experience to look down at the clouds in the valley below and then ski down the hill into that same cloud. Which brings me to a confession: I had a minor fall, made worse because I foolishly had a camera in my shirt pocket, which got knocked into my ribs, leaving me with one bruised or broken. Yesterday I had a new sympathy for James, finding myself with bone pain, difficulty in breathing deeply, a stinking headache, and nausea. All on a very minor, temporary, and insignificant scale compared to James, sending me to the med cupboard to look for some of James' pills while reminding me how extraordinary his achievement was to keep up such a cheerful and positive attitude despite the load he carried.

So we are back home, much refreshed, having gained a new perspective of our new life. The time away has helped us see what is important and to remember what our core values are. God bless!   Syd

SUBJECT: LIFE CONTINUES
SENT: JUNE 28, 2002 6:32 AM

I keep thinking that an update from the Birrells is hardly of interest six months after James has gone. However, it is 3:56 a.m., a traditional hour for writing a James update, so I will give it a go. And I will not be offended if you wish to be removed from the mailing list—just let me know.

Recently I read that Sir Winston Churchill and his wife lost a much-loved daughter about the same age as James. Now, in times past I have read many Churchill volumes, so I can only assume that this detail cannot have been new to me, yet it was. I guess that in my pre children-dying-of-cancer world it just did not register. The biographer noted that the tragedy was rarely spoken of again, that the door was firmly shut, and that the family blocked off the tragedy with a wall of silence. That's not the conventional wisdom of today, but I don't pretend to have mastered the business of grieving, so I will allow that although it may have worked for Churchill and company, it isn't the route for me. In fact, I welcome the chance to remember James and to talk about him, though it often brings tears. Ben and Rebecca hate to see us cry, but I think they are quite secure in knowing that life these days is mostly about them and that we are a happy family, always looking for adventures and fun, and that tears for James now and then are all right, as long as it's not in public!

I have not yet succeeded in getting past the constant pain of losing James. So far we have chosen not to sell the house, move to another community, change careers and start over (and I don't think we will), so the daily triggers are many. Every day circumstance dictates that I drive past the IGA store, scene of the soapbox derby, that day of unbelievably powerful memories. Sometimes I drive to the starting line, stop, release the brakes, and coast down the hill to see if I can match the 51 km per hour he clocked by the time we reach the IGA store at the bottom of the hill. I never can. Every time I sit at the organ, I remember that James delighted to sit next to me on the bench, pulling out the stops for me, keeping me company, especially in the days of Pam's cancer treatment. And though I love to see Ben and

Rebecca running up and down the sidewalk playing with the neighborhood kids, there is always the feeling that the scene is incomplete without cheerful, noisy, inventive James and that his best buddy Cam is still looking for his place in this new order.

Coming out of James' death, Pam and I found ourselves setting some goals. Top of the list was our family, carrying a hidden pain that mirrored James' own appalling suffering. In fact, by December 18th, 2001, the shock of watching James suffer was much greater than dealing with his death. I marvel how we ever lived through those frightful times. Six months later, I think we are only just moving beyond the searing memory of his suffering and dealing instead with our loss. So family matters headed the list of our priorities. We took a long-overdue holiday together and visited the cousins in Vancouver. Pam and I had a wonderful visit to Montreal. We don't think twice about pulling the children from school for an adventure day, and there have been lots of those. Just last week, for her tenth birthday, I took Rebecca to Halifax by overnight train for a five-day daddy/daughter holiday. That was an amazing adventure that deserves an email all to itself. Best moment for me was when at supper in the dining car an elderly couple asked how many children I have. "Two children," I said, but Rebecca quickly spoke up and said, "No, there are three children, but my brother James died!" The Halifax trip was the fulfillment of an old promise to Rebecca that she too, like James, could have an overnight train trip. Ben of course was very jealous, but he knows that when he is ten he too can have a train holiday. He is already planning, and right now he favors the famous Silverton-Durango mountain railway in the States.

Syd and Rebecca at Peggy's Cove

I hope that you don't think that we see family time only in terms of exciting holidays. One of the great pleasures of life is to spend an evening at home with the family. "There's nothing on the calendar; shall we get a movie?" Great. Or a walk by the river, or a family bike ride, or a picnic. We place great value in these simple things. Soon we will disappear to the cottage for our summer holidays, to our cancer-free zone, where each day is full of time for each other. Rebuilding our physical health has been another focus. The children have excelled at their swimming lessons, and they love their weekly soccer games. Pam is now regularly out to yoga. I have begun early-morning running again. On the work front, it has been wonderful to have the mental energy to think about my career again. I love my musical vocation, and how good it has been to throw myself back into the church and into the Peterborough Singers. And in a different way, it has been fun to be an active landlord again and to have the option of fixing the broken toilets or door handles or stoves instead of calling in the repair guys.

The James Fund has emerged as a big part of our lives. It gives a sense of purpose to our tragedy to see the fund grow and to see more neuroblastoma research projects funded and awareness of the disease raised. It gives us a chance to stay connected with many new friends that we made throughout James' illness. Turning the James emails into a book is on the agenda this summer. Pam and I find ourselves frequently giving inspirational/motivational speeches, so it will be interesting to see how this unfolds. And now I see it is already 6:28 a.m. I seem to be losing my ability to write fast and furiously in between medical crises. My best wishes to you all.   Syd

SUBJECT: THE YELLOW TOOLBOX
SENT: JULY 18, 2002 11:17 PM

Today I stumbled across a memory. I tried to forget about it; after all it's an old story now, dating back to last November, and I should be over these things by now. But there it was, that happy, bright yellow toolbox that James, after much deliberation, had chosen on one of our trips to Home Depot. I found it this evening in the basement while looking for something else. I gazed at it for a moment, knowing that I was facing one of those grief choices: walk away and be safe or stay and face the memories. Go on! Dare to remember! After three weeks at the cottage, that wonderful cancer-free zone, I thought I had made some good progress on the James front. So I paused, kept my eyes on the yellow toolbox, and remembered. Then I reached out and touched it. And the tears flowed.

You see, James and I shared (or do I say, share?) a fascination with tools, and in the last few months of his life, when he was well enough, I would invent an excuse to take a trip to Home Depot and ask James if he'd like to come. He always said yes. Rebecca and Ben would be at school, so it would be with a certain amount of guilt that I would wheel James along in his wheelchair to the tool section, and together we would admire all those beautiful shiny tools before choosing one to add to his growing collection. "What's that tool for, Dad?" he might say. Or "Why do these pliers cost more than the other ones?" You could buy a set of ten cheap screwdrivers for $5.99, or just one first class screwdriver for $8.99. And so we would discuss the merits of one over the other, and inevitably we would buy the expensive one. How do you say "no" to your dying child? Was it foolishness, buying high-quality tools for a dying boy who would never use them? Now they sit in his bright yellow toolbox with its drawers and trays, a toolbox James carefully chose over several dozen other ones. How proud he was as he held it on his lap and we wheeled off to the cashier! How I wish I could remember his exact words as he excitedly told the cashier about his new toolbox and all the tools he was going to keep in it.

Later Pam would very reasonably say, "And what did you get for Rebecca and Ben?" I confess I wasn't very good at answering that question, but in my defense I will say that I am trying hard these days to make up the lost ground with Rebecca and Ben, and I am enjoying doing so. In fact, we are all enjoying each other in a way that was not possible back in the panic stricken days of neuroblastoma. Some time ago, Pam decided that we should spend this summer at the cottage, and now we are experiencing the wisdom of that decision. The pace is undeniably slow, so slow that we forget what day it is. We have been racing for a long time—too long. The cottage has always been a place of healing for us and never more than the last few weeks.

Often in times past, the writing of a James update had its cathartic effect. I don't know what message for Syd there is in the yellow toolbox tonight. But I feel better, having written, so thank you for bearing with me. Good night!   Syd

SUBJECT: FIRST DAY OF SCHOOL, ONCE AGAIN
SENT: SEPTEMBER 3, 2002 12:01 AM

Ben and his good friend Nicholas were playing down at the river while the two dads were standing by, idly skipping rocks across the surface. It was a hot summer evening. The water level was low and much of the riverbed was exposed, so the boys were rearranging rocks, making little canals and streams, generally having a wonderful time. Suddenly Ben let out a cry, and we turned towards him to see him holding up his hand, the fingernail ripped right off one finger, dangling by a thread of skin. I scooped him up, and we headed for the car. Ben was being very brave and wasn't crying, but he struck right to my heart by whispering in a scared little voice, "Dad, am I going to die?"

Ben, you have seen too much in your short six years! Our hurt has gone too deep. Just when we thought how well you have been dealing with James' death, you come out with a line like that.

The local hospital soon had Ben's finger x-rayed and patched up (yes, broken finger), so we thought we would drop by Nicholas's house to let him know that his buddy was doing just fine. There we heard Part Two, as related earlier by Nicholas to his dad. "Is Ben going to the same hospital that James used to go to?" "Yes," his dad replied. "Then I know Ben is going to die, because that hospital couldn't do anything for James!" The indisputable logic of a six year old. How your life is changed forever when you watch your friend die.

So we got the message, loud and clear. The children are still very fragile. On the surface, our Rebecca and Ben look like two well-adjusted, happy children, but just below the surface lurks the grief. Oddly enough, the incident turned out to be the clincher in a very difficult decision we were facing about schooling. Despite six very good years at Armour Heights School, years where we received tremendous support from staff and students, it was becoming clear that Rebecca needed more than the school could offer. We decided to switch both Ben and Rebecca over to Rhema Christian School. We made the application and got accepted. Rebecca is very happy. "Now I won't have to pretend I have a stomach ache when I don't want to go to school!" she confided.

And so it was this morning that we found ourselves re-enacting the Birrell First Day of School ritual. It began with a big cooked breakfast, and then it was time to find those brand new backpacks, put on the new shoes, and head for the front garden for the traditional First Day of School photo. Oh well, Ben never did like the picture-taking ceremony, but I did manage to catch one good shot in between his scowls. Off to the new school we drove, and as we did so, it seemed that an emotion that had been quietly brewing for some days was at last coming to the surface. After the outdoor welcome that was held in the school playground, we were invited to see our kids into their classrooms. Breathe deeply; keep smiling. Rebecca was quickly surrounded by girls eager to welcome her and know who she was. She studiously ignored me, everything under control, don't need parents, thank you very much, so I headed down to join Pam at the grade two class to see Ben get settled in. He looked just fine too, so we swallowed hard and headed towards the exit. Tears. Pam appeared to be on the verge of a meltdown. Then me, I realized, as I stole her Kleenex. Another parent drew near to comfort us and, misinterpreting our emotion, said "Ben will be all right, don't worry!" Oh, how much could be said in response, but all I could get out was a stifled, "It's not Ben; it's James!" A year ago today there were not two but three smiling Birrell children eagerly going to school. "No, Dad, I can carry my own backpack!" said James with great determination. And he did. By some miracle he was well enough for school that day. It was the first of just three days that he was able to attend grade three. Three days culminating in the most magnificent of days, the soapbox derby, of which much could be said.

But today there are just two children, and quite unexpectedly we were finding The First Day of School experience about as hard as it gets.

Actually, I thought we had been doing pretty well in putting life together after James, but today was a permissible exception, I guess. It seems that grieving has no timetable. For us, January to June seemed to be all about learning to live without James while getting back into society. July and August followed, and the lazy, idyllic eight weeks of the summer seemed to be about seeking stability, about reconnecting with each other and openly facing the pain, without the crutch of being busy, in the stillness and beauty of our cottage getaway.

Pam and I got home from the school and had another cry and a good hug. I found last year's photo album, and maybe it was a bit unwise, but I pulled the 2001 First Day of School photo, figuring that we are already crying and looking at a photo can't make things worse. Let's have a real pity party. There was Rebecca, glowing, smiling, happy as can be; and there was Ben, intent on escape, scowling fiercely; and in the middle was James, one arm firmly around Ben and the other around Rebecca, grinning from ear to ear.

Oddly enough, I feel much better for putting these thoughts into words. Now I am debating whether to click the Send button, adding more sadness to the world. Ben and Rebecca, as it turned out, had a terrific day at school. "Fun, fun, fun!" said Ben. "Oh yes, I like my new school very much," Rebecca said. Later in the evening Pam sang beautifully for the opening staff chapel at Lakefield College, while I reacquainted myself with the art of finding middle C on the organ and playing hymns. The ordeal of The First Day of School has come and gone. An ordeal that all parents face in one way or another. Thanks for listening.   Syd

I will put in a disclaimer right at the start. This is a late-night email and may suffer from a lack of logic. Here goes.

I just figured out that James died 285 days ago. Perhaps I did the calculation in an attempt to shed some light on the perplexing and exhausting business of grieving. I promise that I will not keep count hereafter, making it a daily ritual, in the style of the prisoner scratching a mark on the wall of his cell once a day, because I suspect that road leads nowhere useful. But having discovered today's number, I might as well use it. For example, can the number 285 help me discover why grief is so wearying? I shed tears five times today (only got caught once). A fairly average day for crying. So, 5 x 285 = 2,280. I guess that two thousand two hundred and eighty weeps could be quite tiring. Yes, that bit of arithmetic brings comfort. On the other hand, another part of me is appalled that after 285 days my heart remains broken. Open heart surgery heals in a tenth of that time. Let's dig deeper.

Day 285 was a fairly typical post-James day, lots of nice moments; lots of sad ones, too. The day began with a jolt at 4:58 a.m. A dream about James playing with a puppet on his hand, laughing hilariously and mischievously, left me sitting up in bed crying with bitter disappointment, for I woke to find the picture was unreal, just a phantom. So I got up, did some emails, shuffled some papers. Now every night as I kiss Rebecca good night, she tells me that if I have trouble sleeping, then I am welcome to come to her bed. So I did, and I woke with her a few hours later to the wonderful smell of French toast floating up from the kitchen. Pam and Ben had already eaten, so Rebecca and I shared a delightful Sunday breakfast together. One of the really nice moments of the day. Had a visit with Ben to some interesting Web sites of the world's best roller coasters, something of a passion with him these days. Sunday church followed, still a yo-yo experience, very uplifting at times but then full of poignant memories, as in when my junior choir sang, missing one child these days. Then there are the prayers for the sick, James no longer on the list, but nevertheless a vivid reminder of where we were in times past. To play a cheerful Bach fugue for the postlude is definitely an up time, until there arrives the sudden recollection of James faithfully sitting on the organ bench next to me. But a pleasant family lunch puts things right. Two o'clock saw me back on the organ bench to play a funeral, and there I quietly lost things as Psalm 23 was read. Many times James asked us to read us that psalm as he lay in bed dying. How often I have thought that the organist's job is so much easier than the singer's. I can choke up and cry yet still make music with my fingers and feet. I don't know how Pam manages to sing.

Home for the bike ride. By contrast this is an absolutely magical time. I thought this was the first time we had ever done a family bike ride, but Pam tells me there actually was one other earlier this spring. Certainly there never was one while James was still alive, so today felt like a milestone event. Four Birrells riding our bikes together in Jackson Park. What a wonderful thing to do on a Sunday afternoon. Look at us! Maybe we are winning in our quest to find out what normal families do together. Then a stunning thought came: What's to stop Pam and I going for a bike ride together some time? What a novel idea. The possibilities are endless now that we are freed from palliative care. Actually, I must confess that Pam and I find ourselves very curious about what normal families do together. We have six years of catching up to do.

Well, the bike ride was followed by a supper with friends at their home, still a rare event, as I suspect many would find the Birrells an emotional challenge. Then we headed home for a game of Monopoly and some reading of Rudyard Kipling to Ben. Good night, Rebecca! It's Mummy and Daddy time! Go to bed! So Pam and I chat, and surprise! surprise! we find ourselves talking about James again. Rebecca soon returns, in tears, worried about the house burning down, but we see through that one and send her back to bed. Pam and I talk some more, but then it's my turn to get the boot, Pam ready for sleep.

So has day 285 been a more successful day in coping with life than day 284, or, for that matter, day 184? Just how long does this battle last? Surely our friends will tire of our endless need to talk through our grief. Outwardly we put on a pretty good show, active and upbeat at work, involved with the family at home, excited about the children's new school. But why are we still so fragile, 285 days after James left us? I spoke to 1200 high school students just last Monday, to launch their Terry Fox campaign, and by all reports my James speech was a stunner. How could it be otherwise, when you have had the privilege of being dad to a little boy who says to you, "Dad, I've been thinkin' that every day is like a precious gift. You gotta use each day!" But why did I shed tears as I took the podium? I think that Pam and I are doing a good job of making our lives focus around Rebecca and Ben and each other. The challenge seems to be finding the right balance between the need to look back and process our memories of James and, at the same time, move ahead and give Ben and Rebecca all we gave to James.

Do write me your comments if you wish. Over the months and years your thoughts have been a big part of surviving. I am so grateful that I have such easy access to a community that brings our family so much comfort. Tell me what normal families do on a Sunday afternoon.   Sincerely, Syd

P.S. *My Big Fat Greek Wedding* is definitely the movie to see. Pam and I loved it.

P.P.S. Please note from P.S. that I took Pam to the movies. Syd scores extra points.

SUBJECT: WHAT YOU SAID
SENT: OCTOBER 6, 2002 6:24 AM

Last Monday I sent out my Day 285 email. I printed off a copy for Nanny, who, I have to admit, seems to have a life despite her refusal to buy a computer and get on-line. The family photo printed off too, because, as usual, I forgot to click on the Selection button. More wasted expensive color cartridge, I thought. But then on a whim, I found a spare three-ring binder, got out the three-hole punch, and put the photo in it. So when all your wonderful responses started arriving, the obvious thing to do was to put them in the binder too. It has gotten quite full.

I want to thank you for that gift. Pam and I keep picking up the binder for another read, and it has brought us great comfort this week. And I want you to know that our week has been shaped by your thoughts and brought us a new sense of stability and direction. You have helped us put to rest a number of issues. In grieving there are times when the unanswered questions become a babble of noise in your head that is overwhelming. You have calmed that storm. Then there were those niggling decisions to make that have been put off for months, the indecision and inaction adding to one's sense of failure. The tombstone was one of them. James' grave is still without one, as we hum and haw about the design. But three of you mentioned the Jewish tradition of unveiling the tombstone on the first anniversary. Not only did that get us down to the monument place to finalize the details, but now we know what we will be doing on December 18th—a gift in itself, I can tell you. Another friend tentatively suggested attending a bereavement class for the family. Coincidentally (maybe not) a new session was starting on Wednesday, so we were there, all four of us (sorry—five, one of James' good friends came too), and while the kids worked through some art therapy, Pam and I shared in the parent session next door. Then there was the idea of building all sorts of new family memories, memories that can stand proud next to all those James' adventures. That concept has given us the push to welcome new friends and experiences. Pam has accepted an invitation to adjudicate a Kiwanis music festival, a first for her. And we finally caved in to the children's wish to see Niagara Falls, so off we go later this month for a three-day visit. We are doing lots of things to build our new family unit; speaking of which, we all went to the bowling alley yesterday afternoon and decided that five pin was okay while ten pin was brutal. Glad no one was watching us do the latter.

Some of you shared your Sunday afternoon normality with us. Actually, some sounded delightfully abnormal. I could fill a book with Sunday afternoon anecdotes. Did you know how many people look forward to their Sunday afternoon nap? Just to read of what other folk do I found very soothing.

You sent us some words so profound that I want to share a few. Your responses have made a deep impression on Pam and me. Many of you have written out of your own grief, and perhaps sharing these words helps us all. I can't thank you enough for taking the time to write.

"There is no time limit on grief, especially a child, your own child."

"Memories become a torment before they become a treasure."

"Believe that your dream of a happy James is an affirmation that he is indeed ecstatically happy in his House in Heaven with Jesus."

"I use my calendar to heal. I plan things and do them. I have lunches with friends. I have get-togethers and parties. I have my son, daughter-in-law, and grandchildren here for barbecues and lots of visits. I don't allow myself too much time to slip into depression."

"James Barrie created Peter Pan. He had a brother who died when he was a child, and he grew up to create the beloved boy who never became an adult. He enriched generations of people with the depiction of a boy who doesn't develop. It prob-

ably didn't stop him from grieving his brother, but it turned a loss into a gain...I think you're doing that already."

"Your updates have been such an important part of my life for the past couple of years."

"I don't think we ever completely 'get over' losing a loved one. I'm not sure we're supposed to. I think what we do is surprise ourselves by discovering that we can indeed laugh and have fun in between those bittersweet times of missing our loved one. Then, gradually, we find that we have more times of laughter and fun, and the times of missing seem less like a sharp pain and more like a wistful mixture of both fond memories and the sadness that the person isn't there to share the fun."

"Grief is very much a roller coaster."

"Is it a surprise that Ben is fascinated by roller coasters? He has been on the Birrell roller coaster for a long time."

"I think you are doing what every family who has suffered a tragic loss does—laugh in between the grieving. Don't worry, soon you will be grieving in between the laughs, and you will be the better for it."

So we are not alone on this path, and it brings meaning to our loss to think that sharing our walk might encourage others too. In a moment I will print off a copy of this email for Nanny. Actually, two copies. The second I will place at the back of my binder, to remind me in times to come of what I have learned this week. And I will end with a quote from a mom in Australia, because I can't do better. And I very much empathize.

> *"Well, I think I've said enough; you and your family take care, and when you find normal, please email it to me."*

They say the first year is particularly hard because you are facing all the firsts—the first day of school without James, the first family holiday—so many firsts. This week brought the first Halloween without James. Just two instead of three children on the staircase for the annual Halloween photo. And the very next day, November 1st, is The Birthday, what would have been James' ninth.

What to do? Pam thought maybe we should sit at the kitchen table and cry all day. But Rebecca and Ben didn't like that idea. They said we should think about the things James liked to do. For example: trains. Okay, let's take a train somewhere. How about Toronto on the GO Train? Sure! said Ben. Sick Kids Hospital? Right from our first visit the children have always loved Sick Kids, with its exciting atrium, the yellow elevators, the cafeteria next to the indoor fountain, lots of good memories. Who should we invite? Well, Rebecca's best friend Rebecca, and Ben's friend Clayton, and of course Clayton's brother Cameron, who is James' best friend, and James' other best friend, Austin. And their families. And Big James, and Dave from Camp Ooch. Since we were going to be at the hospital, we thought we could invite some of our medical friends. Our friends in the foundation offered us a room for the party. James was very generous, so Ben and Rebecca decided that people could bring presents and we would give them to the kids battling cancer in the bone marrow transplant ward at Sick Kids. James wanted very much to see the James Fund help find a cure for neuroblastoma, so we decided to invite the researchers who have won awards, along with his friends in the foundation. And the docs and nurses and nuclear medicine technicians. And our Toronto friends. And Posy the clown. Mustn't forget Granny and Nanny. So at lunchtime on November 1st, eighteen of us arrived at the Oshawa Go station. Great excitement. Bea was there to welcome us with gift bags for all the children. Bea is the ticket seller lady whom James and I got to know on our many train trips to Sick Kids, one of the countless encouragers we met along the difficult road of cancer. GO Transit had heard we were coming and generously provided free tickets. Naturally, the children chose to ride upstairs on the GO Train, and there the children discovered that the gift bags included whistles, so we had the upstairs pretty much to ourselves all the way to Toronto. For us small-town Peterborough dwellers, the last stretch of the train ride is always a great thrill as the CN Tower and the skyscrapers slide into view. We took the subway up to the hospital, and there the party began.

The Bear Theatre is a great place for a party. Posy the clown was there to entertain the children. Years ago we first met Posy, James just diagnosed and very sick. James had more or less shut down, no longer responding to the world, when Posy arrived at his bedside. At first he closed his eyes tight shut, but Posy didn't give up, and somehow she pulled him back from the brink. James smiled, the first smile in many a day, and the will to live returned. It was very right to have Posy with us on James' birthday. So as Posy amused the children, we were able to meet countless friends, brought together through the legacy James has left us. We showed a short video that we had put together the day before, full of photos of James and family and friends, full of hugs and adventures.

Later I asked Ben, "Did you like the video?"

"No, because every time I saw James smiling it made me cry."

I must admit there were few dry eyes in the room. Cameron told me they were the okay kind of tears, when you are remembering good things. Then Malcolm, our good friend from the Foundation, spoke of James and all the good things the James Fund has achieved and then gave Pam and I a framed letter of recognition, which we shall always treasure. A very generous check was handed over to the James Fund by Melody Homes, a Peterborough builder, and then a young girl who knew James brought forward a donation from part of her bat mitzvah money. How appropriate it seemed to me that we were able to have both donations made today, representing both the corporate world and the world of a young woman. The story of James knows no boundaries, something that never ceases to amaze me. Some other surprise donations brought the day's total to over $12,000, taking the fund well over $200,000. When we get to $250,000, they will have to move James' plaque on the donor wall downstairs into the next category, as I was plainly told by the kids when we went to find James' name later on.

Five-thirty p.m. and some would have called it a day, but in true James spirit there was still time for more fun. The same good friends that had arranged the special screening of *The Lord of the Rings* for James last year had arranged complimentary tickets for us to see the Two Towers exhibit just opened at the ROM, in the planetarium. It's a magnificent walk-through display taking you right into the Two Towers movie, about to be released, the second in the trilogy. I can highly recommend it. The girls loved the dresses and the boys loved the weapons, and we all loved the incredible sets. Almost as exciting was the subway ride to Union Station that followed. This time, when we got to the subway ticket booth and said, "Seven kids, two teens, six adults and three grandmothers," the ticket man just said, "How be we just say it's twelve dollars?"—which was fine with us. By the way, keeping a cool head on the subway with seven kids, two teens, six adults, and three grandmothers is not easy. But we made it safely to Union Station, where GO Transit had a second set of goodie bags for us, even some for the adults. But no whistles. Another cool train ride, the children making rude noises with balloons this time, some fast food at McDonald's, the health-conscious moms now beyond caring about such things, and we arrived home tired but happy.

Pam: "It was a wonderful way to spend James' birthday."

Rebecca: "It was a great day."

Ben: "At the next James' birthday party, can we make the subway part a lot longer?"

Syd: "A perfect day." Thanks, everyone!

The big anniversary is fast approaching, and many of you have been gently providing advance support. Thank you. And you have been asking how we are doing. There's a lot to share. Pam and I have long since given up making any predictions about our grieving, so I can't tell if the sense of impending doom in my head is a natural thing or a self-fulfilling prophecy. Why should December 18th, the day James died, be any harder, for example, than the day he was diagnosed? Anyway, I find that lately I have gotten into the habit of rereading the email narratives of a year ago, each one an anniversary of a sort. November 25th, the last good day, great day. November 28th, the Cadd pump hooked up for pain control. December 2nd, "Cancer gets you ready to go to heaven," says James. December 4th, "Dad, I've been thinkin' that every day is like a precious gift. You gotta use each day." December 8th, James makes his last outing, to see the special screening of *The Lord of the Rings* that had been arranged for him. December 10th, the Ring is indeed very heavy as James walks through Mordor. On December 12th, I read, James and I talked about Frodo, who deserved a long and happy life after fulfilling his mission, but it wasn't to be. The wounds were incurable, and he left instead for the Havens. "Just like James," I whisper, and James nods his head. December 14th, "Read me more Bible stories, please." December 16th, "I love you, James." "I love you too, Dad." What great words to remember. December 17th, James' best friend Cam comes over. "I've come to say good-bye, James…I love you, James…I'm going to miss you very much…" December 17th, I leave home for three hours to conduct Handel's *Messiah*, to date the most powerful musical experience of my life. "Comfort ye my people," the soloist sings, the first of many familiar words that take on stunning new meaning for me.

And then December 18th, "James just died."

So here I am, having another middle-of-the-night weep, wondering if this remembering is foolish self-pity or a necessary catharsis. December is a church musician's busiest month, full of concerts, carol services, exciting musical events to plan and perform. To that we have added a major James Fund event, the early screening of the second *The Lord of the Rings* movie, right bang on the anniversary of last year's screening. I bet that's going to be a lot more for the Birrells than raising money for the James Fund. Then there's the James Fund newsletter, much more work than it sounds, in the mail Monday morning. Work on the James Fund, by the way, we find profoundly satisfying. Is all this busyness a way of hiding from reality or a healthy tool to deal with the first anniversary?

On the private side, we are spending lots of time together as a family. We have decided to celebrate Ben's birthday, next week, in extravagant fashion, to make up for the dismal feel of last year's party. "How many kids can I invite to my birthday party?" Traditionally in our family we have strict rules, a matter of parental self-preservation. "You can invite as many kids as you want!" Eighteen, I believe, is the tally. (Help! Are we crazy?) And then we are making plans for the unveiling of the tombstone, following the advice of our Jewish friends, on the anniversary day itself.

As I read those emails, I can hardly believe that we found so much meaning in those terrible days. But my own words force me to acknowledge so many good and powerful memories. Pam and I conclude that we are still dealing with two issues: the trauma of watching your child die a gruesome death, and then the actual loss itself. We conclude that we have yet to leave the former behind, and it still remains the big challenge. Yet rereading those emails leaves me astounded that we found so much of beauty and significance in such a difficult time.

I started this email an hour ago, and now I hear Rebecca's CD player starting up, playing Rhonda Larson's beautiful flute music, so I will go and have a cuddle. My best to you all, and thanks to you for listening.   Syd

SUBJECT: HUGS
SENT: DECEMBER 18, 2002 1:06 AM

I find myself quite restless on the eve of my son's death. What should I be doing? What ought I be thinking? A feeling of panic as the hour approaches. Perhaps I am looking for a rite or ceremony to guide me through the coming hours. Earlier in the evening we had a brief family discussion on the matter, cheerful and upbeat, and we decided to cuddle up and read one of James' favorite stories. It's called the *Polar Express*, all about a child who keeps believing in Christmas and can still hear Santa's bell. Granny is here visiting us today, so we asked her to read the story. Bigsby was having a Tigger moment, tearing around the bedroom with one of his stuffed toys, eager to play, but eventually he calmed down. We lit a candle first, as candles seem to go with ceremony. The candlestick is made with wood from the floor of the old chapel at Lakefield College School where I play the organ, a floor that James walked across many a time to join me on the organ bench. So you can see that an attempt was being made to use some tangibles to help remember the intangible.

Like a broken record, the searing memory of James' suffering plagues both Pam and me. Try as we might, the trauma of watching James die is still with us. I said to Pam this evening, "Why are we commemorating such a sad day? Why not choose one of James' happiest days and celebrate that instead?"

Her response: "We cannot deal with the trauma of his suffering unless we face it." So tonight we are remembering the last terrible eight hours of James' life, from the time the seizures started in earnest, the breathing turned to noisy gasps, the pain became completely uncontrollable...

Has it really been a year? It all seems so fresh, the memories so strong and vivid. I wonder if I will be able to sleep tonight. I wonder if I will awake at 5:30 a.m. and make my way to the very place in the family room where he died. Part of me wants to see a great drama unfold tonight, but another voice urges me to turn the page and begin a new chapter. I weary of second-guessing my emotions; I weary of the unending process of grieving. Tomorrow we will go to the cemetery and unveil the new tombstone, another ritual to carry us through The Day. Ben will bring his prayer book, and we will no doubt cry a bit. We will take great comfort from friends and family, and afterwards we will return home for soup and hugs, two special emblems from those difficult days. Soup was dropped off at the house for us almost daily, made by loving hands, providing far more than mere sustenance. Hugs—well, a book could be written about those hugs James gave us. If you ever experienced a James hug, and many of you have, you know what I mean. Hugs that lasted half a minute; hugs that warmed you till your heart glowed within you; hugs that later we understood to mean, "This is a special hug because I am going soon. I love you!"

There, now I know why I had to write this email. I don't have a lot of words left in me tonight, and I think it's because I have found the answer I need. Think of the hugs. Thank you, James.

SUBJECT: ANOTHER ANNIVERSARY
SENT: DECEMBER 18, 2002 5:15 AM

I didn't mean to wake up, but Ben stumbled into our bedroom an hour ago, sleepwalking again, so here I am. Everyone else is fast asleep. For some reason it's cold downstairs. As I walked past the window I saw the moon, so full and bright, yet so unreachable. James loved the moon, and it always held a fascination for him. Maybe that's why Apollo 13 movie and the Tom Hanks series about the Apollo program held such a strong place in his mind. Maybe it was something to do with achieving the unachievable. We loved to cuddle up and watch them together.

I awoke to find half a dozen emails waiting for me, all full of comfort and wisdom. Light a candle, said my friend. So I did. And as I thought of candles, I realized that I wanted to do something bigger than a candle, and I remembered how much James loved to light the wood stove at the cottage or make a bonfire and then sit around, poke it with a stick, enjoy the warmth. So I prepared the fire, and as the very moment arrived, in the very room that he died in, I lit it. I found the ritual I was searching for a few hours ago. Soon the warmth filled the room, a physical comfort. Then I watched the birthday video, positioning the rocking chair to be in the exact spot where a year ago at this moment James took one huge raspy breath and died. The birthday video is very powerful and is made up of images of James interspersed with some of those extraordinary one-liners that he used come up with, along with two of his favorite songs to accompany the visuals. What a great smile James had! Just one thing to do to complete the circle, and that's to write an email and connect with you all. It's going to be a good day. After all, "Ya can't let cancer ruin your day!"

SUBJECT: ANOTHER CHRISTMAS
SENT: DECEMBER 25, 2002 4:39 AM

This is very odd. I am awake; it's 4 a.m.; I am at the computer; but I am completely without inspiration. I suppose I could look up my Christmas emails from last year, and the year before, and the year before that, stir up some memories, and cook up something. Or I could reach over to the bookcase next to the computer and pull out one of the many photo albums packed with images of a smiling boy no longer with us. That's always good for a few tears. But contrary to what you might think reading my Birrell updates, which tend to be introspective stuck-in-the-past kind of things, the Birrells actually spend a lot of time looking ahead. We consider ourselves a very lucky family, despite the cancer setbacks, or maybe because of the cancer challenges, and the future is looking very exciting. Those cheerful people who tell you that the pain of the loss will diminish are right. Maybe that's not saying a lot, because the kind of grief you have when you lose a child is so big that even a fair bit of diminishing still leaves you with an unbelievable, in-your-face, moment-by-moment load to carry. There is not a bereaved parent I have spoken to who does not echo the same sentiment. We are a preoccupied lot. By the way, there are lots of those people in my life; they are a wonderful bunch; and they have been a great help. But life is full of choices. You can choose to draw aside the curtains that keep you closeted in your grief, and, surprise, surprise, there other people out there with big problems too. Another one of those balancing acts: yes, you have to deal with the pain and the loss, but you have to look ahead, too. And if you get too analytical about it all, that spoils the fun too.

All of this is a preamble to saying that having awoken early on this Christmas day, which I am sure is going to erupt in megakid noise and excitement very soon, I am wanting to send a message to all our friends to say that we are all right. Maybe time does heal. I think we are learning to cope, that the Birrell decisions of the past year, made so fearfully at the time, have turned out to be good ones (especially the children's new school!), and that we do see a future ahead of us. I am glad to say that future does include James and his legacy in many areas, but there are lots of categories that are new ones, James free, and for that we need not apologize. I also want to acknowledge the impact of your support for our family. Not a day goes by that I do not marvel at this army of encouragers who stand by, offering words and deeds to encourage us. Each one of you has brought your own unique gifts to us. I really hope that you understand how much that means to us, and I wish there was another, bigger, better, superlative couple of words that could convey the full depth of our gratitude. There isn't, so here goes. Thank you!   Syd

I've been waiting for this dream. The other parents have all had the same dream, so I know a bit about what to expect. Those "other" parents of course are my Internet friends who have also lost a child. It's just that I seem to be slower than the others, at Day 404, instead of perhaps the six-month mark of other parents. Actually, there is hardly a day goes by that I do not hear from another grieving parent— and a most helpful thing it has been, I must say. Behind the cheerful facade that we have built between ourselves and the world, we do a lot of wonderfully strange things in order to cope. We try hard to understand and do what is "normal," thinking that maybe this will help the pain, but secretly we do all kinds of bizarre things to cope with the daily explosions that characterize life with one child missing. Personally, I find it very helpful to discover that wandering into James' bedroom daily to say good morning and good night is quite acceptable. One mom has kept her daughter's email account and sends her emails, which I think is a great idea. We do whatever we have to do to get through another day.

So the dream goes like this: I am very busy doing important busy stuff (so important that I can't for the life of me remember what the stuff is) when it comes to my attention that James is actually still alive, in hospital. So, consumed with guilt at this parental neglect, I rush to the hospital (one I have never seen before) and find him in a ward with many other sick children (James never had anything other than a private room). He is lying on his side, greatly wasted away (that part accurate), but his face is strangely different. He manages his trademark "Hi Dad!" that I miss so much, but he is too sick for much more than that. I know I should do something, and as I wonder vaguely about calling a doctor or nurse, the dream ends. I wake up and head down to the computer, thinking that it wouldn't hurt to write an email to clear my head (common enough; sleeping the night through is still pretty rare for me). Often I write an email not knowing if I will send it, which is where I am right now.

My good friend Robin sends back brilliant responses to my rambling words, and I know that the very least she will say is that when grieving any dream tends to be better than no dream at all. I have gained a certain confidence as time moves on, the kind of confidence that lets you do or think what you need to in order to get through another day. Grieving people have to learn not to be too hard on themselves. At Day 404, life without James is brutal, which is quite an improvement over the absolutely unbearably brutal feeling of the six-month mark. Now what triggered tonight's dream I cannot say. Perhaps it was yesterday's early morning visit to Big James' hangar where we built the soapbox derby racer. More likely it was the recording session with my Peterborough Singers later in the day, for we taped "House in Heaven" several times. That, by the way, is a good example of time improving one's coping mechanisms. James' happy face grins at you from the front cover, hiding for a moment the unbelievable memory of a terminally sick child in terrible pain, comforting his mother with the whispered words, "Jesus is building me a house in heaven." I find these days that it is possible to catch yourself when you start walking into one of those powerfully charged places, and as you start to fall to pieces, if you are quick, you can close the door and run away. Which I did as I conducted, though I confess to leaving the door open maybe a crack, as I really wanted remember all I could. Grieving is all about choices, so it seems.

The door idea reminds me of another recent experience. My mother was visiting, and I took her to the children's new school to check it out. The principal, Ray, is always pleased to welcome guests and show them around, especially grand-mothers, and we walked right into both the grade two and the grade five classrooms to see what Ben and Rebecca were doing. No problem. Then, as we continued the tour, Ray took us in to see the grade four class. And there I experi-enced one of those grief explosions, a completely unex-pected moment where you fall to pieces. As the door was opened and Granny and Ray entered, it was as though an invisible but powerful force field was blocking me. The words that we found in one of James' grade-three journal books came crashing down on me—words penned in response to the question, "What are your goals for this year?"—and the enthusiastic answer, "I just want to get to grade four!" Here is the classroom that James should have been in, full of happy, exuberant, pain-free, nine-year-old boys. When other children are complaining about school, I can't help thinking of James' wish. How I wish that I could have seen James through the open door in that class!

I guess one of the ways to deal with all those unfulfilled wishes and dreams is to look around you and seek new dreams and memories. Take the sad, and make it glad. I am blessed with an amazing family. Every day I am thankful for them and the richness they bring. Never will I take family for granted! Tragedy has a wonderful way of teaching you what really is important in life. I hope that I never forget the lessons I have learned. At the Birrell home we have allowed grieving to be whatever it is. No rules, no expectations, no timetable, no guilt. Looking back from the thirteen-month mark, I see huge highs and terrible lows. The breaking of one's heart in some way enlarges it so you have more room to treasure and understand family, friends, and the beautiful things in life.   Sincerely, Syd

SUBJECT: PAM, SYD, AND SCIENTISTS
SENT: MARCH 3, 2003 12:49 AM

There we were, Pam and I, in a room full of doctors and scientists gathered under the auspices of the James Birrell Neuroblastoma Research Fund Working Group to hear one of the James Fund award winners present a paper to the group. The group meets once a month. We felt very honored and privileged to be there at the Hospital for Sick Children with them. Something that had been just a bright idea some months ago had now been taken through the "proof of principle" stage, and the results were both promising and exciting. Another potential weapon to use in the treatment of neuroblastoma. Dr. Helen He, under the direction of

James' friend Dr. Ray Reilly, has found that switching the isotope of a radiopharmaceutical drug results in much less damage to bone marrow stem cells in mice while still killing off certain types of neuroblastoma cells. Many neuroblastoma treatments, or cancer treatments in general, can nicely kill off all the cancer cells in a patient, but unfortunately the high dose required to do this also kills the patient, often through irreparable damage to the bone marrow, the starting place of your immune system. Now if you think I'm getting too technical here, try sitting in a room full of the brightest and best as they excitedly toss question after question at Dr. He and Dr. Reilly, and the ideas flow, and the group grapples with the challenge of taking this research to where it really matters, the kids dying of neuroblastoma.

So what's it like to be a parent of a child who recently died of neuroblastoma and find yourself in a highly technical discussion about radiopharmaceutical drug and its impact on neuroblastoma cell lines? Well, every now and then you feel the tears pushing though, so you try to concentrate on the abstract and, mustering all the logic you can, to tell yourself that this is how we are going to beat this disease. Actually, a good deal of the emotion comes from knowing that here is another example of the legacy of James. The James Fund has paid for this research, thanks to so many people's support, and James himself has inspired these scientists to look at this ghastly disease, an orphan disease that has been ignored for too long. As James himself once said to me about his fund, "With all this experimenting, they'll get it figured out, and then all the kids in Canada with neuroblastoma will be able to survive." I am always struggling to find meaning in James' suffering and death, and I must say that it was very therapeutic to be there in that room, to watch and listen as a completed James Fund research project was presented to the James Fund Working Group. How grateful I am that so much good has come out of James' short life.

It was a busy week. On Tuesday I did a James speech to 500 students at Notre Dame High School in Ajax. An hour goes by very quickly when you are talking about James. I had decided to go with the theme "You gotta use every day!" And then on Thursday it was Pam's turn to speak, to the students of Bethany Hills School. It is very humbling and at the same time very soul satisfying to be able to speak words that make a deep impact on people. Every week we hear from somewhere around the world that our family's story has helped someone be a better parent or face their own cancer challenges. It is starting to sink in that the James story is not over.

I suppose that after that kind of week, it was hardly surprising that I had the dream again. Pam tells me that she is both jealous and relieved that I had the dream this time, and not her. In the dream James was in remission, which means no detectable cancer: you are full of hope, yet also living in deadly fear of a relapse. In the dream, James and I were playing together, laughing. The dream process had somehow adjusted his age appropriately, so that he was nine years old and bigger than when he left us. Then we were walking along, side by side. It was just as I realized that he really was pain free and that I could hug him as hard as I liked and just as I was reaching out to put an arm around him that I woke up. And then, just as all you grieving parents have told me happens, I was so disappointed, I could do nothing but cry. Never have I so wanted to be able to return to a dream.

Two dreams. One is about our loss, and the other is about finding a cure for neuroblastoma. It really is a dream come true to see the James Fund thriving, to see the research moving ahead. The paradox is that out of tragedy so much opportunity and happiness and excitement has come. Life is all about choices, as my wife frequently tells Rebecca, Ben, and me. If you want to, you can choose to make the world a better place.

I have gotten a little too profound for the hour. I now choose sleep. Good night!   Syd

SUBJECT: BEN'S TRAIN TRIP
SENT: MARCH 21, 2003 10:50 AM

Last year Rebecca and I took the train to Halifax to celebrate her tenth birthday. Great trip. So good that I couldn't wait for Ben's tenth birthday. There is something very special about one-on-one parent/child holidays. Last week Ben and I caught the train to Halifax, three years ahead of schedule. I don't know who was more excited, Ben or me. Of course the train motif has been a regular Birrell adventure theme, something that James got us into, and now it's a legacy. Pam and I recently did a train trip to Montreal with friends and are looking forward to using the free tickets that have come out of the Ben-and-Dad Halifax trip. But I am getting ahead of myself.

The thing about the Halifax trip is that you get a chance to settle in, explore the train, enjoy the dome car, eat a couple of meals in the dining car, and make the most of the double bedroom. Not to mention no emails, no phone calls, no faxes—no business, period. Ben had my undivided attention, and that gave me great pleasure. It's about twenty hours from Montreal to Halifax in the special train called "The Ocean," plus the train ride from Cobourg to Montreal. Rebecca and I had spent three days exploring Halifax once we got there, but for Ben the attraction was the train ride, so we went to Halifax, spent a night in a hotel, and caught the very next train back. Everyone we met on the train to Halifax had a reason for going there, many for something called "The Brier," all about a curling championship apparently, but we just wanted a train ride together. So while everyone else was groaning about the train being three hours late, Ben and I were enjoying the unexpected free extra time together on the train.

We had decided that we would take *The Lord of the Rings* for reading material. But when I asked Ben whether he would like to wear his VIA train hat, he said, "No, that would remind me of James and make me sad." Likewise he instructed me not to bring any photos of James, because this was his trip, not James'. It was good to settle that before we left and know that the focus was Ben and me. Ben really has come into his own since James died, and I try very hard not to look for James in Ben. Rebecca was very close to James, and the memories are still very close to the surface, but she is not a boy, does not look like James, and was sixteen months older. But Ben is now very much the age of James as we remember him best and shares many of James' passions and interests, and daily I catch myself making comparisons, which I quickly delete.

Ben following in his brother's footsteps
on the steps to the dome car

We caught the lunchtime train from Cobourg, which gave us four hours to sit next to each other and talk. I don't know when I was last able to do that. Seven year olds have a lot of interesting stuff in their heads, and sometimes daily life finds you too busy to connect. Four hours allowed us to cover a lot of unexpected ground, for example, multiplication, and at one point Ben was testing me on the squares, up to nineteen times nineteen, grinning with glee if I got the wrong answer. I think those four hours also allowed me to begin adjusting to the holiday way of doing things together.

Instead of barking parental orders—"Now we are doing this, this and this,"—it was, "Ben, what would you like to do?" Part of the charm of the trip was seeing how good Ben is at weighing up a situation and making decisions.

In Montreal we had time to eat supper with Uncle Rodney before catching the overnight train. This is the classic train with the dome car that has been a feature of Canadian train travel for fifty years. I will never forget Ben's excitement as we settled into our bedroom and watched our attendant Ross magically transform the sitting room by pulling down our beds from the ceiling and the wall. There was time to climb up and down the ladder, unpack, and master all seven light switches. I delighted in watching Ben's delight. And then of course it was off to the dome car to take in our departure from Montreal. Later we read some of *The Lord of the Rings* together, first from the top bunk and then from the lower bunk, reading about the pursuit of the Orcs from Rauros as we sped across the snowy countryside. After Ben fell asleep, I sat and gazed at him for some time, thinking many things.

Next morning we ate breakfast in the dome car bullet lounge, where I discovered Ben is quite safe at filling up his cup with boiling water, adding a tea bag, milk, and sugar, all the while alarming the clucking old ladies. Actually they were very nice ladies, and later one decided Ben was ready to learn how to tell the time. As she was carefully explaining about the big hand, he politely informed her that it was twenty-seven minutes after nine. Lunch we took in the dining car, which is quite a walk. Young boys can move a lot faster down the narrow corridors than dads. It was at lunch that we learned that we running three hours late, which suited us just fine. More train time. Approaching Halifax at sunset, seated upstairs in the dome car, we were treated to a panoramic view of the harbor.

Lots more could be said of our eighteen hours in Halifax, two swims in the hotel pool, the whirlwind taxi ride around the city in the morning, making sure we crossed both suspension bridges, the container terminals, the oil rigs, the warships, the citadel, the Maritime museum. On the train ride back we were tickled to hear the flustered conductor on the PA saying, "Ladies and gentlemen, we are insanely late!" Thanks to that kind of insanity, VIA Rail gives us our next trip half price, so Pam and I are looking for an opening in our schedule. I got to thinking that many of us are insanely on time, and as a result we miss many of the important things of life. Here I was, spending four days with my son and having the time of my life. A wise friend told me that bringing up children is all about creating memories. Enough said.   Syd

SUBJECT: SAILING
SENT: NOVEMBER 1, 2003 2:36 AM

Some time ago Rebecca said to Pam and me, "You two are always remembering days that happened." It wasn't an accusation, just an observation. She is quite right about this "remembering the days" habit that her parents exhibit. Today, November 1st, is one of those days, for it is the birthday of James, and for the grieving parent there is no way to avoid wondering about what kind of boy James would have been on his tenth birthday had he lived.

The world moves on, and almost two years later I feel left behind, the "grieving parent" label still firmly attached. "Ancient History" is how I interpret the silence around me, and likely that is the way it should be. For Rebecca and Ben are thriving, happy, growing, loving, maturing, embracing life, and I am very proud of them. But I am learning that to be a grieving parent is not a phase of life that you pass through and then leave behind you, but rather it is your new identity. Every day forever I will be torn in two by the loss of my son. Word reached me of a ninety-year-old woman in a nursing home who thinks daily of her young son, snatched so many years ago by the same disease that took James. You hide your grief; you get on with things; but you just can't escape the reality that your child is gone. It is a very lonely road, for you find that this bit of ancient history has a limited shelf life with many of your friends. When you write an email, or talk on the phone, or walk into a room, the last thing you want is for your friends to think of you as a dark cloud, best avoided if they don't want to spoil their day. Sometimes I think I am like an amputee who has lost, say, a hand. One is equipped with a prosthetic, learns to use it, and gets on with life. But you are an amputee, and part of you is undeniably missing. Likewise I think I have successfully picked up the threads of life, I think I am making a contribution to the world around me. I experience moments of great happiness, fulfillment and satisfaction, but...life is full of buts these days.

I dreamt of James and then woke. I didn't remember the dream at first, but something triggered my memory, and there it was. I was in a boat on a warm summer's day, and as I looked back, I saw a small sailboat, actually a sailboard (though that doesn't sound reasonable to my daytime

338

logic), and I could see at once that it was being sailed by a small boy, and that the boy was James. At first I couldn't see his face very well, but as I screwed up my eyes, suddenly I saw very clearly that it was indeed James, a confident, happy, and very healthy-looking James, a shock of brown curly hair and those engaging brown eyes, full of delight. James, sailing with supreme confidence. And that was it. No sooner had I figured out that the sailor boy was James than the dream ended. I thought I would tell Pam about my dream, but I found that even the first steps towards putting the dream into words unleashed powerful emotions, my throat choking up, tears welling, so I decided instead to type. Same problem, but more manageable.

The sailing dream is a gift, I have no doubt. "Tomorrow would have been James' tenth birthday," said Pam to the children at supper last night, "and there is no way that we can avoid thinking about that. I think that we should do something to remember him and to celebrate his birthday. But we don't want you children to think that your parents think James' birthday is more important than your birthdays. We can't do anything too exciting."

The response was immediate. "Oh, we don't mind that! Let's go for a train ride! We always go on a train on James' birthday," said Rebecca and Ben. Last year's celebrations did indeed include a train ride, and a rather spectacular day it was. So we will catch the GO Train to Toronto later this morning, embrace the adventure of the day, and I will try to shed the grieving parent label and think instead of sailing.   Syd

POSTSCRIPT:...*AND I'M HERE!*

It's been a while since I composed one of these emails. I was feeling that, really, it's almost two years; you can't go on like this indefinitely, forever moping about your son who died. After all, you have a wife and two children, and they deserve your best. So I didn't write, and what do you know, I found myself slipping into what might be labeled depression. I try not to look back too much. I have a feeling that successful grieving involves making choices, rather than letting the emotions lead the way. One should choose to look ahead, right? and not follow the self indulgent path of constantly revisiting the photo albums, videos, and diaries. After all, that's just another futile attempt at finding James. Like returning to his bedroom, vaguely looking for something new that I might have missed on previous visits to his room. There again, the first rule in the book of rules about grieving is that there are no rules, so perhaps I can be allowed to follow this whim that has caught my attention and share an old story that has taken on new meaning for me. I see the date is March 23, 2000. Here it is, an excerpt from an email I wrote some time ago:

> *This story involves buying new bikes for the children, as they have outgrown their old clunkers. "But*

what's the point in spending money on one for James if he's going to be dead by year end?" spoke one of the voices in my head. Well, I ignored that voice and listened to the one that said, "Buy that nice, shiny red one over there with the training wheels."

James tried it out in the store, got things all adjusted nicely, and, it being a warm spring day, we went to the park to try it out. "Careful! Your platelets are low; you mustn't get a cut or bruise; stay on the right side of the path!" Then winter returned, so it wasn't till yesterday that we were able to go bike riding again.

Off we went. With great confidence James zoomed around, and as he zoomed he said, "Dad, when can I take my training wheels off?"

"Right now," I said quickly, before the sensible voice in my head could register an objection. Off came the wheels, and then came that back-killer business for the parent where you grip the saddle and stagger along, desperately trying to avert disaster. So far, so good. All the time I'm thinking, He's on Acutane; his skin is compromised from the drug; can we afford a spill, a scraped knee, hand, or face? But his platelet count was good that week, so I took courage and let go. This, I suppose, is a priceless moment for all parents, because the letting go goes far further than just the bike-riding thing, but for me and James the stakes seemed so much higher. I watched, enchanted, aghast at my foolhardiness, thrilled at my daring, convinced that a terrible accident was seconds away, savoring the moment. But

James just kept riding around the parking lot, feeding instructions to the non-existent dad behind him, until he looked up and saw me on the other side of the parking lot. "Dad, you're there, and I'm here!" "Dad, I can ride without training wheels all by myself!" "Look at me, Dad!"

I have a copy of this email pasted on a huge blowup photo of James riding his bike, Pam just behind, huge grins on both their faces, and it gives me mostly great pleasure but also a little sadness to look at it. If I recall correctly, the photo was taken after we had returned home triumphantly from the first ride, found Pam, told her the news, and headed outside to prove the point.

So here's what grabbed me today, just another day in the endless quest of trying to make sense of life without one of my children. *"Dad, you're there, and I'm here!"* Spoken from the other side of the parking lot, I know, but today I reach for another meaning. This is the boy who said, "Jesus is building me a house in heaven,"…*"and I'm here!"*

"Look at me, Dad!" I'm looking, James, wanting to get beyond the pain, wanting to believe that there is something better. *"Dad, I can ride without training wheels all by myself!"* The training wheels of this life. I need them for a while yet. Yes, James, and somehow tonight I think I have heard your voice. *"Dad, you're there, and I'm here!"*

THE JAMES FUND

For Neuroblastoma Research at Sick Kids

AT THE HOSPITAL FOR SICK CHILDREN, TORONTO, CANADA
HONORARY PATRON: TOM HANKS

The James Fund was founded by the Birrell family and friends in 2001 and has become one of North America's leading neuroblastoma research initiatives. Neuroblastoma is a rare but deadly childhood cancer, killing about one Canadian child every week, one American child every sixteen hours. Through the James Fund, a number of significant research projects have been mounted in Canada and the USA. As a result of the James Fund, Toronto has taken its place as one of the leaders in the global effort to find a cure for neuroblastoma.

Donations can be made on-line at:
www.JamesFund.ca

Syd Birrell may be contacted at *info@greentrainbooks.com*

**A portion of the proceeds of this book
supports the James Fund.**

A WORD FROM OUR HONORARY PATRON

THE JAMES FUND

For Neuroblastoma Research at Sick Kids

James Birrell was a good kid. He was a cheerful voice on the phone and a diligent pen pal who was a big fan of spaceships and railroad trains. When neuroblastoma took James away, that word was new and ugly.

Now, before other families have to learn its meaning, there is a duty to raise money for neuroblastoma research and care. There is also honor to be found in being connected with the research fund bearing James' name.

TOM HANKS
Honorary Patron
The James Fund